D0251652

12 SERMONS ON PRAISE

Charles H. Spurgeon

BAKER BOOK HOUSE
Grand Rapids, Michigan 49506

Library
Oakland S.U.M.

13184

Reprinted 1982 by
Baker Book House
from the edition issued by
Passmore & Alabaster

ISBN: 0-8010-8218-8

PHOTOLITHOPRINTED BY CUSHING - MALLOY, INC.
ANN ARBOR, MICHIGAN, UNITED STATES OF AMERICA

Library
Oakland S.U.M.

Contents

1. "Magnificat"

" Awake, awake, Deborah; awake, awake, utter a song; arise, Barak, and lead thy captivity captive, thou son of Abinoam."—Judges v. 12.

MANY of the saints of God are as mournful as if they were captives in Babylon, for their life is spent in tears and sighing. They will not chant the joyous psalm of praise, and if there be any that require of them a song, they reply, "How can we sing the Lord's song in a strange land?" But, my brethren, we are not captives in Babylon; we do not sit down to weep by Babel's streams; the Lord hath broken our captivity, he hath brought us up out of the house of our bondage. We are freemen; we are not slaves; we are not sold into the hand of cruel taskmasters, but we that have believed do enter into rest:" Heb. iv. 3. Moses could not give rest to Israel; he could bring them to Jordan, but across the stream he could not conduct them; Joshua alone could lead them into the lot of their inheritance, and our Joshua, our Jesus, has led us into the land of promise. He hath brought us into a land which the Lord our God thinketh on; a land of hills and valleys; a land that floweth with milk and honey; and though the Canaanites still be in the land, and plague us full sore, yet is it all our own, and he hath said unto us, "All things are yours, whether Paul, or Apollos, or Cephas, or the world, or life, or death, or things present, or things to come, all are yours, and ye are Christ's, and Christ is God's:" 1 Cor. iii. 21-23. We are not, I say, captives, sold under sin; we are a people who sit every man under his own vine and his own fig-tree, none making us afraid. We dwell in "a strong city, salvation will God appoint for walls and bulwarks:" Isa. xxvi. 1. We have come unto Zion, the city of our solemnities, and the mourning of Babylon is not suitable to the palace of the great King, which is beautiful for situation, the joy of the whole earth. "Let us serve the Lord with gladness, and come before his presence with singing:" Ps. c. 2. Many of God's people live as if their God were dead. Their conduct would be quite consistent if the promises were not yea and amen; if God were a faithless God. If Christ were not a perfect Redeemer; if the Word of God might after all turn out to be untrue; if he had not power to keep his people, and if he had not love enough with which to hold them even to the end, then might they give way to mourning and to despair; then might they cover their heads with ashes, and wrap their loins about with sackcloth. But while God is Jehovah, just and true; while his promises stand as fast as the eternal mountains; while the heart of Jesus is true to his spouse; while the arm of God is unpalsied, and his eye undimmed; while his covenant and his oath are unbroken and unchanged; it is not comely, it is not seemly for the upright to go mourning all their days. Ye children of God, refrain yourselves from weeping, and make a joyful noise unto the

Rock of your salvation ; let us come before his presence with thanksgiving, and show ourselves glad in him with psalms.

> " Your harps, ye trembling saints,
> Down from the willows take ;
> Loud to the praise of love divine,
> Bid every string awake."

First, I shall urge upon you *a stirring up of all your powers to sacred song* "Awake, awake, Deborah ; awake, awake, utter a song." In the *second* place, I shall persuade you to *practise a sacred leading of your captivity captive.* " Arise, Barak, and lead thy captivity captive, thou son of Abinoam."

I. First, then, A STIRRING UP OF ALL OUR POWERS TO PRAISE GOD, according to the words of the holy woman in the text, "Awake, awake,"—repeated yet again " Awake, awake."

1. WHAT is there that we need to awaken if we would praise God ? I reply, we ought to arouse all the *bodily* powers. Our flesh is sluggish ; we have been busy with the world, our limbs have grown fatigued, but there is power in divine joy to arouse even the body itself, to make the heavy eyelids light, to re-animate the drowsy eye, and quicken the weary brain. We should call upon our bodies to awake, especially our tongue, "the glory of our frame." Let it put itself in tune like David's harp of old. A toilworn body often makes a mournful heart. The flesh has such a connection with the spirit, that it often boweth down the soul. Come, then, my flesh, I charge thee, awake. Blood, leap in my veins ? Heart, let thy pulsings be as the joy-strokes of Miriam's timbrel ! Oh, all my bodily frame, stir up thyself now, and begin to magnify and bless the Lord, who made thee, and who has kept thee in health, and preserved thee from going down into the grave.

Surely we should call on all our *mental* powers to awake. Wake up my *memory* and find matter for the song. Tell what God has done for me in days gone by. Fly back ye thoughts to my childhood ; sing of cradle mercies. Review my youth and its early favours. Sing of longsuffering grace, which followed my wandering, and bore with my rebellions. Revive before my eyes that gladsome hour when first I knew the Lord, and tell o'er again the matchless story of the "Streams of mercy never ceasing," which have flowed to me since then, and which "Call for songs of loudest praise." Awake up my *judgment* and give measure to the music. Come forth my understanding, and weigh his lovingkindness in scales, and his goodness in the balances. See if thou canst count the small dust of his mercies. See if thou canst understand the riches unsearchable which he hath given to thee in that unspeakable gift of Christ Jesus my Lord. Reckon up his eternal mercies to thee—the treasures of that covenant which he made on thy behalf, ere thou wast born. Sing, my understanding, sing aloud of that matchless wisdom which contrived—of that divine love which planned, and of that eternal grace which carried out the scheme of thy redemption. Awake, my *imagination,* and dance to the holy melody. Gather pictures from all worlds. Bid sun and moon stay in their courses, and join in thy new song. Constrain the stars to yield the music of the spheres ; put a tongue into every mountain, and a voice into every wilderness ; translate the lowing of the cattle and the scream of the eagle ; hear thou the praise of God in the rippling of the rills, the dashing of the cataracts, and the roaring of the sea, until all his works in all places of his dominion bless the Lord.

But especially let us cry to all the *graces of our spirit*—" awake." Wake up, my *love,* for thou must strike the key-note and lead the strain. Awake and sing unto thy beloved a song touching thy well-beloved. Give unto him choice canticles, for he is the fairest among ten thousand, and the altogether lovely. Come forth then with thy richest music, and praise the name which is as ointment poured forth. Wake up, my *hope,* and join hands with thy sister—love ; and sing of blessings yet to come. Sing of my dying hour, when he shall be with me on my couch. Sing of the rising morning,

6

when my body shall leap from its tomb into her Saviour's arms! Sing of the expected advent, for which thou lookest with delight! And, O my soul, sing of that heaven which he has gone before to prepare for thee, "that where he is, there may his people be." Awake my love—awake my hope—and thou my *faith*, awake also! Love has the sweetest voice, hope can thrill forth the higher notes of the sacred scale; but thou, O faith—with thy deep resounding bass melody—thou must complete the song. Sing of the promise sure and certain. Rehearse the glories of the covenant ordered in all things, and sure. Rejoice in the sure mercies of David! Sing of the goodness which shall be known to thee in all thy trials yet to come. Sing of that blood which has sealed and ratified every word of God. Glory in that eternal faithfulness which cannot lie, and of that truth which cannot fail. And thou, my *patience,* utter thy gentle but most gladsome hymn. Sing to-day of how he helped thee to endure in sorrows' bitterest hour. Sing of the weary way along which he has borne thy feet, and brought thee at last to lie down in green pastures, beside the still waters. Oh, all my graces, heaven-begotten as ye are, praise him who did beget you. Ye children of his grace, sing unto your Father's name, and magnify him who keeps you alive. Let all that in me is be stirred up to magnify and bless his holy name.

Then let us wake up the *energy* of all those powers—the energy of the body, the energy of the mind, the energy of the spirit. You know what it is to do a thing coldly, weakly. As well might we not praise at all. You know also what it is to praise God passionately—to throw energy into all the song, and so to exult in his name. So do ye, each one of you, this day; and if Michal, Saul's daughter, should look out of the window and see David dancing before the ark with all his might, and should chide you as though your praise were unseemly, say unto her, "It was before the Lord, which chose me before thy father, and before all his house, therefore will I play before the Lord:" 2 Samuel vi. 21. Tell the enemy that the God of election must be praised, that the God of redemption must be extolled,—that if the very heathen leaped for joy before their gods, surely they who bow before Jehovah must adore him with rapture and with ecstacy. Go forth, go forth with joy then, with all your energies thoroughly awakened for his praise.

2. But you say unto me, "WHY and wherefore should we this day awake and sing unto our God?" There be many reasons; and if your hearts be right, one may well satisfy Come, ye children of God, and bless his dear name; for *doth not all nature around you sing?* If you were silent, you would be an exception to the universe. Doth not the thunder praise him as it rolls like drums in the march of the God of armies? Doth not the ocean praise him as it claps its thousand hands? Doth not the sea roar, and the fulness thereof? Do not the mountains praise him when the shaggy woods upon their summits wave in adoration? Do not the lightnings write his name in letters of fire upon the midnight darkness? Doth not this world, in its unceasing revolutions, perpetually roll forth his praise? Hath not the whole earth a voice, and shall we be silent? Shall man, for whom the world was made, and suns and stars were created,—shall he be dumb? No, let him lead the strain. Let him be the world's high priest, and while the world shall be as the sacrifice, let him add his heart thereto, and thus supply the fire of love which shall make that sacrifice smoke towards heaven.

But, believer, *shall not thy God be praised?* I ask thee. Shall not *thy God be* praised? When men behold a hero, they fall at his feet and honour him. Garibaldi emancipates a nation, and lo, they bow before him and do him homage. And thou Jesus, the Redeemer of the multitudes of thine elect, shalt thou have no song? Shalt thou have no triumphal entry into our hearts? Shall thy name have no glory! Shall the world love its own, and shall not the Church honour its own Redeemer? Our God *must* be praised. He shall be. If no other heart should ever praise him, surely mine *must.* If creation should forget him, his redeemed must remember him. Tell us to be silent? Oh, we cannot. Bid us restrain our holy mirth? Indeed you bid us do an impossibility. He is God, and he must be extolled ; he is our God, our gracious, our tender, our faithful God, and he must have the best of our songs.

Thou sayest, believer, why should I praise him ? Let me ask thee a question too. *Is it not heaven's employment to praise him ?* And what can make earth more like heaven, than to bring down from heaven the employment of glory, and to be occupied with it here ! Come, believer, when thou prayest, thou art but a man, but when thou praisest, thou art as an angel. When thou asketh favour, thou art but a beggar, but when thou standest up to extol, thou becomest next of kin to cherubim and seraphim. Happy, happy day, when the glorious choristers shall find their numbers swelled by the addition of multitudes from earth ! Happy day when you and I shall join the eternal chorus. Let us begin the music here. Let us strike some of the first notes at least ; and if we cannot sound the full thunders of the eternal hallelujah, let us join as best we may. Let us make the wilderness and the solitary place rejoice, and bid the desert blossom as the rose.

Besides, Christian, dost thou not know that *it is a good thing for thee to praise thy God ?* Mourning weakens thee, doubts destroy thy strength ; thy groping among the ashes makes thee of the earth, earthy. Arise, for praise is pleasant and profitable to thee. "The joy of the Lord is our strength." "Delight thyself in the Lord and he will give thee the desire of thine heart." Thou growest in grace when thou growest in holy joy ; thou art more heavenly, more spiritual, more Godlike, as thou gettest more full of joy and peace in believing on the Lord Jesus Christ. I know some Christians are afraid of gladness, but I read, "Let the children of Zion be joyful in their King." If murmuring were a duty, some saints would never sin, and if mourning were commanded by God they would certainly be saved by works, for they are always sorrowing, and so they would keep his law. Instead thereof the Lord hath said it, "Rejoice in the Lord always, and again I say, rejoice ;" and he has added, to make it still more strong, "Rejoice evermore."

But I ask you one other question, believer. Thou sayest, "Why should I awake, this morning to sing unto my God ?" I reply to thee, *"Hast thou not a cause ?"* Hath he not done great things for thee, and art thou not glad thereof ? Hath he not taken thee out of the horrible pit, and out of the miry clay ; hath he not set thy feet upon a rock and established thy goings, and is there no new song in thy mouth ? What, art thou bought with blood, and yet hast thou a silent tongue ? Loved of thy God before the world began and yet not sing his praise ! What, art thou his child, an heir of God and joint heir with Jesus Christ, and yet no notes of gratitude ! What ! has he fed thee this day ? Did he deliver thee yesterday out of many troubles ? Has he been with thee these thirty, these forty, these fifty years in the wilderness, and yet hast thou no mercy for which to praise him ? O shame on thy ungrateful heart, and thy forgetful spirit ; come pluck up courage, think of thy mercies and not of thy miseries, forget thy pains awhile and think of thy many deliverances. Put thy feet on the neck of thy doubts and thy fears, and God the Holy Ghost, being thy Comforter, begin from this good hour to utter a song.

3. "But," saith one, "WHEN shall I do this ? When shall I praise my God ?" I answer, praise ye the Lord all his people, at all times, and give thanks at every remembrance of him. Extol him even when your souls are drowsy and your spirits are inclined to sleep. When we are awake there is little cause to say to us four times, "Awake, awake, awake, awake, utter a song ;" but when we feel most drowsy with sorrow and our eyelids are heavy, when afflictions sore are pressing us down to the very dust, then is the time to sing psalms unto our God and praise him in the very fire. But this takes much grace, and I trust brethren you know that there is much grace to be had. Seek it of your divine Lord, and be not content without it ; be not easily cast down by troubles, nor soon made silent because of your woes ; think of the martyrs of old, who sang sweetly at the stake ; think of Ann Askew, of all the pains she bore for Christ, and then of her courageous praise of God in her last

8

moments. Often she had been tortured, tortured most terribly; she lay in prison expecting death, and when there she wrote a verse in old English words and rhyme,

> " I am not she that lyst
> My anker to let fall,
> For every dryslynge myst;
> My shippe's substancyal."

Meaning thereby, that she would not stop her course and cast her anchor for every drizzling mist; she had a ship that could bear a storm, one that could break all the waves that beat against it, and joyously cut through the foam. So shall it be with you. Give not God fine weather songs, give him black tempest praises; give him not merely summer music, as some birds will do and then fly away; give him winter tunes. Sing in the night like the nightingales, praise him in the fires, sing his high praises even in the shadow of death, and let the tomb resound with the shouts of your sure confidence. So may you give to God what God may well claim at your hands.

When shall you praise him? Why, praise him when you are full of doubts, even when temptations assail you, when poverty hovers round you, and when sickness bows you down. They are cheap songs which we give to God when we are rich; it is easy enough to kiss the hand of a giving God, but to bless him when he takes away—this is to bless him indeed. To cry like Job, "though he slay me yet will I trust in him," or to sing like Habukkuk, "Although the fig tree shall not blossom, neither shall fruit be in the vines; the labour of the olive shall fail, and the fields shall yield no meat: the flocks shall be cut off from the fold, and there shall be no herd in the stalls: yet will I rejoice in the Lord, I will joy in the God of my salvation." Oh Christian, thou askest me when thou shalt rejoice, I say *to-day*, "Awake, awake, O Deborah, awake, awake, utter a song."

4. Yet once more, you reply to me, "But HOW can I praise my God?" I will be teacher of music to thee, and may the Comforter be with me. Wilt thou think this morning how great are thy mercies. Thou art not blind, nor deaf, nor dumb; thou art not a lunatic; thou art not decrepid; thou art not vexed with piercing pains; thou art not full of agony caused by disease; thou art not going down to the grave; thou art not in torments, not in hell. Thou art still in the land of the living, the land of love, the land of grace, the land of hope. Even if this were all, there were enough reason for thee to praise thy God. Thou art not this day what thou once wert, a blasphemer, a persecutor and injurious; the song of the drunkard is not on thy lips, the lascivious desire is not in thy heart. And is not this a theme for praise. Remember but a little while ago, with very many of you, all these sins were your delight and your joy. Oh! must not you praise him, ye chief of sinners, whose natures have been changed, whose hearts have been renewed. Ye sons of Korah, lead the sacred song! Bethink you of your iniquities, which have all been put away, and your transgressions covered, and none of them laid to your charge; think of the privileges you this day enjoy; elect, redeemed, called, justified, sanctified, adopted, and preserved in Christ Jesus. Why man, if a stone or rock could but for a moment have such privileges as these, the very adamant must melt and the dumb rock give forth hosannas. And will you be still when your mercies are so great? Let them not lie—"Forgotten in unthankfulness, and without praises die." Bethink thee yet again how little are thy trials after all. Thou hast not yet resisted unto blood striving against sin. Thou art poor, it is true, but then thou art not sick; or thou art sick, but still thou art not left to wallow in sin; and all afflictions are but little when once sin is put away. Compare thy trials with those of many who live in thine own neighbourhood. Put thy sufferings side by side with the sufferings of some whom thou hast seen on their dying bed; compare thy lot with that of the martyrs who have entered into their rest; and oh I say, thou wilt be compelled to exclaim

with Paul, " These light afflictions which are but for a moment are not worthy to be compared to the glory which shall be revealed in us." Come, now, I beseech you, brethren, by the mercies of God, be of good cheer, and rejoice in the Lord your God, if it were for no other reason than that of the brave-hearted Luther. When he had been most slandered—when the Pope had launched out a new bull, and when the kings of the earth had threatened him fiercely—Luther would gather together his friends, and say, " Come let us sing a psalm and spite the devil." He would ever sing the most psalms when the world roared the most. Let us to-day join in that favourite psalm of the great German, "God is our refuge and strength, a very present help in trouble. Therefore will we not fear, though the earth be removed and though the mountains be carried in the midst of the sea ; though the waters thereof roar and be troubled, though the mountains shake with the swelling thereof."—Psalm xlvi. I say, then, sing to make Satan angry. He has vexed the saints ; let us vex him.

Praise ye the Lord to put the world to the blush. Never let it be said that the world can make its votaries more happy than Christ can make his followers. Oh, let your songs be so continual, and so sweet, that the wicked may be compelled to say, "That man's life *is* happier than mine ; I long to exchange with him. There is a something in his religion which my sin and my wicked pleasures can never afford me." O praise the Lord ye saints, that sinners' mouths may be set a watering after the things of God. Specially praise him in your trials, if you would make the world wonder—strike sinners dumb, and make them long to know and taste the joys of which you are a partaker.

" Alas !" said one, " but I cannot sing ; I have nothing to sing of, nothing without for which I could praise God." It is remarked by old commentators that the windows of Solomon's temple were narrow on the outside, but that they were broad within, and that they were so cut, that though they seemed to be but small openings, yet the light was well diffused. (See Hebrew of 1 Kings vi. 4.) So is it with the windows of a believer's joy. They may look very narrow without, but they are very wide within ; there is more joy to be gotten from that which is within us than from that which is without us. God's grace within, God's love, the witness of his Spirit in our hearts, are better themes of joy than all the corn and wine, and oil, with which God sometimes increases his saints. So if thou hast no outward mercies, sing of inward mercies. If the water fail without, go to that *fons perennis*, that perpetual fountain which is within thine own soul. "A good man shall be satisfied from himself." Prov. xiv. 14. When thou seest no cheering providence without, yet look at grace within. " Awake, awake, Deborah ! awake, awake, utter a song."

II. I now turn to the second part of my subject, upon which very briefly. I know not whether you feel as I do, but in preaching upon this theme, I mourn a scantiness of words, and a slowness of language. If I could let my heart talk without my lips, methinks with God's Spirit I could move you indeed with joy. But these lips find that the language of the heart is above them. The tongue discovereth that it cannot reach the fulness of joy that is within. Let it beam from my face, if it cannot be spoken from my mouth.

And now the second part of the subject. " ARISE, BARAK, AND LEAD THY CAPTIVITY CAPTIVE, THOU SON OF ABINOAM."

You understand the exact picture here. Barak had routed Sisera, Jabin's captain, and all his hosts. She now exhorts Barak to celebrate his triumph. "Mount, mount thy car, O Barak, and ride through the midst of the people. Let the corpse of Sisera, with Jael's nail driven through its temples, be dragged behind thy chariot. Let the thousand captives of the Canaanites walk all of them with their arms bound behind them. Drive before thee the ten thousand flocks of sheep, and herds of cattle which thou hast taken as a spoil. Let their chariots of iron, and all their horses be led captive in grand procession. Bring up all the treasures and the jewels of which thou hast stripped the slain ; their armour, their shields, their spears, bound up as glorious trophies. Arise, Barak, lead captive those who led thee captive, and celebrate thy glorious victory."

Beloved, this is a picture which is often used in Scripture. Christ is said to have led captivity captive, when he ascended on high. He led principalities and powers captive at his chariot-wheels. But here is a picture for us—not concerning Christ, but concerning ourselves. We are exhorted to-day to lead captivity captive. Come up, come up, ye great hosts of *sins*, once my terror and dismay. Long was I your slave, O ye Egyptian tyrants ; long did this back smart beneath your lash when conscience was awakened, and long did these members of my body yield themselves as willing servants to obey your dictates. Come up ye sins, come up for ye are prisoners now ; ye are bound in fetters of iron, nay, more than this, ye are utterly slain, consumed, destroyed ; you have been covered with Jesu's blood ; ye have been blotted out by his mercy ; ye have been cast by his power into the depths of the sea, yet would I bid your ghosts come up, slain though ye be, and walk in grim procession behind my chariot. Arise, celebrate your triumph, oh ye people of God. Your sins are many, but they are all forgiven. Your iniquities are great, but they are all put away. Arise and lead captive those who led you captive—your blasphemies, your forgetfulness of God, your drunkenness, your lust, all the vast legion that once oppressed you. They are all clean destroyed. Come and look upon them, sing their death psalm, and chant the life psalm of your grateful joy ; lead your sins captive this very day.

Bring hither in bondage another host who once seemed too many for us, but whom by God's grace we have totally overcome. Arise my *trials ;* ye have been very great and very numerous ; ye came against me as a great host, and ye were tall and strong like the sons of Anak. Oh ! my soul, thou hast trodden down strength ; by the help of our God have we leaped over a wall ; by his power have we broken through the troops of our troubles, our difficulties, and our fears. Come now, look back, and think of all the trials you have ever encountered. Death in your family ; losses in your business ; afflictions in your body ; despair in your soul ; and yet here you are, more than conquerors over them all. Come, bid them all walk now in procession. To the God of our deliverances—who has delivered us out of deep waters—who has brought us out of the burning, fiery furnace, so that not the smell of fire has passed upon us—to him be all the glory, while we lead our captivity captive.

Arise and let us lead captive all our *temptations.* You, my brethren, have been foully tempted to the vilest sins. Satan has shot a thousand darts at you, and hurled his javelin multitudes of times ; bring out the darts and snap them before his eyes, for he has never been able to reach your heart. Come, break the bow and cut the spear in sunder ; burn the chariot in the fire. "Thy right hand, O Lord, thy right hand O Lord, hath dashed in pieces the enemy ; thou hast broken, thou hast put to confusion them that hated us ; thou hast scattered the tempters, and driven them far away." Come, ye children of God, kept and preserved where so many have fallen, lead now this day your temptations captive.

I think that you as a church, and I as your minister, can indeed lead captivity captive this day. There has been no single church of God existing in England for these fifty years which has had to pass through more trial than we have done. We can say, " Men did ride over our heads." We went through fire and through water, and what has been the result of it all ? God hath brought us out into a wealthy place and set our feet in a large room, and all the devices of the enemy have been of none effect. Scarce a day rolls over my head in which the most villainous abuse, the most fearful slander is not uttered against me both privately and by the public press ; every engine is employed to put down God's minister—every lie that man can invent is hurled at me. But hitherto the Lord hath helped me. I have never answered any man, nor spoken a word in my own defence, from the first day even until now. And the effect has been this: God's people have believed nothing against me: they who feared the Lord have said often as a new falsehood has been uttered, " This is not true concerning that man ; he will not answer for himself, but God will answer for him." They have not checked our usefulness as a church ; they have not thinned our congregations ; that which was to be but a spasm—an enthusiasm which it was hoped would only last an hour—God has daily increased ; not because of me, but because of that gospel which I preach ; not because there was anything in me, but because I came out as the exponent of plain, straight-forward, honest Calvinism, and because I seek to speak the Word simply, not according to the critical dictates of man, but so that the poor may comprehend what I have to say. The Lord has helped us as a church ; everything has contributed to help us ; the great and terrible catastrophe invented by Satan to overturn us, was only blessed of God to swell the stream ; and now I would not stay a liar's mouth if I could, nor would I stop a slanderer if it were in my power, except it were that he might not sin, for all these things tend to our profit, and all these attacks do but widen the stream of usefulness. Many a sinner has been converted to God in this hall who was first brought here, because of some strange anecdote, some lying tale which had been told of God's servant, the minister. I say it boasting in the Lord my God, this morning, though I become a fool in glorying, I do lead in God's name my captivity captive. Arise ! arise ! ye members of this church, ye who have followed the son of Barak, and have gone up as the thousands at his feet ; arise and triumph for God is with us, and his cause shall prosper ; his own right arm is made bare in the eyes of all the people, and all the ends of the earth shall see the salvation of our God.

As it is in this single church, and in our own individual sphere, so shall it be in the church at large. God's ministers are all attacked ; God's truth is everywhere assailed. A terrible battle awaits us ; but oh ! Church of God, remember thy former victories. Awake, ministers of Christ, and lead your captivity captive. Sing how the idols of Greece tottered before you. Say, " Where is Diana ? Where now the gods that made glad Ephesus of old ?" And thou, O Rome, was not thine arm broken before the majesty of the Church's might ? Where now is Jupiter, where Saturn, where Venus ? They have ceased to be. And thou Juggernaut—thou Bramah—ye Gods of China and Hindostan—ye too must fall, for this day the sons of Jehovah arise and lead their captivity captive. " Come, behold the works of the Lord, what desolations he hath made in the earth. He breaketh the bow, he cutteth the spear in sunder ; he burneth the chariots in the fire. Be still and know that I am God ; I will be exalted among the heathen ; I will be exalted in the earth." Church of God, come forth with songs, come forth with shouting to your last battle. Behold the battle of Armageddon draweth nigh. Blow ye the silver trumpets for the fight, ye soldiers of the cross. Come on, come on, ye leagured hosts of hell. Strong in the strength of God most High, we shall dash back your ranks as the rock breaketh the waves of the sea. We shall stand against you and triumph, and tread you down as ashes under the soles of our feet. " Arise, Barak, and lead thy captivity captive, thou son of Abinoam."

Would to God that the joy of heart which we feel this morning may tempt some soul to seek the like. It is to be found in Christ at the foot of his dear cross. Believe on him, sinner, and thou art saved.

2. The Power of Prayer and the Pleasure of Praise

" Ye also helping together by prayer for us, that for the gift bestowed upon us by the means of many persons thanks may be given by many on our behalf. For our rejoicing in this, the testimony of our conscience, that in simplicity and godly sincerity, not with fleshly wisdom, but by the grace of God, we have had our conversation in the world, and more abundantly to you-ward."—2 Corinthians, i. 11, 12.

THE apostle Paul had, by singular providences, been delivered from imminent peril in Asia. During the great riot at Ephesus, when Demetrius and his fellow shrine-makers raised a great tumult against him, because they saw that their craft was in danger, Paul's life was greatly in jeopardy, so that he writes, "We were pressed out of measure, above strength, insomuch that we despaired even of life.' The apostle attributes to God alone his singular preservation; and if he referred also to the occasion when he was stoned and left for dead, there is much appropriateness in his blessing " God which raised the dead." The apostle, moreover, argues from the fact that God had thus delivered him in the past, and was still his helper in the present, that he would be with him also in the future. Paul is a master at all arithmetic, his faith was always a ready-reckoner, we here find him computing by the believer's *Rule of Three* ; he argues from the past to the present, and from the present to things yet to come. The verse preceding our text is a brilliant example of this arriving at a comfortable conclusion by the *Rule of Three*— "Who delivered us from so great a death, and doth deliver : in whom we trust that he will yet deliver us." Because our God is " the same yesterday, to-day, and for ever ;" his love in time past is an infallible assurance of his kindness to-day, and an equally certain pledge of his faithfulness on the morrow ; whatever our circumstances may be, however perplexed may be our pathway, and however dark our horizon, yet if we argue by the rule of " he hath, he doth, he will," our comfort can never be destroyed. Courage, then, O ye afflicted seed of Israel ; if ye had a changeable God to deal with, your souls might be full of bitterness, but because he is " the same yesterday, to-day, and for ever," every repeated manifestation of his grace should make it more easy for you to rest upon him ; every renewed experience of his fidelity should confirm your confidence in his grace. May the most blessed Spirit teach us to grow in holy confidence in our ever-faithful Lord.

Although our apostle thus acknowledged God's hand, and God's hand alone, in his deliverance, yet he was not so foolish as to deny or under-value the second causes. On the contrary, having first praised the God of all comfort, he now remembers with gratitude the earnest prayers of the many loving intercessors. Gratitude to God must never become an excuse for ingratitude to man. It is true that Jehovah shielded the apostle of the Gentiles, but he did it in answer to prayer: the chosen vessel was not broken by the rod of the wicked, for the out-stretched hand of the God of heaven was his defence, but that hand was out-stretched because the people of Corinth and the saints of God every-where had prevailed at the throne of grace by their united supplications. With gratitude those successful pleadings are mentioned in the text, "Ye also helping together by prayer for us," and he desires the brethren now to unite their praises with his, "that for the gift bestowed upon us by the means of many persons thanks may be given by many on our behalf," for he adds that he has a claim upon their love, since he was not as some who were unfaithful to their trust, but his conscience was clear that he had preached the Word simply and with sincerity.

While speaking upon these topics may the anointing Spirit now descend to make them profitable to us. We shall, first, *acknowledge the power of united prayer;* secondly, *excite you to united praise;* and then, in the third place, *urge our joyful claim upon you—a claim which is not our's alone, but belongs to all ministers of God who in sincerity labour for souls.*

I. First, then, dear friends, it is my duty and my privilege this morning to ACKNOWLEDGE THE POWER OF UNITED PRAYER.

It has pleased God to make prayer the abounding and rejoicing river through which most of our choice mercies flow to us. It is the golden key which unlocks the well-stored granaries of our heavenly Joseph. It is written upon each of the mercies of the covenant, "For this will I be inquired of by the house of Israel to do it for them." There are mercies which come unsought, for God is found of them that sought not for him; but there are other favours which are only bestowed upon the men who ask, and therefore receive; who seek, and therefore find; who knock, and therefore gain an entrance. Why God has been pleased to command us to pray at all it is not difficult to discover, for prayer *glorifies God,* by putting man in the humblest posture of worship. The creature in prayer acknowledges his Creator with reverence, and con-fesses him to be the giver of every good and perfect gift; the eye is lifted up to behold the glory of the Lord, while the knee is bent to the earth in the lowliness of acknowledged weakness. Though prayer is not the high-est mode of adoration, or otherwise it would be continued by the saints in heaven, yet it is the most humble, and so the most fitting, to set forth the glory of the perfect One as it is beheld by imperfect flesh and blood. From the "Our Father," in which we claim relationship, right on to "the kingdom, and the power, and the glory," which we ascribe to the only true God, every sentence of prayer honours the Most High. The groans and tears of humble petitioners are as truly acceptable as the continual "Holy, holy, holy," of the Cherubim and Seraphim; for in their very essence all truthful confessions of personal fault are but a homage paid to the infinite perfections of the Lord of hosts. More honoured is the Lord by our prayers than by the unceasing smoke of the holy incense of the altar which stood before the veil. Moreover, the act of prayer *teaches us our unworthiness*, which is no small blessing to such proud beings as we are. If God gave us favours without constraining us to pray for them we should never know how poor we are, but a true prayer is an inventory of wants, a catalogue of necessities, a suit *in formâ pauperis*, an exposure of secret wounds, a revelation of hidden poverty. While it is an application to divine wealth, it is a confession of human emptiness. I believe that the most healthy state of a Christian is to be always empty, and always depending upon the Lord for supplies; to be always poor in self and rich in Jesus; weak as water personally, but mighty through God to do great exploits; and hence the use of prayer, because while it adores God, it lays the creature where he should be, in the very dust. Prayer is in itself, apart from the answer which it brings, a great benefit to the Christian. As the runner gains strength for the race by daily exercise, so for the great race of life we acquire energy by the hallowed labour of prayer. Prayer plumes the wings of God's young eaglets, that they may learn to mount above the clouds. Prayer girds the loins of God's warriors, and sends them forth to combat with their sinews braced and their muscles firm. An earnest pleader cometh out of his closet, even as the sun ariseth from the chambers of the east, rejoicing like a strong man to run his race. Prayer is that uplifted hand of Moses which routs the Amalekites more than the sword of Joshua ; it is the arrow shot from the chamber of the prophet foreboding defeat to the Syrians. What if I say that prayer clothes the believer with the attributes of Deity, girds human weakness with divine strength, turns human folly into heavenly wisdom, and gives to troubled mortals the serenity of the immortal God. I know not what prayer cannot do ! I thank thee, great God, for the mercy-seat, a choice gift of thy marvellous lovingkindness. Help us to use it aright !

As many mercies are conveyed from heaven in the ship of prayer, so *there are many choice and special favours which can only be brought to us by the fleets of united prayer*. Many are the good things which God will give to his lonely Elijahs and Daniels, but if two of you agree as touching anything that ye shall ask, there is no limit to God's bountiful answers. Peter might never have been brought out of prison if it had not been that prayer was made without ceasing by *all* the Church for him. Pentecost might never have come if *all* the disciples had not been "with one accord in one place," waiting for the descent of the tongues of fire. God is pleased to give many mercies to one pleader, but at times he seems to say—"Ye shall all appear before me and entreat my favour, for I will not see your face, unless even your younger brethren be with you." Why is this, dear friends ? I take it that thus our gracious Lord sets forth his own esteem for the communion of saints. "I believe in the communion of saints" is one article of the great Christian creed, but how few there are who understand it. Oh! there is such a thing as real union among God's people. We may be called by different names—

> "But all the servants of our King
> In heaven and earth are one."

We cannot afford to lose the help and love of our brethren. Augustine says—"The poor are made for the rich and the rich are made for the poor." I do not doubt but that strong saints are made for weak saints, and that the weak saints bring special benedictions upon the full-grown believers. There is a fitness in the whole body; each joint owes something to every other, and the whole body is bound together and compacted by that which every joint supplieth. There are certain glands in the human body which the anatomist hardly understands. He can say of the liver, for instance, that it yields a very valuable fluid of the utmost value in the bodily economy, but there are other secretions whose distinct value he cannot ascertain; yet, doubtless, if that gland were removed, the whole body might suffer to a high degree: and so, beloved friends, there may be some believers of whom we may say—"I do not know the use of them; I cannot tell what good that Christian does; yet were that insignificant and apparently useless member removed, the whole body might be made to suffer, the whole frame might become sick and the whole heart faint." This is probably the reason why many a weighty gift of heaven's love is only granted to combined petitioning—that we may perceive the use of the whole body, and so may be compelled to recognize the real vital union which divine grace has made and daily maintains among the people of God. Is it not a happy thought, dear friends, that the very poorest and most obscure Church-member can add something to the body's strength. We cannot all preach; we cannot all rule; we cannot all give gold and silver, but we can all contribute our prayers. There is no convert, though he but two or three days old in grace, but can pray. There is no bed-ridden sister in Jesus who cannot pray; there is no sick, aged, imbecile, obscure, illiterate, or penniless believer, who cannot add his supplications to the general stock. This is the Church's riches. We put boxes at the door that we may receive your offerings to God's cause—remember there is a spiritual chest within the Church, into which we should all drop our loving intercessions, as into the treasury of the Lord. Even the widow, without her two mites, can give her offering to this treasury. See, then, dear friends, what union and communion there are among the people of God, since there are certain mercies which are only bestowed when the saints unitedly pray. How we ought to feel this bond of union! How we ought to pray for one another! How, as often as the Church meets together for supplication, should we all make it our bounden duty to be there! I would that some of you who are absent from the prayer-meeting upon any little excuse would reflect how much you rob us all. The prayer-meeting is an invaluable institution, ministering strength to all other meetings and agencies. Are there not many of you who might by a little pinching of your time and pressing of your labours come among us a little oftener? And what if you should lose a customer now and then, do you not think that this loss could be well made up to you by your gains on other days? Or if not so, would not the spiritual profit much more than counterbalance any little temporal loss? "Not forgetting the assembling of yourselves together as the manner of some is."

We are now prepared for a further observation. *This united prayer should specially be made for the ministers of God.* It is for them peculiarly that this public prayer is intended. Paul asks for it—"Brethren, pray for us;" and all God's ministers to the latest time will ever confess that this is the secret source of their strength. The prayers of the people must be the might of the ministers. Shall I try to show you why the minister more than any other man in the Church needs the earnest prayers of the people? Is not *his position the most perilous?* Satan's orders to the hosts of hell are—"Fight neither with small nor great, save only with the ministers of God." He knows if he can once smite through the heart one of these, there will be a general confusion, for if the champion be dead, then the people fly. It is around the standard-bearer that the fight is thickest. There the battle-axes ring upon the helmets; there the arrows are bent upon the armour, for the foeman knows that if he can cut down the standard, or cleave the skull of its bearer, he will strike a heavy blow and cause deep discouragement. Press around us, then, ye men at arms! Knights of the red cross rally for our defence, for the fight grows hot. We beseech you if you elect us to the office of the ministry, stand fast at our side in our hourly conflicts. I noticed on returning from Rotterdam, when we were crossing the bar at the mouth of the Maas, where by reason of a neap tide and a bad wind the navigation was exceedingly dangerous, that orders were issued—"All hands on deck!" So methinks the life of a minister is so perilous, that I may well cry—"All hands on deck;" every man to prayer; let even the weakest saint become instant in supplication. The minister, standing in such a perilous position, has, moreover, *a solemn weight of responsibility resting on him.* Every man should be his brother's keeper in a measure, but woe to the watchmen of God if they be not faithful, for at their hands shall the blood of souls be required; at their door shall God lay the ruin of men if they preach not the gospel fully and faithfully. There are times when this burden of the Lord weighs upon God's ministers until they cry out in pain as if their hearts would burst with anguish. I marked the captain as we crossed that bar throwing the lead himself into the sea; and when one asked why he did not let the sailors do it, he said, "At this point, just now, I dare not trust any man but myself to heave the lead, for we have hardly six inches between our ship and the bottom." And, indeed, we felt the vessel touch once or twice most unpleasantly. So there will come times with every preacher of the gospel, if he be what he should be, when he will be in dread suspense for his hearers, and will not be able to discharge his duty by proxy, but must personally labour for men, not even trusting himself to preach, but calling upon his God for help since he is now overwhelmed with the burden of men's souls. Oh, do pray for us. If God gives us to you and if you accept the gift most cheerfully, do not so despise both God and us as to leave us penniless and poverty-stricken because your prayers are withheld. Moreover, the preservation of the minister *is one of the most important objects to the Church.* You may lose a sailor from the ship, and that is very bad, both for him and for you; but if the pilot should fall over, or the captain should be smitten with sickness, or the helmsman be washed from the wheel, then what is the vessel to do? Therefore, though prayer is to be put up for every other person in the

17

Church, yet for the minister is it to be offered first and foremost, be-cause of the position which he occupies. And then, *how much more is asked of him than of you?* If you are to keep a private table for indi-vidual instruction, he is, as it were, to keep a public table, a feast of good things for all comers; and how shall he do this unless his Master give him rich provisions? You are to shine as a candle in a house: the minister has to be as a lighthouse to be seen far across the deep, and how shall he shine the whole night long unless he be trimmed by his Master, and fresh oil be given, him from heaven? His influence is wider than yours: if it be for evil, he shall be a deadly upas, with spreading boughs poisoning all beneath his shadow; but if God make him a star in his right hand, his ray of light shall cheer with its genial influence whole nations and whole periods of time. If there be any truth in all this, I implore you yield us generously and constantly the assistance of your prayers.

I find that in the original, the word for "helping together," implies very earnest WORK. Some people's prayers have no work in them; but the only prayer which prevails with God is a real working-man's prayer—where the petitioner, like a Samson, shakes the gates of mercy, and labours to pull them up rather than be denied an entrance. We do not want finger-end prayers, which only touch the burden, we need shoulder-prayers, which bear a load of earnestness and are not to be denied their desire. We do not want those dainty run-away knocks at the door of mercy, which professors give when they show off at prayer-meetings, but we ask for the knocking of a man who means to have, and means to stop at mercy's gate till it opens and all his need shall be supplied. The energetic, vehement violence of the man who is not to be denied, but intends to carry heaven by storm until he wins his heart's desire—this is the prayer which ministers covet of their people. Melancthon, it is said, derived great comfort from the information that certain poor weavers, women and children, had met together to pray for the Reformation. Yes, Melancthon, there was solid ground for comfort here. Depend on it, it was not Luther only, but the thousands of poor persons who sung psalms at the plough-tail, and the hundreds of serving men and women who offered supplications, that made the Reformation what it was. We are told of Paulus Phagius, a celebrated Hebrew scholar, very useful in introducing the Reformation into this country, that one of his frequent requests of his younger scholars, was that they would continue in prayer, so that God might be pleased to pour out a blessing in answer to them. Have I not said a hundred times, that all the blessing that God has given us here, all the increase to our Church, has been due, under God, to your earnest, fer-vent supplications? There have been heaven-moving seasons both in this house and at New Park Street. We have had times when we have felt we could die sooner than not be heard; when we carried our Church on our bosom as a mother carrieth her child; when we felt a yearning and a travailing in birth for the souls of men. "What hath God wrought?" we may truly say, when we see our Church daily increasing, and the multitudes still hanging upon our lips to listen to the Word. Shall we now cease from our prayers? Shall we now say unto the

Great High Priest, "It is enough?" Shall we now pluck the glowing coals from the altar and quench the burning incense? Shall we now refuse to bring the morning and evening lambs of prayer and praise to the sacrifice? O children of Ephraim, being armed and carrying bows, will ye turn your backs in the day of battle? The flood is divided before you; the Jordan is driven back; will you refuse to march through the depths? God, even your God, goeth up before you; the shout of a King is heard in the midst of your hosts; will you now be recreant and refuse to go up and possess the land? Will you now lose your first love? Shall "Ichabod" be written upon the forefront of this tabernacle? Shall it be said that God hath forsaken you? Shall the day come in which the daughters of Philistia shall rejoice and the sons of Syria shall triumph? If not, to your knees again, with all the force of prayer! If not, to your vehement supplications once more! If not, if you would not see good blighted and evil triumphant, clasp hands again, and in the name of him who ever liveth to intercede, once more be prevalent in prayer that the blessing may again descend. " Ye also helping together by prayer for us."

II. We must now EXCITE YOU TO PRAISE.

Praise should always follow answered prayer; the mist of earth's gratitude should rise as the sun of heaven's love warms the ground. Hath the Lord been gracious to thee, and inclined his ear to the voice of thy supplication? Then praise him as long as thou livest. Deny not a song to him who hath answered thy prayer and given thee the desire of thy heart. To be silent over God's mercies is to incur the guilt of shocking ingratitude, and ingratitude is one of the worst of crimes. I trust, dear friends, you will not act as basely as the nine lepers, who after they had been healed of their leprosy, returned not to give thanks unto the healing Lord. To forget to praise God, is to refuse to benefit ourselves, for praise, like prayer, is exceedingly useful to the spiritual man. It is a high and healthful exercise. To dance, like David, before the Lord, is to quicken the blood in the veins and make the pulse beat at a healthier rate. Praise gives to us a great feast, like that of Solomon, who gave to every man a good piece of flesh and a flagon of wine. Praise is the most heavenly of Christian duties. The angels pray not, but they cease not to praise both day and night. To bless God for mercies received is to benefit our fellow-men; "the humble shall hear thereof and be glad." Others who have been in like circumstances, shall take comfort if we can say, "Oh! magnify the Lord with me, and let us exalt his name together; this poor man cried, and the Lord heard him." Tongue-tied Christians are a sad dishonour to the Church. We have some such, some whom the devil has gagged, and the loudest music they ever make is when they are champing the bit of their silence. I would, my brethren, that in all such cases the tongue of the dumb may sing.

To go a step further here. As praise is good and pleasant, blessing man and glorifying God, *united praise has a very special commendation.* United praise is like music in concert. The sound of one instrument is exceeding sweet, but when hundreds of instruments, both wind and stringed, are all combined. then the orchestra sendeth forth a noble

19

volume of harmony. The praise of one Christian is accepted before God like a grain of incense; but the praise of many is like a censer ful' of frankincense smoking up before the Lord. Combined praise is an anticipation of heaven, for in that general assembly they altogether with one heart and voice praise the Lord.

> " Ten thousand thousand are their tongues,
> But all their joys are one."

Public praise is very agreeable to the Christian himself. How many burdens has it removed ; I am sure when I hear the shout of praise in this house it warms my heart. It is at times a little too slow for my taste, and I must urge you to quicken your pace, that the rolling waves of majestic praise may display their full force, yet with all drawbacks, to my heart there is no music like yours. My Dutch friends praise the Lord so very slowly that one might very well go to sleep, lulled by their lengthened strains. Even there, however, the many voices make a grand harmony of praise. I love to hear God's people sing when they really do sing, not when it is a *drawling* out somewhere between harmony and discord. O for a sacred song, a shout of lofty praise in which every man's soul beats the time, and every man's tongue sounds the tune, and each singer feels a high ambition to excel his fellow in gratitude and love. There is something exceedingly delightful in the union of true hearts in the worship of God, and when these hearts are expressed in song, how sweet the charming sounds. I think we ought to have a praise-meeting once a week. We have a prayer meeting every Monday, and a prayer-meeting every Saturday, and a prayer-meeting every morning, but why do we not have a *praise-meeting?* Surely seasons should be set apart for services made up of praise from beginning to end. Let us try the plan at once.

As I said about united prayer, that it should be offered specially for ministers, *so should united praise often take the same aspect*, the whole company should praise and bless God for the mercy rendered to the Church through its pastors. Hear how our apostle puts it again—" That for the gift bestowed upon us by the means of many persons, thanks may be given by many on our behalf." Brethren, we ought to praise God for good ministers *that they live*, for when they die much of their work dies with them. It is astonishing how a reformation will press on while Luther and Calvin live, and how it will cease directly the reformers die. The spirits of good men are immortal only in a sense. The Churches of God in this age are like the Israelites in the times of the judges, when the judges died they went after graven images again. And it is so now. While God spares the man the Church prospers, but when the man dies the zeal which he blew to a flame smoulders among the ashes. In nine cases out of ten, if not in ninety-nine out of every hundred, the prosperity of a Church rests on the minister's life. God so ordains it to humble us. There should be gratitude, then, for spared life ; but there should be great gratitude for *preserved character*, for oh! when a minister falls, what a disgrace it is ! Why, when you read in the police-reports the sad case of the Rev. Mr. ———, who chose to call himself a Baptist minister, everybody says, " What a shocking thing !

what a bad set the Baptists must be." Now, any fool in the world may call himself a Baptist minister. Our liberty is so complete that no law or order exists. Any man who can get a dozen to hear him, is a minister at least to them; therefore you cannot suppose but what there will be some hypocrites who will take the name in order to get some sort of reputation. If the true minister be kept, and made to hold fast his integrity, there should be constant gratitude to God on his behalf. If the minister be kept *well supplied with goodly matter;* if he be like a springing well; if God give him to bring out of his treasury things both new and old to feed his people, there should be hearty thanks. And if he be kept *sound,* if he go not aside to philosophy on the one hand, nor to a narrowness of doctrine on the other, there should be thanksgiving there. If God give to the masses the will to hear him, and above all, if souls be converted, and saints be edified, there should be never-ceasing honour and praise to God. Ah! I am talking now about what you all know, and you just nod your heads to it, and think there is not much in it, but if you were made to live in Holland for a little time you would soon appreciate these remarks. While travelling there, I stayed in houses with godly men, men of God with whom I could hold sweet communion, who cannot attend what was once their place of worship. Why not? "Sir," they say, "can I go to a place of worship when the most of the ministers deny every word of Scripture; not those of the Reformed Church only, but of every sect in Holland; how can I listen to the traitors who swear to the Calvinistic or Lutheran articles, and then go into the pulpit and deny the reality of the resurrection, or assert that the ascension of Jesus is a mere spiritual parable?" I find that in the Netherlands they are fifty years in advance of us in infidelity. We shall soon catch up with them if gentlemen of a certain school I know of are suffered to multiply. The Dutch divines have taken great strides in Neologianism, till now the people love the truth, and there are multitudes that are willing to hear it, but these are compelled absolutely to refuse to go to church at all, lest by any means they should give countenance to the heretical and false doctrines which are preached to them every Sabbath-day. Ah! if God were once to take away from England the ministers who preach the gospel boldly and plainly, you would cry to God to give you the candlestick back again. We may indeed say of England—

"With all thy faults I love thee still."

We have a colonial bishop who avows his unbelief; we have a few men of all denominations who are quietly sliding from the truth; but thank God they are nothing as yet; they are but as a drop in a bucket compared to the Churches of Christ, and those among us who are not quite as Calvinistic as we might wish, I thank God, never dispute the inspiration of Scripture, nor doubt the great truth of justification by faith. We have still preserved amongst us men that are faithful to God, and preach the whole truth as it is in Jesus. Be thankful for your ministers, I say again, for if you were placed where some believers are, you would cry out to your God—"Lord, send us back thy prophets; send us a famine of bread or a famine of water, but send us not a famine of the Word of God!"

I ask for myself this morning, as your minister, your thanksgivings

21

to be mingled with mine in praising God for the help which he has vouchsafed to me in the very arduous work of the last fortnight. Praise be to God for the acceptance which he gave me in that country among all ranks of the people. I speak to his praise, and not to mine, for this has been a vow with me; that if God will give me a harvest, I will not have an ear of corn of it, but he shall have it all. I found in all the places where I went great multitudes of people; crowds who could not understand the preacher, but who wanted to see his face, because God had blessed his translated sermons to their souls; multitudes who gave me the grip of brotherly kindness, and, with tears in their eyes, invoked, in the Dutch language, every blessing upon my head. I hoped to preach to some fifties and hundreds, and instead of that there were so many that the great cathedrals were not too large. This surprised me and made me glad, and caused me to rejoice in God, and I ask you to rejoice with me. I thank God for the acceptance which he gave me among all ranks of the people. While the poor crowded to shake hands, till they almost pulled me in pieces, it pleased God to move the heart of the Queen of Holland to send for me, and for an hour and a quarter I was privileged to talk with her concerning the things which make for our peace. I sought no interview with her, but it was her own wish; and then I lifted up my soul to God that I might talk of nothing but Christ, and might preach to her of nothing but Jesus; and so it pleased the Master to help me, and I left that very amiable lady, not having shunned to declare the whole counsel of God. Gratified was I, indeed, to find myself received cordially by all denominations, so that on the Saturday at Amsterdam I preached in the Mennonite Church in the morning, and at the Old Dutch Reformed Church in the evening; the next Sunday morning in the English Presbyterian Church, and then again in the evening in the Dutch Free Church; sometimes in the great cathedrals, as in the Dom Kirk, at Utrecht, and in Peter's Kirk, at Leyden, not having the poor only, but the nobility and the gentry of the land, who of course could understand English better than most of the poor, who have had no opportunity of learning it. I felt while going from town to town the Master helping me continually to preach. I never knew such elasticity of spirit, such bounding of heart in my life before; and I come back, not wearied and tired, though preaching twice every day, but fuller of strength and vigour than when I first set out. I give God the glory for the many souls I have heard of who have been converted through the reading of the printed sermons, and for the loving blessings of those who followed us to the water's edge with many tears, saying to us—" Do thy diligence to come again before winter," and urging us once more to preach the word in that land. There may be mingled with this some touch of egotism; the Lord knoweth whether it be so or not, but I am not conscious of it. I do praise and bless his name, that in a land where there is so much philosophy, he has helped me to preach the truth so simply, that I never uttered a word as a mere doctrinalist, but I preached Christ, and nothing but Christ. Rejoice with me, my dear brethren. I must have you rejoice in it, or if you will not, I must rejoice alone, but my loaf of praise is too great for me to eat it all.

III. And now we come to a close. I have to urge THE JOYFUL CLAIMS which the apostle gives in the twelfth verse, as a reason WHY THERE SHOULD BE PRAYER AND PRAISE.

"For our rejoicing is this, the testimony of our conscience, that in simplicity and godly sincerity, not with fleshly wisdom, but by the grace of God, we have had our conversation in the world, and more abundantly to you-ward." Ah! after all, a man's comfort must come, next to the finished salvation of God, from the testimony of his own conscience, and to a minister what a testimony it is that he has preached the gospel in simplicity, to which there are two senses: preached it not with double mindedness—saying one thing and meaning another; preached it, not as watermen row, looking one way and pulling another, but preached it meaning what he said, having a single heart, desiring God's glory and the salvation of men. And what a blessing to have preached it simply, that is to say, without hard words, without polished phrases, never studying elocutionary graces, never straining after oratorical embellishments. How accursed must be the life of a man who profanes the pulpit to the dignity of eloquence; how desperate will be his death-bed, when he remembers that he made an exhibition of his powers of speech rather than of the solid things which make for the winning of souls. That conscience may well be easy that can speak of having dealt with God's truth in simplicity. The apostle says, also, that he had preached it with sincerity, that is, he had preached it meaning it, feeling it, preached it so that none could accuse him of being false. The Greek word has something in it of sunlight, and he is the true minister of God who preaches what he would wish to have hung up in the sunlight, or who has the sunlight shining right through him. I am afraid we are none of us like white glass, most of us are coloured a little, but he is happy who seeks to get rid of the colouring matter as much as possible, so that the light of the gospel may shine right straight clear as it comes from the Sun of Righteousness, through him. Paul had preached with simplicity and sincerity. And he adds, "Not with fleshly wisdom." Oh! what stories have I heard of what fleshly wisdom will do, and I have learned a lesson during the last fortnight which I would that England would learn. There are three schools of theological error over yonder, and each one leaps over the back of its fellow, some of them holding that all the facts of Scripture are only myths, others of them saying that there are some good things in the Bible, though there are a great many mistakes, and others going further still, and flinging the whole Bible away altogether as to its inspiration, though they still preach it, and still lean on it, saying that they do that merely for the edification of the vulgar, merely holding it up for the sake of the masses, though I ought to add merely to get their living as well. Sad! sad! sad! that the Church has gone to such a length as that—the Old Dutch Reformed Church, the very mirror of Calvinism, standing fast and firm in its creeds to all the doctrines we love, and yet gone astray to latitudinarian and licentious liberty. Oh! how earnestly should we decry fleshly wisdom! I am afraid, dear friends, sometimes that some of you when you hear a minister, you like him to put it pretty well, and you find fault unless he shows some degree of talent. I wonder whether that is

23

not a sin? I am half inclined to think it is. I sometimes think whether we ought not to look less every day to talent, and more and more to the matter of the gospel that is preached; whether if a man be blessed with elocutionary power we may perhaps be more profited by him—whether that is not a weakness, whether we had not better go back to the days of fishermen once again, and give men no sort of education whatever, but just send them to preach the truth simply, rather than go the length they are now going, giving men, I know not what, of all sorts of learning that is of no earthly use to them, but which only helps them to pervert the simplicity of God. I love that word in my text—"Not with fleshly wisdom."

And now I lay my claim, as my conscience bears me witness—I lay my claim to this boasting of our apostle. I have preached God's gospel in simplicity; I do not know how I can preach it more simply, nor can I more honestly declare it. I have preached it sincerely—the Searcher of all hearts knows that; and I have not preached it with fleshly wisdom, and that for one excellent reason—that I have not any, and have been compelled to keep to the simple testimony of the Lord. But if I have done aught, it has been done by the grace of God. If any success has been achieved, it has been grace that has done it all. "And more especially to you-ward;" for though our word has gone forth to many lands, and our testimony belts the globe, yet "more especially to you-ward." You have we warned; you have we entreated; you have we exhorted; with you have we pleaded; over you have we wept; for you have we prayed; to some of you we have been a spiritual parent in Christ; to many of you as a nursing father; to many of you as a teacher and an edifier in the gospel; and we hope to all of you a sincere friend in Christ Jesus. Therefore do I claim your prayers—*yours* more than any other people's; and though there will be not a few who will remember us in their supplications, I do conjure *you*, inasmuch as it has been "especially to you-ward," let us specially have your prayers. Some will say that it is unkind even for me to suppose that you do not pray. Well, I do not so suppose it out of unkindness, but there may be some who forget—some who forget to plead. Oh! do pray for us still! The whole congregation is not saved yet. There are some that hear us that are not yet converted. Plead with God for their sakes. There are some hard hearts unbroken; ask God to make the hammer strike; and while there are some still unmelted, pray God to make the word like a fire. This great London needs to be stirred from end to end. Pray for all your ministers, that God may make them mighty. The Church wants more still of the loud voice of God to wake it from its sleep. Ask God to bless all his sent servants. Plead with him with divine energy, that so his kingdom may come, and his will may be done on earth as it is in heaven.

O that you all believed in Jesus; for until you do, you cannot pray nor praise! O that you all believed in Jesus! Remember, this is the only way of salvation. Trust Jesus, for he that believeth on him is not condemned, but he that believeth not is condemned already, because he believeth not on the Son of God. Trust Jesus and you shall be saved. May Christ accept you now, for his own love's sake. Amen.

24

3. Praise Thy God, O Zion

"And when he was come nigh, even now at the descent of the mount of Olives, the whole multitude of the disciples began to rejoice and praise God with a loud voice for all the mighty works that they had seen; Saying, Blessed be the King that cometh in the name of the Lord: peace in heaven, and glory in the highest. And some of the Pharisees from among the multitude said unto him, Master, rebuke thy disciples. And he answered and said unto them, I tell you that, if these should hold their peace, the stones would immediately cry out."—Luke xix. 37—40.

THE Saviour was "a man of sorrows," but every thoughtful mind has discovered the fact that down deep in his innermost soul he must have carried an inexhaustible treasury of refined and heavenly joy. I suppose that of all the human race there was never a man who had a deeper, purer, or more abiding peace than our Lord Jesus Christ. "He was anointed with the oil of gladness above his fellows." Benevolence is joy. The highest benevolence must from the very nature of things have afforded the deepest possible delight. To be engaged in the most blessed of all errands, to foresee the marvellous results of his labours in time and in eternity, and even to see around him the fruits of the good which he had done in the healing of the sick and the raising of the dead, must have given to such a sympathetic heart as that which beat within the bosom of the Lord Jesus Christ much of secret satisfaction and joy. There were a few remarkable seasons when this joy manifested itself. "At that hour Jesus rejoiced in spirit and said, I thank thee, O Father, Lord of heaven and earth." Christ had his songs though it was night with him; and though his face was marred, and his countenance had lost the lustre of earthly happiness, yet sometimes it was lit up with a matchless splendour of unparalleled satisfaction, as he thought upon the recompense of the reward, and in the midst of the congregation sang his praise unto God.

In this, the Lord Jesus is a blessed picture of his Church on earth. This is the day of Zion's trouble: at this hour the Church expects to walk in sympathy with her Lord along a thorny road. She is without the camp—through much tribulation she is forcing her way to the crown. She expects to meet with reproaches. To bear the cross is her office, and to be scorned and counted an alien by her mother's children is her lot. And yet the Church has a deep well of joy, of which none can drink but her own children. There are stores of wine, and oil,

25

and corn, hidden in the midst of our Jerusalem, upon which the saints of God are evermore sustained and nurtured; and sometimes, as in our Saviour's case, we have our seasons of intense delight, for "there is a river, the streams whereof make glad the city of our God." Exiles though we be, we rejoice in our King, yea in him we exceedingly rejoice: while in his name we set up our banners.

This is a season with us as a Church when we are peculiarly called upon to rejoice in God. The Lord Jesus, in the narrative before us, was going to Jerusalem, as his disciples fondly hoped, to take the throne of David and set up the long-expected kingdom. Well might they shout for joy, for the Lord was in their midst, in their midst in state, riding amidst the acclamations of a multitude who had been glad partakers of his goodness. Jesus Christ is in our midst to-day: the kingdom is securely his. We see the crown glittering upon his brow; he has been riding through our streets, healing our blind, raising our dead, and speaking words of comfort to our mourners. We, too, attend him in state to-day, and the acclamations of little children are not wanting, for from the Sabbath school there have come songs of converted youngsters, who sing gladly, as did the children of Jerusalem in days of yore, "Hosanna! Blessed is he that cometh in the name of the Lord!"

I want, dear friends, this morning, to stir up in all of us the spirit of holy joy, because our King is in our midst; that we may welcome him and rejoice in him, and that while he is working his mighty deeds of salvation throughout this congregation so graciously, he may not lack such music as our feeble lips can afford him. I shall therefore invite your attention to these four verses, by way of example, that we may take a pattern for our praise from this inspired description. We shall observe four things: first, *delightful praise;* secondly, *appropriate song;* thirdly, *intrusive objections;* fourthly, *an unanswerable argument.*

I. First, we shall observe here DELIGHTFUL PRAISE.

In the thirty-seventh verse every word is significant, and deserves the careful notice of all who would learn aright the lesson of how to magnify the Saviour. To begin with, the praise rendered to Christ was *speedy praise.* The happy choristers did not wait till he had entered the city, but "when he was come nigh, even now, at the descent of the mount of Olives, they began to rejoice." It is well to have a quick eye to perceive occasions for gratitude. Blind unbelief and blear-eyed thanklessness allow the favours of God to lie forgotten in unthankfulness, and, without praises, die; they walk in the noonday of mercy and see no light to sing by; but a believing, cheerful, grateful spirit, detects at once the rising of the Sun of mercy, and begins to sing, even at the break of day. Christian, if thou wouldst sing of the mercy thou hast already, thou wouldst soon have more. If twilight made thee glad, thou shouldst soon have the bliss of noon. I am certain that the Church in these days has lost much, by not being thankful for little. We have had many prayer-meetings, but few, very few, praise-meetings; as if the Church could cry loud enough when her own ends were to be answered, but was dumb as to music for her Lord. Her King acts to her very much as he did with the man with the pound. That man put not out the pound to interest, and therefore it was taken away. We have not thanked him for little mercies, and therefore even these have been removed, and Churches have become barren and deserted by the Spirit of God. Let *us* lift up the voice of praise to our Master, because he has blessed us these twelve years. We have had a continual stream of revival. The cries of sinners have sounded in our ears—every day we have seen souls converted—I was about to say almost every hour of the week, and that by the space of these twelve years, and of late, we have had a double portion. Benjamin's mess has been set near our place at the table; we have been made to feast on royal dainties, and have been filled with bread even to the fill. Shall we not then praise God? Ah! let us not require twice telling of it, but let our souls begin to praise him, even now, that he comes nigh unto Jerusalem.

It strikes us at once, also, that this was *unanimous* praise. Observe, not only the multitude, but the *whole multitude* of the disciples rejoiced, and praised him; not one silent tongue among the disciples—not one who withheld his song. And yet, I suppose, those disciples had their trials as we have ours. There might have been a sick wife at home, or a child withering with disease. They were doubtless poor, we know they were, indeed; and poverty is never without its pinches. They were men of like passions with ourselves; they had to struggle with inbred sin, and with temptation from without, and yet there seems to have been no one who on those grounds excluded himself from the choir of singers on that happy day. Oh, my soul, whatever thou hast about thee which might bow thee down, be thou glad when thou rememberest that Jesus Christ is glorified in the midst of his Church. Wherefore, my brother, is that harp of thine hanging on the willows? Hast thou nothing to sing about? Has he done nothing for thee? Why, if thou hast no personal reason for blessing God, then lend us your heart and voice to help *us*, for we have more praise-work on hand than we can get through alone—we have more to praise him for than we are able to discharge without extra aid. Our work of praise is too great for us, come and help us; sing on our behalf, if thou canst not on thine own; and then, mayhap, thou wilt catch the flame, and find something after all for which thou, too, must bless him.

I know there are some of you who do not feel as if you could praise God this morning: let us ask the Master to put your harp in tune. Oh be not silent! Be not silent! Do bless him! If you cannot bless him for temporals, do bless him for spirituals; and if you have not of late experimentally enjoyed many of these, then bless him for what he is. For that dear face, covered with the bloody sweat; for those pierced hands, for that opened side, will you not praise him? Why, surely, if he had not died for me, yet I must love him, to think of his goodness in dying for others. His kindness, the generosity of his noble heart in dying for his enemies might well provoke the most unbelieving to a song. I am, therefore, not content unless all of you will contribute your note. I would have every bird throw in its note, though some cannot imitate the lark or nightingale; yea, I would have every tree of the forest clap its hands, and even the hyssop on the wall wave in adoration. Come, beloved, cheer up. Let dull care and dark fear be gone. Up with harps and down with doubts. It must be praise from "the whole multitude." The praise must be unanimous—not one chord out of order to spoil the tune.

27

Next, it was *multitudinous*. "The whole multitude." There is something most inspiriting and exhilarating in the noise of a multitude singing God's praises. Sometimes, when we have been in good tune, and have sung "Praise God from whom all blessings flow," our music has rolled upward like thunder to yon dome and has reverberated peal on peal, and these have been the happiest moments some of us have ever known, when every tongue was praise, and every heart was joy. Oh, let us renew those happy times; let us anticipate the season when the dwellers in the East and in the West, in the North and in the South, of every age and of every clime, shall assemble on the celestial hill-tops and swell the everlasting song, extolling Jesus Lord of all. Jesus loves the praise of many; he loves to hear the voices of all the bloodwashed.

> " Ten thousand thousand are their tongues,"
> But all their joys are one."

We are not so many as that, but we are counted by thousands, and let us praise his name—the whole multitude.

Still it is worthy of observation that, while the praise was multitudinous, it was quite *select*. It was the whole multitude "*of the disciples.*" The Pharisees did not praise him—they were murmuring. All true praise must come from true hearts. If thou dost not learn of Christ, thou canst not render to him acceptable song. These disciples, of course, were of different sorts. Some of them had but just enlisted in the army—just learned to sit at his feet. Some had worked miracles in his name, and, having been called to the apostolic office, had preached the word to others; but they were all disciples. I trust that in this congregation there is a vast majority of disciples : well, then, all of you, you who have lately come into his school, you who have long been in it, you who have become fathers in Israel, and are teaching others, the whole multitude of disciples, I hope, will praise God. I could wish—God grant the wish—I could wish that those who are not disciples might soon become so. "Take my yoke upon you," saith he, "and learn of me, for I am meek and lowly in heart." A disciple is a learner. You may not know much, but you need not know anything in coming to Christ. Christ begins with ignorance, and bestows wisdom. If thou dost but know that thou knowest nothing, thou knowest enough to become a disciple of Christ Jesus. There is no matriculation necessary in order to enter into Christ's college. He takes the fools, and makes them know the wonders of his dying love. Oh that thou mayest become a disciple! "Write my name down, sir," say thou to the writer with the inkhorn by his side, and be thou henceforth a humble follower of the Lamb. Now, though I would not have those who are not disciples close their mouths when ever others sing, yet I do think there are some hymns in which they would behave more honestly if they did not join, for there are some expressions which hardly ought to come from unconverted lips; better far would it be if they would pray, "Lord, open thou my lips, and my mouth shall shew forth thy praise." You may have a very sweet voice, my friend, and may sing with admirable taste and in exquisite harmony any of the parts, but God does not accept the praise where the heart is absent. The best tune in the book is one called *Hearts*. The whole

28

multitude of the disciples whom Jesus loves are the proper persons to extol the Redeemer's name. May you, dear hearer, be among that company!

Then, in the next place, you will observe that the praise they rendered was *joyful praise.* "The whole multitude of the disciples began to rejoice." I hope the doctrine that Christians ought to be gloomy will soon be driven out of the universe. There are no people in the world who have such a right to be happy, nor have such cause to be joyful as the saints of the living God. All Christian duties should be done joyfully; but especially the work of praising the Lord. I have been in congregations where the tune was dolorous to the very last degree; where the time was so dreadfully slow that one wondered whether they would ever be able to sing through the 119th Psalm; whether, to use Watts's expression, eternity would not be too short for them to get through it; and altogether, the spirit of the people has seemed to be so damp, so heavy, so dead, that we might have supposed that they were met to prepare their minds for hanging rather than for blessing the ever-gracious God. Why, brethren, true praise sets the heart ringing its bells, and hanging out its streamers. Never hang your flag at half-mast when you praise God; no, run up every colour, let every banner wave in the breeze, and let all the powers and passions of your spirit exult and rejoice in God your Saviour. They *rejoiced.* We are really most horribly afraid of being too happy. Some Christians think cheerfulness a very dangerous folly, if not a ruinous vice. That joyous Hundredth Psalm has been altered in all the English versions.

> " All people that on earth do dwell,
>   Sing to the Lord with cheerful voice,
> Him serve with fear, his praise forth tell,
>   Come ye before him and rejoice."

" Him serve with fear," says the English version; but the Scotch version has less thistle and far more rose in it. Listen to it, and catch its holy happiness:—

> " Him serve with *mirth*, his praise forth tell;
>   Come ye before him and rejoice."

How do God's creatures serve him out of doors? The birds do not sit on a Sunday with folden wings, dolefully silent on the boughs of the trees, but they sing as sweetly as may be, even though the rain-drops fall. As for the new-born lambs in the field—they skip to his praise, though the season is damp and cold. Heaven and earth are lit up with gladness, and why not the hearts and houses of the saints? "Him serve with mirth." Well saith the Psalmist; "before him exceedingly rejoice." It was *joyful* praise.

The next point we must mention is, that it was *demonstrative* praise. They praised him with their voices, and with a *loud* voice. Propriety very greatly objects to the praise which is rendered by Primitive Methodists at times; their shouts and hallelujahs are thought by some delicate minds to be very shocking. I would not, however, join in the censure, lest I should be numbered among the Pharisees who said, " Master, rebuke thy disciples." I wish more people were as earnest and even as vehement as the Methodists used to be. In our

Lord's day we see that the people expressed the joy which they felt; I am not sure that they expressed it in the most tunable manner, but at any rate they expressed it in a hearty, lusty shout. They altogether praised with a *loud* voice. It is said of Mr. Rowland Hill that, on one occasion, some one sat on the pulpit stairs, who sang in his ears with such a sharp shrill voice, that he could endure it no longer, but said to the good woman, " I wish you would be quiet;" when she answered, " It comes from my heart." " Oh," said he, " pray forgive me—sing away: sing as loudly as you will." And truly, dear friends, though one might wish there were more melody in it, yet if your music comes from the heart, we cannot object to the loudness, or we might be found objecting to that which the Saviour could not and would not blame. Must we not be loud? Do you wonder that we speak out ? Have not his mercies a loud tongue? Do not his kindnesses deserve to be proclaimed aloud ? Were not the cries upon the cross so loud that the very rocks were rent thereby, and shall our music be a whisper? No, as Watts declares, we would—

> " Loud as his thunders shout his praise,
> And sound it lofty as his throne."

If not with loud voices actually in sound, yet we would make the praise of God loud by our actions, which speak louder than any words; we would extol him by great deeds of kindness, and love, and self-denial, and zeal, that so our actions may assist our words. " The whole multitude praised him with a loud voice." Let me ask every Christian here to do something in the praise of God, to speak in some way for his Master. I would say, speak to-day; if you cannot with your voice, speak by act and deed; but do join in the hearty shout of all the saints of God while you praise and bless the name of our ever-gracious Lord.

The praise rendered, however, though very demonstrative, was very *reasonable;* the reason is given—" for all the mighty works that they had seen." My dear friends, we have seen many mighty works which Christ has done. I do not know what these disciples had happened to see. Certain it is, that after Christ entered into Jerusalem, he was lavish of his miracles. The blind were healed, the deaf had their ears opened, many of those possessed with devils were delivered, and incurable diseases gave way at his word. I think we have the like reason in a spiritual sense. What hath God wrought? It has been marvellous—as our elders would tell you, if they could recount what God has done—the many who have come forward during the last fortnight to tell what God has done for their souls. The Holy Spirit has met with some whom hitherto no ministry had reached. Some have been convinced of sin who were wrapped up in self-righteous rags; others have been comforted whose desponding hearts drew nigh unto despair. I am sure those brethren who sat to see enquirers must have been astonished when they found some hundreds coming to talk about the things that make for their peace. It was blessed work, I doubt not, for them. They, therefore, would lead the strain. But you have all in your measure seen something of it. During the meetings we have held we have enjoyed an overpowering sense of the Divine presence. Without excitement there has been a holy bowedness of spirit, and yet a blessed lifting up of hope, and joy, and holy fervour. The Master has cast sweet smiles upon his Church, he has come near to his beloved, he has given her the tokens of his affection, and made her to rejoice with joy unspeakable. Any joy which we have towards Christ, then, will be reasonable enough, for we have seen his mighty works.

With another remark, I shall close this first head—the reason for their joy was a *personal* one. There is no praise to God so sweet as that which flows from the man who has tasted that the Lord is gracious. Some of you have been converted during the last two or three months. Oh! you *must* bless him, you *shall;* you must take the front rank now, and bless his name for the mighty work which you have seen in yourself. The things which once were dear to you you now abhor, and those things which seemed dry and empty are now sweet and full of savour. God has turned your darkness into light. He has brought you up out of the horrible pit, and out of the miry clay, and has set your feet upon a rock; shall not your established goings yield him a grateful song? You shall bless him. Others here present have had their own children saved. God has looked on one family and another, and taken one, and two, and three. He has been pleased to lay his hand upon the elders among us, and bless their families. Oh sing unto his name! Sing praises for the mighty works which we have seen.

This will be common-place talk enough to those of you who have not seen it; but those who have, will feel the tears starting to their eyes as they think of son and daughter, of whom they can say, "Behold, he prayeth." Saints of God, I wish I could snatch a firebrand from the altar of praise that burns before the great throne of God: I wish I could fire your hearts therewith, but it is the Master's work to do it. Oh! may he do it now. May every one of you feel as if you could cast your crown at his feet; as if you could sing like the cherubim and the seraphim, nor yield even the first place of gratitude to the brightest spirit before the eternal throne. This morning may it be truly said, "The whole multitude of the disciples rejoiced with a loud voice for all the mighty things which they had seen."

> "O come, loud anthems let us sing,
> Loud thanks to our Almighty King;
> For we our voices high should raise,
> When our salvation's rock we praise.
>
> Into his presence let us haste,
> To thank him for his favours past;
> To him address, in joyful songs,
> The praise that to his name belongs."

II. I shall now lead you on to the second point—their praise found vent for itself in AN APPROPRIATE SONG. "Blessed be the King that cometh in the name of the Lord. Peace in heaven, and glory in the highest."

It was an appropriate song, if you will remember that *it had Christ for its subject.* "My heart is inditing of a good matter: I speak of the things which I have made touching the king." No song is so sweet from believing lips as that which tells of him who loved us and who gave himself for us. This particular song sings of Christ in his character of King—a right royal song then—a melody fit for a coronation day. Crown him! crown him Lord of all! That was the refrain —"Blessed be the King." It sang of that King as commissioned by the Most High "who cometh in the name of the Lord." To think of Christ as bearing divine authority, as coming down to men in God our Father's name, speaking what he has heard in heaven, fulfilling no self-espoused errand, but a mission upon which the divine Father sent him according to his purpose and decree; all this is matter for music. Oh bless the Lord, ye saints, as ye remember that your Saviour is the Lord's anointed: he hath set him on his throne; he Jehovah, who was pleased to bruise him, has said, "Yet have I set my King upon my holy hill of Sion." See the Godhead of your Saviour. He whom you adore, the Son of Mary, is the Son of God. He who did ride upon a colt the foal of an ass, did also ride upon a cherub and did fly; yea, he rode upon the wings of the wind. They spread their garments in the way, and brake down branches; it was a humble triumph, but long ere this the angels had strewn his path with adoring songs. Before him went the lightnings, coals of fire were in his track, and up from his throne went forth hailstones and coals of fire. Blessed be the King! Oh praise him this day: praise the King, divine, and commissioned of his Father. The burden of their song was, however, of Christ *present in their midst*. I do not think they would have rejoiced so loudly and sweetly if *he* had not been there. That was the source and centre of their mirth—the King riding upon a colt the foal of an ass—the King triumphant. They could not but be glad when he revealed himself. Beloved, our King is here. We sang at the beginning of this visitation, "Arise, O King of grace, arise, and enter to thy rest!" You remember our singing the verse—

> "O thou that art the Mighty One,
> Thy sword gird on thy thigh."

And King Jesus has done so in state: he has ridden prosperously, and out of the ivory palaces his heart has been made glad; and the King's daughter, all-glorious within, standing at his right hand, cannot but be glad too. Loud to his praise wake every string of your heart, and let your souls make the Lord Jesus the burden of their song.

This was an appropriate song, in the next place, because *it had God for its object ;* they extolled God, God in Christ, when they thus lifted up their voices. They said, "Peace in heaven, and glory in the highest." When we extol Christ, we desire to bless the infinite majesty that gave Christ to us. Thanks be unto the Father for his unspeakable gift. O thou eternal God, we thy creatures in this little world do unfeignedly bless thee for that great purpose and decree, by which thou didst choose us to be illustrious exhibitions of thy majesty and love. We bless thee that thou didst give us grace in Christ thy Son before the starry sky was spread abroad. We praise thee, O God, and magnify thy name as we enquire, "What is man, that thou art mindful of him, or the son of man, that thou visitest him?" How couldst thou deign to stoop from all the glory of thine infinity, to be made man, to suffer, to bleed, to die for us? "Give unto the Lord, O ye mighty, give unto the Lord glory and strength. Give unto the Lord the glory that is due unto his name." Oh that I

32

could give place to some inspired bard, some seer of old, who standing before you with mouth streaming with holy eloquence, should extol him that liveth but once was slain, and bless the God who sent him here below that he might redeem unto himself a people who should show forth his praise.

I think this song to have been very appropriate for another reason, namely, because *it had the universe for its scope.* It was not praise within walls as ours this morning: the multitude sung in the open air with no walls but the horizon, with no roof but the unpillared arch of heaven. Their song, though it was from heaven, did not stay there but enclosed the world within its range. It was, " Peace in heaven; glory in the highest." It is very singularly like that song of the angels, that Christmas carol of the spirits from on high when Christ was born; but it differs, for the angels' song was, " Peace on earth," and this at the gates of Jerusalem was, " Peace in heaven." It is the nature of song to spread itself. From heaven the sacred joy began when angels sang, and then the fire blazed down to earth in the words, " Peace on earth;" but now the song began on earth, and so it blazed up to heaven with the words, " Peace in heaven: glory in the highest." Is not it a wonderful thing that a company of poor beings, like us here below, can really affect the highest heavens? Every throb of gratitude which heaves our hearts glows through heaven. God can receive no actual increase of glory from his creature, for he has infinite glory and majesty, but yet the creature manifests that glory. A grateful man here below, when his heart is all on fire with sacred love, warms heaven itself. The multitude sung of peace in heaven, as though the angels were established in their peaceful seats by the Saviour, as though the war which God had waged with sin was over now, because the conquering King was come. Oh let us seek after music which shall be fitted for other spheres! I would begin the music here, and so my soul should rise. Oh for some heavenly notes to bear my passions to the skies! It was appropriate to the occasion, because the universe was its sphere.

And it seems also to have been most appropriate, because it had *gratitude for its spirit.* They cried aloud, *"Blessed"*—" Blessed be the King." We cannot bless God, and yet we do bless him, in the sense in which he blesses us. Our goodness cannot extend to him, but we reflect the blessedness which streams from him as light from the sun. Blessed be Jesus! My brethren, have you never wished to make him happier? Have you not wished that you could extol him? Let him be exalted! Let him sit on high! I have almost wished even selfishly that he were not so glorious as he is, that we might help to lift him higher. Oh! if the crushing of my body, soul, and spirit would make him one atom more glorious, I would not only consent to the sacrifice, but bless his name that he counted me worthy so to do. All that we can do bringeth nothing unto him. Yet, brethren, I would that he had his own. Oh that he rode over our great land in triumph! Would that King Jesus were as well known here now as he was once in puritanic times! Would that Scotland were as loyal to him as in covenanting periods! Would that Jesus had his majesty visible in the eyes of all men! We pray for this, we seek for this; and among the chief joys our chiefest joy is to know that God hath highly exalted

33

him, and given him a name which is above every name, that at the name of Jesus every knee should bow. We have thus said something about the appropriateness of the song; may you, each of you, light upon such hymns as will serve to set forth your own case and show forth the mercy of God in saving you, and do not be slack in praising him in such notes as may be most suitable to your own condition.

III. Thirdly, and very briefly—for I am not going to give much time to these men—we have INTRUSIVE OBJECTIONS. " Master, rebuke thy disciples." We know that voice—the old grunt of the Pharisee. What could he do otherwise? Such is the man, and such must his communications be. While he can dare to boast, " God, I thank thee that I am not as other men are," he is not likely to join in praises such as other men lift up to heaven.

But why did these Pharisees object? I suppose it was first of all because *they thought there would be no praise for them.* If the multitude had been saying, " Oh these *blessed* Pharisees! these excellent Pharisees! What broad phylacteries ! What admirable hems to their garments ! How diligently and scrupulously they tithe their mint and their anise and their cummin! What a wonder that God should permit us poor vile creatures to look upon these super-excellent incarnations of virtue!" I will be bound to say there would not have been a man among them who would have said, "Master, rebuke thy disciples." A proud heart never praises God, for it hoards up praise for itself.

In the next place, *they were jealous of the people.* They did not feel so happy themselves, and they could not bear that other people should be glad. They were like the elder brother who said, " Yet thou never gavest me a kid, that I might make merry with my friends." Was that a reason why nobody else should be merry? A very ill reason truly! Oh, if we cannot rejoice ourselves, let us stand out of the way of other people. If we have no music in our own hearts, let us not wish to stop those who have.

But I think the main point was that they were *jealous of Jesus;* they did not like to have Christ crowned with majesty. Certainly this is the drift of the human heart. It does not wish to see Jesus Christ extolled. Preach up morality or dry doctrine, or ceremonies, and many will be glad to hear your notes; but preach Jesus Christ up, and some will say, " Master, rebuke thy disciples !" It was not ill advice of an old preacher to a young beginner, when he said, " Preach nothing down but sin, and preach nothing up but Christ." Brethren, let us praise nothing up but Christ." Have nothing to say about your Church, say nothing about your denomination, hold your tongue about the minister, but praise Christ, and I know the Pharisees will not like it, but that is an excellent reason to give them more of it, for that which Satan does not admire, he ought to have more of. The preaching of Christ is the whip that flogs the devil; the preaching of Christ is the thunderbolt, the sound of which makes all hell shake. Let us never be silent then; we shall put to confusion all our foes, if we do but extol Christ Jesus the Lord. " Master, rebuke thy disciples!" Well, there is not much of this for Jesus Christ to rebuke in the Christian Church in the present day. There used to be—there used to be a little of what the world calls fanaticism. A consecrated cobbler once set forth to

34

preach the gospel in Hindoostan. There were men who would go preaching the gospel among the heathen, counting not their lives dear unto them. The day was when the Church was so foolish as to fling away precious lives for Christ's glory. Ah! she is more prudent now-a-days. Alas! alas! for your prudence. She is so calm and so quiet—no Methodist's zeal now—even that denomination which did seem alive has become most proper and most cold. And we are so charitable too. We let the most abominable doctrines be preached, and we put our finger on our lip, and say, "There's so many good people who think so." Nothing is to be rebuked now-a-days. Brethren, one's soul is sick of this! Oh, for the old fire again! The Church will never prosper till it comes once more. Oh, for the old fanaticism, for that indeed was the Spirit of God making men's spirits in earnest! Oh, for the old doing and daring that risked everything and cared for nothing, except to glorify him who shed his blood upon the cross! May we live to see such bright and holy days again! The world may murmur, but Christ will not rebuke.

IV. We come now to the last point, which is this—AN UNANSWERABLE ARGUMENT. He said, "If these should hold their peace, the very stones would cry out."

Brethren, I think that is very much our case; if we were not to praise God, the very stones might cry out against us. We *must* praise the Lord. Woe is unto us if we do not! It is impossible for us to hold our tongues. Saved from hell and be silent! Secure of heaven and be ungrateful! Bought with precious blood, and hold our tongues! Filled with the Spirit and not speak! Restrain, from fear of feeble man, the Spirit's course within our souls! God forbid. In the name of the Most High, let such a thought be given to the winds. What, our children saved; the offspring of our loins brought to Christ! What, see them springing up like willows by the water courses, and no awakening of song, no gladness, no delight! Oh, then we were worse than brutes, and our hearts would have been steeled and become as adamant. We must praise God! What, the King in our midst, King Jesus smiling into our souls, feasting us at his table, making his word precious to us, and not praise him. Why if Satan could know the delight of Christ's company he might begin to love; but we, we were worse than devils if we did not praise the name of Jesus! What! the King's arm made bare, his enemies subdued, his triumphant chariot rolling through our streets, and no song! Oh Zion, if we forget to sing let our right hand forget her cunning; if we count not the King's triumph above our chiefest joy. What, the King coming! His advent drawing nigh, the signs of blessing in the sky and air around, and yet no song! Oh, we must bless him! Hosanna! Blessed is he that cometh in the name of the Lord!

But could the stones ever cry out? Yes, that they could, and if they were to speak they would have much to talk of even as we have this day. If the stones were to speak they could tell of their *Maker;* and shall not we tell of him who made us anew, and out of stones raised up children unto Abraham? They could speak of ages long since gone; the old rocks could tell of chaos and order, and the handiwork of God in various stages of creation's drama; and cannot we talk of God's decrees, of God's great work in ancient times, and all that he did for his Church? If the

35

stones were to speak they could tell of their *breaker*, how he took them from the quarry, and made them fit for the temple; and cannot we tell of our Creator and Maker, who broke our hearts with the hammer of his word that he might build us into his temple? If the stones were to speak, they would tell of their *builder*, who polished them and fashioned them after the similitude of a palace; and shall not we talk of our Architect and Builder, who has put us in our place in the temple of the living God? Oh, if the stones could speak, they might have a long, long story to tell by way of *memorial*, for many a time hath a great stone been rolled as a memorial unto God; and we can tell of Ebenezers, stones of help, stones of remembrance. The broken stones of the law cry out against us, but Christ himself, who has rolled away the stone from the door of the sepulchre, speaks for us. Stones might well cry out, but we will not let them: we will hush their noise with ours, we will break forth into sacred song, and bless the majesty of the Most High all our days. Let this day and to-morrow be especially consecrated to holy joys, and may the Lord in infinite mercy fill your souls right full of it, both in practical deeds of kindness and benevolence and works of praise! Blessed be his name who liveth for ever and ever!

4. A New Song for New Hearts

"And in that day thou shalt say, O Lord, I will praise thee: though thou wast angry with me, thine anger is turned away, and thou comfortedst me."—Isaiah xii. 1.

THIS prophesy is said by some to relate to the invasion by Sennacherib. That calamity threatened to be a very terrible display of divine anger. It seemed inevitable that the Assyrian power would make an utter desolation of all Judea; but God promised that he would interpose for the deliverance of his people, and punish the stout heart of the king of Assyria, and in that day his people should say, "We will praise thee: though thou wast angry with us, and therefore sent the Assyrian monarch to chastise us, thine anger is turned away, and thou comfortedst us." If this be the meaning of it, it is an instance of sanctified affliction, and it is a lesson to us that whenever we smart under the rod, we may look forward to the time when the rod shall be withdrawn; and it is also an admonition to us that when we escape from trial, we should take care to celebrate the event with grateful praise. Let us set up the pillar of memorial, let us pour the oil of gratitude upon it, and garland it with song, blessing the Lord whose anger endureth but for a moment, but whose mercy is from everlasting to everlasting.

It is thought by others, that this text mainly relates to the latter days, and I think it would be impossible to read the eleventh chapter without feeling that such a reference is clear. There is to be a time when the wolf shall dwell with the lamb, the lion shall eat straw like the ox, and the weaned child shall put his hand on the cockatrice den. Then the Lord will set his hand again, the second time, to recover the remnant of his people, and repeat his wondrous works in Egypt and at the Red Sea, so that the song of Moses shall be rehearsed again, "The Lord is my strength and song, and he is become my salvation: he is my God, and I will prepare him an habitation; my father's God, and I will exalt him." In that day the Jewish people upon whose head the blood of Christ has come, who these many centuries have been a people scattered and peeled, and sifted as in a sieve throughout all nations, even these shall be restored to their own land, and the dispersed of Judah from the four corners of the earth; they shall participate in all the glories of the millennial reign, and with joy shall they draw water out of the wells of salvation. In those days, when all Israel shall be saved, and Judah shall dwell safely,

37

the jubilant thanksgiving shall be heard, "O Lord, I will praise thee; for though thou wast angry with me, thine anger is turned away, and thou comfortedst me." The whole people shall sing with such unanimity, with such undivided heart, that they shall speak as though they were but one man, and shall use the singular where their numbers might require the plural, "I will praise thee," shall be the exclamation of the once divided but then united people.

Although both these interpretations are true, and both instructive, the text is many-sided and bears another reading. We shall find out the very soul of the passage if we consider it as an illustration of what occurs to every one of God's people when he is brought out of darkness into God's marvellous light, when he is delivered from the spirit of bondage beneath divine wrath, and led by the spirit of adoption into the liberty wherewith Christ makes him free. In that day I am sure these words are fulfilled; the believer does then say right joyously, "O Lord, I will praise thee: though thou wast angry with me, thine anger is turned away, and thou comfortedst me."

In regarding the text from this point of view, we shall first observe *the prelude* of this delightful song; and then, secondly, we shall listen to *the song itself.*

I. First, I shall ask your consideration of THE PRELUDE of this charming song. Here are certain preliminaries to the music. They are contained in the first line of the text. "*In that day thou shalt say.*" Here we have the tuning of the harps, the notes of the music follow after in the succeeding sentences. Much of instruction is couched in these seven words of prelude.

Note then, first, there is *a time* for that joyous song which is here recorded. "*In that day.*" The term, "that day," is sometimes used for a day of terror, and often for a period of blessing. The common term to both is this, they were both days of the manifestation of divine power. "That day," a day of terrible confusion to God's enemies; "that day"— a day of great comfort to God's friends; the day being in either case the time of the making bare of God's arm, and the manifestation of his strength. Now, the day in which a man rejoices in Christ, is the day in which God's power is revealed on his behalf in his heart and conscience, and the Holy Spirit subdues him to the reign of Christ. It is not always that God works with such effectual power as this in the human heart, he has his set times. Oftentimes the word of human ministry proves ineffectual: the preacher exhorts, the hearer listens, but the exhortation is not obeyed. It sometimes happens that even desires may be excited, and yet nothing is accomplished, for these better feelings prove to be as those spring blossoms on the trees which do not knit, and fall fruitless to the ground. There is, however, an appointed time for the calling of God's elect, a set time in which the Lord visits his chosen with a power of grace, which they cannot effectually resist. He makes them willing in the day of his power. It is a day in which not only is the gospel heard, but our report is believed, because the arm of the Lord is revealed. To everything, according to Solomon, there is a season: a time to break down, and a time to build up; a time of war, and a time of peace; a time to kill, and a time to heal; and even so there is a time for conviction, and a time for consolation. With some who are in great distress of spirit, it may be God's time to wound and to kill. Their self-confidence is yet too vigorous, their carnal righteousness is yet too lively ; their confidences must be wounded; their righteousness must be killed ; for otherwise they will not yield to grace. God does not clothe us till he has stripped us, he does not heal till first he has wounded. How should he make alive those who are not dead ? There is a work of grace in the heart of digging out the foundations, before grace begins to build up our hopes : woe to that man who builds without having the foundation dug out, for his house will fall. Woe to that man who leaps into a sudden peace without ever having felt his need of pardon, without repentance, without brokenness of spirit ; he shall see his hasty fruit wither before his eyes. The time when God effectually blesses is sometimes called "a time of love." It is a time of deep distress to us, but it is a time of love with God, a time wisely determined in the decree and counsel of the Most High, so that healing mercy arrives at the best time to each one who is interested in the covenant of grace. Some one may enquire, "When do you think will be the time when God will enable me to say, 'Thine anger is turned away'?" My dear brother, you can easily discern it. I believe God's time to give us comfort is usually when we are brought low, so as to confess the justice of the wrath which he is pouring upon us. Humbleness of heart is one sure indication of coming peace. A German nobleman some years ago went over the galleys at Toulon. There he saw many men condemned by the French government to perpetual toil at the galley oar on account of their crimes. Being a prince in much repute, he obtained the favour that he should give liberty to some one of the captives. He went about among them, and talked to them, but found in every case that they thought themselves wrongly treated, oppressed, and unrighteously punished. At last he met with one who confessed, " In my case my sentence is a most just and even a merciful one. If I had not been imprisoned in this way I should most likely have long ago been executed for some still greater crime. I have been a very great offender, and the law is doing nothing more than it ought to do in keeping me in confinement for the rest of my life." The German nobleman returned to the manager of the galleys and said, " This is the only man in all this gang that I would wish to set free, and I elect him for liberty." It is so with our great Liberator, the Lord Jesus Christ, when he meets with a soul that confesses its demerit, owns the justice of divine wrath, and has not a word to say for itself, then he saith, " Thy sins which are many are forgiven thee." The time when his anger is turned away is the time when you confess the justice of his anger, and bow down and humbly entreat for mercy. Above all, the hour of grace has struck when you look alone to Christ. While you are looking to any good thing in yourself, and hoping to grow better, or to do better, you are making no advances towards comfort ; but when you give up in despair every hope that can be grounded in yourself, and look away to those dear wounds of his, to that suffering humanity of the Son of God who stooped from heaven for you, then has the day dawned wherein you shall say, " O Lord, I will praise thee." I pray earnestly that this set time to favour you may be now come—the time when the rain is over and gone, and the voice of the turtle is heard in your land.

Looking at the preliminaries of this song again, you notice that a word indicates the singer. "In that day *thou* shalt say." "*Thou*." It is a singular pronoun, and points out one individual. One by one we receive eternal life and peace. "*Thou*, the individual, thou, singled out to feel in thy conscience God's wrath, thou art equally selected to enjoy Jehovah's love. Ah! brethren, it is never a day of grace to us till we are taken aside from the multitude and set by ourselves. Our individuality must come out in conversion, if it never appears at any other time. You fancy, so many of you, that it is all right with you because you live in a Christian nation ; I tell you it is woe unto you, if having outward privileges, they involve you in responsibilities, but bring you no saving grace. Perhaps you fancy that your family religion may somewhat help you, and the erroneous practices of certain Christian churches may foster this delusion, but it is not so; there is no birthright godliness: "Ye must be born again." The first birth will not help you, for, "That which is born of the flesh is flesh; and that which is born of the Spirit is spirit." Still, I know ye fancy that if ye mingle in godly congregations, and sing as they sing, and pray as they pray, it shall go well with you, but it is not so ; the wicket gate of eternal life admits but one at a time. Is it not written, "Ye shall be gathered one by one, O ye children of Israel"? Know ye not that when the fountain is opened in the house of David for sin and for uncleanness, it is declared by the prophet Zechariah, "The land shall mourn, every family apart ; the family of the house of David apart, and their wives apart ; the family of the house of Nathan apart, and their wives apart ; the family of the house of Levi apart, and their wives apart; the family of Shimei apart, and their wives apart; all the families that remain every family apart, and their wives apart"! Ye must each one be brought to feel the divine anger in your souls, and to have it removed from you, that ye may rejoice in God as your salvation. Has it been so with thee, then, dear hearer? art thou that favoured singer? art thou one of that chosen throng who can say, "Thine anger is turned away, and thou comfortedst me"? Away with generals; be not satisfied except with particulars. Little matters it to you that Christ should die for ten thousand men, if you have no part in his death. Little blessing is it to you that there should be joy from myriads of hearts because they are pardoned, if you should die unpardoned. Seek a personal interest in Christ, and do not be satisfied unless in your own heart ye have it satisfactorily revealed that your sin in particular is by an act of grace put away. I like to remember that this word, "thou," is spoken to those who have been by sorrow brought into the last degree of despair. "In that day *thou* shalt say, though thou wast angry with *me*, thine anger is turned away." *Thou* poor down-trodden heart, where art *thou*? Thou woman of a sorrowful spirit, rejoice, for in that day of mercy *thou* shalt sing. Thou broken-hearted sinner, ready to destroy thyself, because of the anguish of conscience, in the day of God's abounding mercy thou shalt rejoice, even thou, and thy note shall be all the sweeter because thou hast had the most sin to be forgiven, and felt most the anger of God burning in thy soul. Dwell on that, ye mourners, and God grant it may be realised personally by yourselves.

The next thing to be noted in the preliminaries is the Teacher. "In that day thou *shalt* say," who says this? It is God alone who can so positively declare, "thou *shalt* say." Who but the Lord can thus command man's heart and speech? It is the Lord alone. He who has made us is master of our spirits; by his omnipotence he ruleth in the world of mind as well as matter, and all things happen as he ordains. He saith, "In that day," that is, in God's own time, "thou shalt say;" and he who thus declares will make good the word. Here is revealed God's will, and what the Lord wills shall be accomplished, what he declares shall be spoken shall assuredly be spoken. Herein is consolation to those feeble folk who fear the word will not be fulfilled. "Thou *shalt* say," is a divine word and cannot fail. The Lord alone can give a man the right to say, "Thine anger is turned away." If any man presumes to say, "God has turned his anger away from me," without a warrant from the Most High, that man lies to his own confusion; but when it is written, "Thou shalt say," it is as though God had said, "I will make it true, so that you shall be fully justified in the declaration." Yet more of comfort is there here, for even when the right to such a blessing is bestowed, we are often unable to enjoy it because of weakness. Unbelief is frequently so great that many things which are true we cannot receive, and under a sense of sin we are so desponding that we think God's mercy too great for us, and therefore we are not able to appropriate the blessing presented to us, though it be inexpressibly delightful. Blessed be God, the Holy Ghost knows how to chase away our unbelief, and give us power to embrace the blessing. He can make us accept the covenant favour and rejoice in it, so as to avow the joy. There are some of you whom I have tried to induce to believe comfortable truths about yourselves, but you have fairly defeated me. I have put the gospel plainly to you, for I have felt sure that its promises were meant for you, and I have said within my heart, "Surely they will be comforted this morning, certainly their broken hearts will be bound up by that gracious word." But oh! I cannot make you say, "Lord, I will praise thee." I am unable to lead you to faith and peace. Here, however, is my joy, my Master can do what his servant cannot. He can make the tongue of the dumb sing. He delights to look after desperate cases. Man's extremity becomes his opportunity. Where the most affectionate words of ours fail, the consolations of his blessed Spirit are divinely efficacious. He cannot merely bring the oil and the wine, but he knows how to pour them into the wounds, and heal the anguish of the contrite spirit. I pray the Master that he who alone can teach us to sing this song, may graciously instruct those of you who have been seeking rest these many months, and finding none, "I am the Lord which teacheth thee to profit." He can put a song into your mouth, for nothing is beyond the range of grace.

Once more, "In that day thou shalt say." Here is another preliminary of the song, namely, *the tone* of it. "Thou shalt *say*, O Lord, I will praise thee." The song is to be an open one, avowed, vocally uttered, heard of men, and published abroad. It is not to be a silent feeling, a kind of soft music whose sweetness is spent within the spirit, but in that day thou shalt say, thou shalt speak it outright, thou shalt testify and bear witness to what the Lord has done for thee. When a man

41

gets his sins forgiven he cannot help revealing the secret. "When the Lord turned again the captivity of Zion, we were like them that dream. Then was our mouth filled with laughter, and our tongue with singing." Even if the forgiven one could not speak with his tongue, he could say it with his eye; his countenance, his manner, his very gait would betray him. The gracious secret would ooze out in some fashion. Spiritual men, at any rate, would find it out, and with thankfulness mark the joyful evidences. I know that before I found the Saviour, had you known me, you would have observed my solitary habits; and if you had tracked me to my chamber, and to my Bible, and my knees, you would have heard groans and sighs, which betokened a sorrowful spirit. The ordinary amusements of youth had in those days few attractions for me, and conversation however cheerful yielded me no comfort. But that very morning that I heard the gospel message, "Look unto me, and be ye saved, all ye ends of the earth," I am certain that no person who knew me could have helped remarking the difference even in my face. A change came over my spirits, which as I remember was even indicated in the way in which I walked, for the heavy step of melancholy was exchanged for a more cheerful pace. The spiritual condition affects the bodily state, and it was evidently so with me. My delight at being forgiven was no ordinary sensation, I could have fairly leaped for joy.

> All through the night I wept full sore,
>   But morning brought relief;
> That hand which broke my bones before,
>   Then broke my bonds of grief.
>
> My mourning he to dancing turns,
>   For sackcloth joy he gives,
> A moment, Lord, thine anger burns,
>   But long thy favour lives.

If I had not avowed my deliverance the very stones must have cried out. It was not in my heart to keep it back, but I am sure I could not have done so if I had desired. God's grace does not come into the heart as a beggar into a barn, and lie hidden away as if it stole a night's lodging; no, its arrival is known all over the house, and every chamber of the soul testifies its presence. Grace is like a bunch of lavender, it discovers itself by its sweet smell. Like the nightingale it is heard where it is not seen. Like a spark which falls into the midst of straw it burns, and blazes, and consumes, and so reveals itself by its own energetic operations. O soul, burdened with sin, if Christ do but come to thee, and pardon thee, I will be bound for it that ere long all thy bones shall say, "Lord, who is like unto thee?" You will be of the same mind as David, "Deliver me from bloodguiltiness, O God, thou God of my salvation: and my tongue shall sing aloud of thy righteousness." You will gladly say with him, "Thy vows are upon me, O God: I will render praise unto thee, for thou hast delivered my soul from death." Not only will you soberly tell what great things grace has wrought for you, but it will be no very unlikely thing that your exuberant joy may lead you beyond the bounds of solemn decorum. The precise and slow-going will condemn you, but you need not mind, for you can offer the same excuse for it as David made to Michal when he danced before the ark.

Far be it from me to condemn you, should you cry, "Hallelujah," or clap your hands. It is our cold custom to condemn every demonstration of feeling, but I am sure Scripture does not warrant us in our condemnation; for we find such passages as these, "O clap your hands, all ye people; shout unto God with the voice of triumph." "Praise him upon the loud cymbals: praise him upon the high sounding cymbals." What if the overflowing of holy joy should seem to be disorderly, what matters it if God accepts it? He who has long been immured in prison, when he gets his liberty may well take a frisk or two, and an extra leap for joy, and who shall grudge him? He who has long been hungry and famished, when he sees the table spread, may be excused if he fall to with more of eagerness than politeness. Oh! yes, they shall say it, they shall say it, "I will praise thee, O Lord." In the very disorderliness of their demonstration, they shall the more emphatically say, "I will praise thee: though thou wast angry with me, thine anger is turned away."

Thus much on the prelude of the song: now let us hear the song itself.

II. In THE SONG ITSELF, I would call to your notice the fact that *all of it is concerning the Lord*. It is all addressed to him. "O Lord, I will praise *thee* : though *thou* wast angry, *thine* anger is turned away."

When a soul escapes from the bondage of sin, and becomes consciously pardoned, it resembles the apostles on the Mount Tabor, of whom we spoke the other Sabbath morning—it sees no man, save Jesus only. While you are seeking grace you think much of the minister, the service, the outward form, but the moment you find peace in God through the precious blood of Christ, you will think of your pardoning God only. Oh, how small everything becomes in the presence of that dear cross, where God the Saviour loved and died ! When we think of all our iniquity being cast into the depth of the sea, we can no more boast of anything that was once our glory. The instrumentality by which peace came to us will be always dear to us, we shall esteem the preacher of the gospel who brings salvation to us to be our spiritual father, but still we shall never think of praising him, we shall give all the glory to our God. As for ourselves, self will sink like lead amidst the waters when we find Christ. God will be all in all when iniquity is pardoned. I have often thought that if some of my brethren, who preach a gospel in which there is little of the grace of God, had felt a little more conviction of sin in being converted, they would be sure to preach a clearer and more gracious gospel. Many nowadays appear to leap into peace without any convictions of sin—they do not seem to have known what the guilt of sin means; but they scramble into peace before the burden of sin has been felt. It is not for me to judge, but I must confess I have my fears of those who have never felt the terrors of the Lord, and I look upon conviction of sin as a good groundwork for a well-instructed Christian. I observe as a rule that when a man has been put in the prison of the law, and made to wear the heavy chains of conviction, and at last obtains his liberty through the precious blood, he is pretty sure to cry up the grace of God, and magnify divine mercy. He feels that in his case salvation must be of grace from first to last, and he naturally favours that system of theology which magnifies most **the** grace of God. Those who have not felt this, whose conversion has been of the more easy kind, produced rather by excitement than by depth of thought, seem to me to choose a flimsy divinity, in which man is more prominent, and God is less regarded. I am sure of this one thing, that I personally desire to ascribe conversion in my own case entirely to the grace of God, and to give God the glory of it; and I dread that conversion which could in any degree deprive God of being in his everlasting decrees the cause of it, by his effectual Spirit the direct agent of it, by his continued working through the Holy Ghost the perfecter of it. Give God the praise, my brethren. You must do so, if you have thoroughly experienced what God's anger means, and what the turning away of it means.

The next thing in this song is, that *it includes repentant memories.* " O Lord, I will praise thee : though thou wast angry with me." There was a time when God was to our consciousness angry with us. When was that, and how did we know that God was angry with us? Outsiders think when we talk about conversion that we are merely talking of sentimental theories, but let me assure you that it is as much matter of fact to us with regard to our spiritual nature, as your feelings of sickness and of recovery are real and actual to you. Time was, when some of us read the word of God, and as we read it, believing it to be an inspired book, we perceived that it contained a law, holy and just, the breach of which was threatened with eternal death. As we read it we discovered that we had broken that law, not in some points, but in all ; and we were obliged, as we read it, to feel that all the sentences of that book against sinners were virtually sentences against us. We may perhaps have read these chapters before, but we had given them no serious thought until on this occasion we were led to see that we stood condemned by the law of God as contained in holy Scripture. Then we felt that God was angry with us. It was not a mere idea of ours, we had this book in evidence of it; if that book were indeed true, we felt we were condemned. We dared not think the old book to be a cunningly-devised fable, we knew it was not, and therefore from its testimony we concluded that God was angry with us. At the same time we learned this terrible truth from the book, our conscience suddenly awoke and confirmed the fact, for it said, " What the book declares is correct. The just God must be angry with such a sinful being as you are." Conscience brought to our recollection many things which we would fain have forgotten. It revealed to us much of the evil of our hearts, which we had no wish to know; and thus as we looked at Scripture by the light of conscience, we concluded in ourselves that we were in a very dreadful plight, and that God was angry with us. Then there entered into us at the same time, over and above all the rest, a certain work of the Holy Spirit called conviction of sin, " When he, the Spirit of truth is come," he shall convince the world of sin. He has come, and he has convinced us of sin, in a way in which the Scripture would not have done apart from him, and conscience would not have done apart from him. But his light shone in upon us, and we felt as we never felt before. Then sin appeared exceeding sinful, as it was committed against infinite love and goodness ; then it appeared to us as though hell must soon swallow us up, and the wrath of God must devour us. Oh, the trembling and the fear, the dismay and the alarm, which then possessed our spirits ; and yet, my brethren, at this very time, the remembrance of it is cause for thankfulness. In the Hebrew, the wording of our text is slightly different from what we get in the English. Our English translators have very wisely put in the word "though," a little earlier than it occurs in the Hebrew. The Hebrew would run something iike this, "O Lord, I will praise thee; thou wast angry with me." Now we do this day praise God that he made us feel his anger. "What," say you, "what, is a sense of anger a cause for praise?" No, my brethren, not if it stood alone, but because it has driven us to Christ. If wrath had been laid up for us hereafter, it would be a cause of horror, deep and dread, but that it was let loose in measure upon us here, and that we were thus condemned in conscience that we might not be condemned at last is reason for much thankfulness. We should never have felt his love if we had not felt his anger. We laid hold on his mercy because of necessity. No soul will accept Christ Jesus until it must. It is not driven to faith until it is driven to self-despair. God's angry face makes Christ's loving face dear to us. We should never look at the Christ of God, unless first of all the God of Christ had looked at us through the tempest and made us afraid. "I will praise thee, that thou didst let me feel thine anger, in order that I might be driven to discover how that anger could be turned away." So you see the song in its deep bass note includes plaintive recollections of sin pressing heavily on the spirit.

The song of our text contains in itself *blessed certainties.* "I will praise thee; though thou wast angry with me, thine anger *is* turned away." Can a man know that? can a man be quite sure that he is forgiven? Ay, that he can, he can be as sure of pardon as he is of his existence, as infallibly certain as he is of a mathematical proposition. "Nay," saith one, "but how is it?" My brother, albeit that this is a matter for spiritual men, yet at the same time it is a matter of certainty as clearly as anything can be ascertained by human judgment. The confidence of a man's being pardoned, and God's anger being turned away from him, is not based upon his merely feeling that it is so, or his merely believing that it is so. You are not pardoned because you work yourself up into a comfortable frame of mind, and think you are pardoned; that may be a delusion. You are not necessarily delivered from God's anger because you believe you are; you may be believing a lie, and may believe what you like, but that does not make it true. There must be a fact going before, and if that fact is not there, you may believe what you choose, but it is pure imagination, nothing more. On what ground does a man know that God's anger is turned away? I answer thus— on the ground of this book, "It is written," is our basis of assurance. I turn to that book, and I discover that Jesus Christ the Son of God came into this world and became the substitute for a certain body of men; that he took their sins, and was punished in their stead, in order that God, without the violation of his justice, might forgive as many as are washed in Christ's blood. My question then is, for whom did Christ die? The moment I turn to the Scriptures, I find very conspicuously on its page this declaration, that "Jesus Christ came into the world to save sinners." I am a sinner, that I am clear of; that gives me some hopes. But I next find that "he that believeth on him is not condemned;" looking to myself I find that I do really believe, that is, I trust Jesus; very well, then I am sure I am not condemned, for God has declared I am not. I read again, "He that believeth and is baptised shall be saved." I know that I have believed, that is to say, trusted—I trust my salvation with Christ ; and have also in obedience to his command been baptised—then I am saved, and shall be saved, for it says so. Now this is a matter of testimony which I receive. He that believeth in Christ, receives the testimony of God, and that is the only testimony he wants. I know it has been thought that you get some special revelation in your own soul, some flash as it were of light, some extraordinary intimation, but nothing of the kind is absolutely needed. I know that the Spirit beareth witness with our spirits that we are born of God, but the first essential matter is God's witness in the word. "He that believeth not God, hath made him a liar ; because he believeth not the record that God gave of his Son." God's witness concerning his Son is this, that if you trust his Son you are saved. His Son suffered for you, his Son bore the punishment that was due to your sins : God declares it, that you are forgiven for Christ's sake. He cannot punish twice for one offence, first his Son and then you. He cannot demand retribution from his law to vindicate his justice, first from your substitute and then from you. Was Christ your substitute ? that is the question. He was if you trust him—your trusting him is the evidence that he was a substitute for you. Now see them, the moment I, being under his anger, have come to trust my soul for ever in the hands of Christ, God's anger is turned away from me, because it was turned upon Christ, and I stand, guilty sinner as I am in myself, absolved before God, and feel that none can lay anything to my charge, for my sins were laid on Christ, and punished upon Christ, and I am clear. And now what shall I say unto the Lord, but, " I will praise thee, for though thou wast angry with me, thine anger is turned away, and thou comfortedst me." It is a matter of certainty, it is not a matter of "ifs," and "ands," and "buts," but of fact. This morning you are either forgiven or you are not; you are either clean in God's sight or else the wrath of God abideth on you ; and I beseech you do not rest till you know which it is. If you find out that you are unforgiven, seek ye the Saviour. " Believe in the Lord Jesus Christ, and thou shalt be saved." But if you believe in him, you are not any longer guilty, you are forgiven. Do not sit down and fret as if you were guilty, but enjoy the liberty of the children of God, and being justified by faith, have peace with God through Jesus Christ your Lord.

Time fails me, but I must add that our song includes *holy resolutions*, " I will praise thee." I will do it with my heart in secret. I will get alone and make my expressive silence hymn thy praise. I will sit and pour out liquid songs in tears of gratitude, welling up from my heart. I will praise thee in the church of God, for I will search out other believers, and I will tell them what God has done for me. I will cast in my lot with thy people : if they are despised, I will bear the shame with them, and count it honour. I will unite myself to them, and help them in their service, and if I can magnify Christ by my testimony among them I will do it. I will praise thee in my life. I will make my business praise thee ; I will make my parlour and my drawing-room, I will make my kitchen and my field praise thee. I will not be content unless all I am and all I have shall praise thee. I will make a harp of the whole universe ; I will make earth and heaven, space and time, to be but strings upon which my joyful fingers shall play lofty tunes of thankfulness. I will praise thee, O my God; my heart is fixed, I will sing and give praise : and when I shall die, or rather pass from this life to another, I who have been forgiven so much sin through such a Saviour, will continue to praise thee.

> " Oh, how I long to join the choir
>   Who worship at his feet !
> Lord, grant me soon my heart's desire !
>   Soon, soon thy work complete !"

Note once more that this is a song which is *peculiar in its character*, and appropriate only to the people of God. I may say of it, " no man could learn this song but the redeemed." He only who has felt his vileness, and has had it washed away in the " fountain filled with blood," can know its sweetness. It is not a Pharisee's song—it has no likeness to " God I thank thee that I am not as other men ; " it confesses, " Thou wast angry with me," and therein owns that the singer was even as others; but it glories that through infinite mercy, the divine anger is turned away, and herein it leans on the appointed Saviour. It is not a Sadducean song, no doubt mingles with the strain. It is not the philosopher's query, " There may be a God, or there may not be," it is the voice of a believing worshipper. It is not, " I may be guilty, or I may not be." It is all positive, every note of it. " Thou wast angry with me "—I know it, I feel it, yet " thine anger is turned away;" of this too I am sure. I believe it upon the witness of God, and I cannot doubt his word. It is a song of strong faith, and yet of humility. Its spirit is a precious incense made up of many costly ingredients. We have here not one virtue alone, but many rare excellences. Humility confesses, " Thou wast angry with me." Gratitude sings, " Thine anger is turned away." Patience cries, " Thou comfortedst me," and while holy joy springs up, and saith, " I will praise thee." Faith and hope, and love, all have their notes here, from the bass of humility up to the highest alto of glorious communion, all the different parts are represented. It is a full song—the swell of the diapason of the heart.

I have done when I have said just these words by way of practical result from the subject. One is a word of *consolation*—consolation to you who are under God's anger this morning. My heart goes out after you. I know what your sorrow is. I knew it by the space of five years at a time, when I mourned the guilt and curse of sin. Ah! poor soul, thou art in a sad plight indeed, but be of good cheer ; thou hast in thy bosom, if thou wilt believe me, a key which will open every lock in doubting castle wherein thou art now confined ; if, man, thou hast but heart to take it out of thy bosom, and out of the word of God, and use it, liberty is near. I will show you that key—look at it, " Him that cometh unto me I will in no wise cast out." " Oh, but that does not happen to fit," say you. Well, here's another: " The blood of Jesus Christ his Son cleanseth from all sin." Does not that meet your case ? Then let me try again : " He is able also to save them to the uttermost that come unto God by him." " To the uttermost"—dwell on that, and be comforted. I never knew God shut a soul up in the prison of conviction, but what he sooner or later released the captive. The Lord will surely bring thee out of the low dungeon of conviction. The worst thing in the world is to go unchastised; to be allowed to sin and eat honey with it, this is the precursor of damnation; but to sin, and have the wormwood of repentance with it, this is the prelude of being saved. If the Lord has embittered thy sin, he has designs of love towards thee. His anger shall yet be turned away." "When the poor and needy seek water, and there is none, and their tongue faileth for thirst, I the Lord will hear them, I the God of Israel will not forsake them."

The next is a word of *admonition*. Some of you have been forgiven, but are you praising God as you should? I have heard say, that in our churches there are not more than five per cent. who are doing any real work for Christ. That is not true of this church; I should be very sorry if it were, but I fear there are more than five per cent. who are doing nothing. Where are you who have felt his anger pass away, and yet are not praising him? Come, bestir yourself, bestir yourself, and seek to serve Jesus. Do you not know that you are meant to be the winners of souls? The American bee-hunter when he wants to collect a hive, catches first a single bee, he puts it in a box with a piece of honeycomb, and shuts the door; after awhile, when it is well fed, he lets it out. It comes back again after more of the sweet, but it brings companions with it; and when they have eaten the honey they always bring yet a more numerous band, so by-and-by there is a goodly muster for the hive. After this fashion ought you to act. If you have found mercy, you ought to praise God and tell others, so that they may believe, and in their turn lead others to Jesus. This is the way the kingdom of God grows. I am afraid you are guilty here. See to it, dear brother, see to it, dear sister, and who can tell of what use you yet may be? There was a dear servant of Christ who was just on the borders of the grave, very old and very ill, and frequently delirious, so that the doctors said no one must go into the chamber except the nurse. A little Sunday-school boy, who was rather curious, peeped in at the door to look at the minister, and the poor dying servant of God saw him, and the ruling passion was strong in death. He called him. "David," said he, "did you ever close in with Christ? I have done so many a time, and I long that you may." Fifty years after, that boy was living and bearing testimony that the dying words of the good man had brought him to Jesus, for by them he was led to close in with Christ. You do not know what half a word might do if you would but speak it. O keep not back the good news that might bring salvation to your wife, to your husband, to your child, to your servant. If thou hast indeed felt the Lord's anger pass away this morning, go home to thy chamber, and on thy knees repeat this vow, "My God, I will praise thee! I have been a sluggard, I have been very silent about thee. I am afraid I have not given thee of my substance as I ought; I am sure I have not given thee of my heart as I should; but oh, forgive the past, and accept thy poor servant yet again. 'Then I will praise thee; for though thou wast angry with me, thine anger is turned away, and thou comfortedst me.'"

God bless you, for Christ's sake.

5. More and More

" But I will hope continually, and will yet praise thee more and more."—
Psalm lxxi. 14.

WHEN sin conquered the realm of manhood, it slew all the minstrels except those of the race of Hope. For humanity, amid all its sorrows and sins, hope sings on. To believers in Jesus there remains a royal race of bards, for we have a hope of glory, a lively hope, a hope eternal and divine. Because our hope abides, our praise continues—" I will hope continually, and will yet praise thee." Because our hopes grow brighter, and are every day nearer and nearer to their fulfilment, therefore the volume of our praise increases. " I will hope continually, and yet praise thee *more and more.*" A dying hope would bring forth declining songs ; as the expectations grew more dim, so would the music become more faint ; but a hope immortal and eternal, flaming forth each day with intenser brightness, brings forth a song of praise which, as it shall always continue to arise, so shall it always gather new force. See well, my brethren, to your faith, and your faith and hope, for otherwise God will be robbed of his praise. It will be in proportion as you hope for the good things which he has promised to your faith, that you will render to him the praise which is his royal revenue, acceptable to him by Jesus Christ, and abundantly due from you.

David had not been slack in praise : indeed, he was a sweet singer in Israel, a very choir-master unto the Lord ; yet he vowed to praise him more and more. Those who do much already, are usually the people who can do more. He was old. Would he praise God more when he was infirm than he had done when he was young and vigorous ? If he could not excel with loudness of voice, yet would he with eagerness of heart ; and what his praise might lack in sound, it should gain in solemn earnestness. He was in trouble too, yet he would not allow the heyday of his prosperity to surpass in its notes of loving adoration the dark hour of his adversity. For him on no account could there be any going back. He had adored the Lord when he was but a youth and kept his father's flock. Harp in hand, beneath the spreading tree, he had worshipped the Lord his Shepherd, whose rod and staff were his comfort and delight. When an exile he had made the rocky fastnesses of Adullam and Engedi resound with the name of Jehovah. In after time, when he had become king in Israel, his psalms had been multiplied, and his harpstrings were daily accustomed to the praises of the God of his salvation. How could that zealous songster make an advance in praise? See him yonder dancing before the ark of the Lord with all his might: what more of joy and zeal can be manifest? Yet he says: "I will yet praise thee more and more." His troubles had been multiplied of late, and his infirmities too, yet for all that, no murmuring escapes him, but he resolved that his praise should rise higher and higher till he continued it in better lands for ever and ever.

Beloved, it is an intense joy to me to address you this morning after so long and sad an absence, and I pray that the Holy Spirit may make my word stimulating to you all. Our subject is that of our praising God *more and more.* I do not intend to exhort you to praise God; but shall take it for granted that you are doing so, though I fear it will be a great mistake in the case of many. We must, however, take that fact for granted in those to whom we address ourselves upon our particular topic; for those who do not praise God at all cannot be exhorted to praise him more and more. To those I direct my speech who now love to praise God; these would I charge to resolve with the psalmist: "I will yet praise thee more and more."

I. Our first business shall be, to URGE OURSELVES TO THIS RESOLUTION. Why should we praise God more and more? Here I am embarrassed with the multitude of arguments which beset me. So many crowd around me that I cannot number them in order, but must seize them somewhat at random.

It is humbling to remember that we may very well praise God more than we have done, for *we have praised him very little as yet.* What we have done, as believers, in glorifying God falls far, far short of his due. Personally, upon consideration, we shall each own this. Bethink thee, my dear brother, or sister, what the Lord has done for thee. Some years ago thou wast in thy sin, and death, and ruin; he called thee by his grace. Thou wast under the burden and curse of sin; he delivered thee. Didst thou not expect in thy first joy of pardon to have done more for him, to have loved him more, to have served him better? What are the returns which thou hast made for the boons which thou hast received? Are they at all fitting or adequate? I look at a field loaded with precious grain and ripening for the harvest: I hear that the husbandman has expended so much in rent, so much upon the ploughing, so much upon enriching the soil, so much for seed, so much more for needful weeding. There is the harvest, and it yields a profit: he is contented. But I see another field: it is my own heart; and, my brother, thine is the same. What has the Husbandman done for it? He has reclaimed it from the wild waste, by a power no less then omnipotent. He has hedged it, ploughed it, and cut down the thorns. He has watered it as no other field was ever watered, for the bloody sweat of Christ has bedewed it, to remove the primeval curse. God's own Son has given his whole self that this barren waste may become a garden.

What has been done it were hard to sum: what more could have been done none can say. Yet what is the harvest? Is it adequate to the labour expended? Is the tillage remunerative? I am afraid if we cover our faces, or if a blush shall serve us instead of a veil, it will be the most fit reply to the question. Here and there a withered ear is a poor recompense for the tillage of infinite love. Let us, therefore, be shamed into a firm resolve, and say with resolute spirit: "By the good help of infinite grace, I, at any rate, having been so great a laggard, will quicken my pace; I will yet praise thee more and more."

Another argument which presses upon my mind is this: that wherein we have praised God up till now, *we have not found the service to be a weariness to ourselves, but it has ever been to us both a profit and a delight.* I would not speak falsely even for God, but I bear my testimony that the happiest moments I have ever spent have been occupied with the worship of God. I have never been so near heaven as when adoring before the eternal throne. I think every Christian will bear like witness. Among all the joys of earth, and I shall not depreciate them, there is no joy comparable to that of praise. The innocent mirth of the fireside, the chaste happinesses of household love, even these are not to be mentioned side by side with the joy of worship, the rapture of drawing near to the Most High. Earth, at her best, yields but water, but this divine occupation is as the wine of Cana's marriage feast. The purest and most exhilarating joy is the delight of glorifying God, and so anticipating the time when we shall enjoy him for ever. Now, brethren, if God's praise has been no wilderness to you, return to it with zest and ardour, and say: "I will yet praise thee more and more." If any suppose that you grow weary with the service of the Lord, tell them that his praise is such freedom, such recreation, such felicity, that you desire never to cease from it. As for me, if men call God's service slavery, I desire to be such a bondslave for ever, and would fain be branded with my Master's name indelibly. I would have my ear bored to the door-post of my Lord's house, and go no more out. My soul joyfully sings—

> "Let thy grace, Lord, like a fetter,
> Bind my wandering heart to thee."

This to me shall be ambition—to be more and more subservient to the divine honour. This shall be gain—to be nothing for Christ's sake. This my all in all—to praise thee, my Lord, as long as I have any being.

A third reason readily suggests itself. We ought surely to praise God more to-day than at any other previous day, because *we have received more mercies.* Even of temporal favours we have been large partakers. Begin with these, and then rise higher. Some of you, dear brethren and sisters, may well be reminded of the great temporal mercies which have been lavished upon you. You are to-day in a similar state with Jacob when he said: "With my staff I passed over this Jordan, and now I am become two bands." When you first left your father's house to follow a toilsome occupation, you had a scant enough purse, and but poor prospects; but where are you now as to temporal circumstances and position? How highly God has favoured some of you! Joseph has risen from the dungeon to the throne, David has gone up from the sheepfolds to a palace. Look back to what you were, and give the Lord his due. He lifts up the poor from the dust, and sets them among princes. You were unknown and insignificant, and now his mercy has placed you in prominence and esteem. Is this nothing? Do you despise the bounty of heaven? Will you not praise the Lord more and more for this? Surely, you should do so, and must do so, or else feel the withering curse which blasts ingratitude wherever it dwells. Perhaps divine providence has not dealt with you exactly in that way, but with equal goodness and wisdom has revealed itself to you in another form. You have continued in the same sphere in which you commenced life, but you have been enabled to pursue your work, have been preserved in health and strength, have been supplied with food and raiment; and what is best, have been blessed with a contented heart and a gleaming eye. My dear friend, are you not thankful? Will you not praise your heavenly Father more and more? We ought not to over estimate temporal mercies so as to become worldly; but I am afraid there is a greater likelihood of our under estimating them, and becoming ungrateful. We must beware of so under estimating them as to lessen our sense of the debt in which they involve us before God. We speak sometimes of *great mercies*. Come now, I will ask you a question: Can you count your great mercies? I cannot count mine. Perhaps you think the numeration easy? I find it endless. I was thinking the other day, and I will venture to confess it publicly, what a great mercy it was to be able to turn over in bed. Some of you smile, perhaps. Yet I do not exaggerate when I say, I could almost clap my hands for joy when I found myself able to turn in bed without pain. This day, it is to me a very great mercy to be able to stand upright before you. We carelessly imagine that there are but a score or two of great mercies, such as having our children about us, or enjoying health and so on; but in trying times we see that innumerable minor matters are also great gifts of divine love, and entail great misery when withdrawn. Sing ye, then, as ye draw water at the nether springs, and as the brimming vessels overflow, praise ye the Lord yet more and more.

But ought we not to praise God more and more when we think of our spiritual mercies? What favours have we received of this higher sort! Ten years ago you were bound to praise God for the covenant mercies you had even then enjoyed; but now, how many more have been bestowed upon you; how many cheerings amid darkness; how many answers to prayer; how many directions in dilemma; how many delights of fellowship; how many helps in service; how many successes in conflict; how many revelations of infinite love! To adoption there has been added all the blessings of heirship; to justification, all the security of acceptance; to conversion, all the energies of indwelling. And, remember, as there was no silver cup in Benjamin's sack till Joseph put it there, so there was no spiritual good in you till the Lord of mercy gave it. Therefore, praise ye the Lord. Louder and louder yet be the song. Praise him on the high-sounding cymbals. Since we cannot hope to measure his mercies, let us immeasurably praise our God. "I will yet praise thee more and more."

Let us now go on a little farther. We have been *proving through a series of years the faithfulness, immutability, and veracity of our God*—proving these attributes by our sinning against God, and their bearing the strain of our misbehaviour—proving them by the innumerable benefits which the Lord has bestowed upon us. Shall all this experience end in no result? Shall there be no advance in gratitude where there is such an increase of obligation? God is so good that every moment of his love demands a life of praise.

It should never be forgotten that *every Christian as he grows in grace should have a loftier idea of God.* Our highest conception of God falls infinitely short of his glory, but an advanced Christian enjoys a far clearer view of what God is than he had at the first. Now, the greatness of God is ever a claim for praise. "Great is the Lord, and"—what follows?—"greatly to be praised." If, then, God is greater to me than he was, let my praise be greater. If I think of him now more tenderly as my Father—if I have a clearer view of him in the terror of his justice—if I have a clearer view of the splendours of his wisdom by which he devised the atonement—if I have larger thoughts of his eternal, immutable love—let every advance in knowledge constrain me to say: "I will yet praise thee more and more." I heard of thee by the hearing of the ear, but now mine eye seeth thee: therefore while I abhor myself in dust and ashes, my praise shall rise yet more loftily; up to thy throne shall my song ascend. I did but see as it were the skirts of thy garment, but thou hast hidden me in the cleft of the rock Christ Jesus, and made thy glory pass before me, and now will I praise thee even as the seraphs do, and vie with those before the throne in magnifying thy name. We learn but little in Christ's school, if the practical result of it all be not to make us cry: "I will yet praise thee more and more."

Still culling here and there a thought out of thousands, I would remind you that it is a good reason for praising God more that *we are getting nearer to the place where we hope to praise him, world without end, after a perfect sort.* Never have we made these walls ring more joyously than when we have united in singing of our Father's house on high, and the tents pitched—

> "A day's march nearer home."

Heaven is indeed the only home of our souls, and we shall never feel that we have come to our rest till we have reached its mansions. One reason why we shall be able to rest in heaven, is because we shall there be able perpetually to achieve the object of our creation. Am I nearer heaven? then I will be doing more of the work which I shall do in heaven. I shall soon use the harp: let me be carefully tuning it: let me rehearse the hymns which I shall sing before the throne; for if the words in heaven shall be sweeter and more rich than any that poets can put together here, yet the essential song of heaven shall be the same as that which we present to Jehovah here below.

> "They praise the Lamb in hymns above,
> And we in hymns below."

The essence of their praise is gratitude that he should bleed: it is the essence of our praise too. They bless Immanuel's name for undeserved favours bestowed upon unworthy ones, and we do the same. My aged brethren, I congratulate you, for you are almost home; be yet more full of praise than ever. Quicken your footsteps as the glory land shines more brightly. You are close to the gate of pearl; sing on, dear brother, though infirmities increase, and let the song grow sweeter and louder until it melts into the infinite harmonies.

Shall I need to give another reason why we should praise God more and more? If I must, I would throw this one into the scale, that surely at this present juncture we ought to be more earnest in the praise of God, because *God's enemies are very earnest in labouring to dishonour him.* These are times when scoffers are boundlessly impudent. Did it not make your blood chill when you heard revolutionists in unhappy Paris talk of having " demolished God"? It struck me as almost a sadder thing when I read the proposition of one of their philosophers who would have them become religious again, that they should bring God back again for ten years at least—an audacious recommendation as blasphemously impertinent as the insolence which had proclaimed the triumph of atheism. But we need not look across the Channel ; perhaps they speak more honestly on that side than we do here; for among ourselves we have abounding infidelity, which pretends to reverence Scripture while it denies its plainest teachings; and we have what is quite as bad, a superstition which thrusts Christ aside for the human priest, and makes the sacraments everything, and simple trust in the great atonement to be as nothing. Now, my brethren, those who hold these views are not sleepers, nor do they relax their efforts. *We* may be very quiet and lukewarm about religion (alas! that we should be); but these persons are earnest propagators of their faith, or no faith— they compass sea and land to make one proselyte. As we think of these busy servants of Satan, we ought to chide ourselves and say : " Shall Baal be diligently served, and Jehovah have such a sleepy advocate? Be stirred, my soul! Awake, my spirit! Arouse thee at once, and praise thy God more and more!"

But, indeed, while I give you these few arguments out of many that come to my mind, the thought cheers my spirit that with those of you who know and love God, there is little need for me to mention reasons, for your own souls are hungering and thirsting to praise him. If you are debarred for a little time from the public service of God, you pant for the assemblies of God's house, and envy the swallows that build their nests beneath the eaves. If you are unable to accomplish service which you were accustomed to perform for Christ's church, the hours drag very wearily along. As the Master found it his meat and his drink to do the will of him that sent him, so when you are unable to do that will, you are like a person deprived of his meat and drink, and an insatiable hunger grows upon you. O Christian brother, do you not pant to praise God? I am sure you feel now: " O that I could praise him better ! " You are perhaps in a position in which you have work to do for him, and your heart is saying, " How I wish I could do this work more thoroughly to his praise!" Or possibly you are in such a condition of life that it is little you can do, and you often wish if God would make a change for you, not that it should be one more full of comfort, but one in which you could be more serviceable. Above all, I know you wish you were rid of sin, and everything which hinders your praising God more and more. Well, then, I need not argue, for your own heart pleads the holy cause.

Suffer me to conclude this head with a fact that illustrates the point. I know one, who has been long privileged to lift his voice in the choir of the great King. In that delightful labour none more happy than he. The longer he was engaged in the work the more he loved it. Now, it came to pass that on a certain day, this songster found himself shut out of the choir; he would have entered to take his part, but he was not permitted. Perhaps the King was angry ; perhaps the songster had sung carelessly; perhaps he had acted unworthily in some other matter; or possibly his master knew that his song would grow more sweet if he were silenced for awhile. How it was I know not, but this I know, that it caused great searching of heart. Often this chorister begged to be restored, but he was as often repulsed, and somewhat roughly too. I think it was more than three months that this unhappy songster was kept in enforced silence, with fire in his bones and no vent for it. The royal music went on without him; there was no lack of song, and in this he rejoiced, but he longed to take his place again. I cannot tell you how eagerly he longed. At last the happy hour arrived, the king gave his permit, he might sing again. The songster was full of gratitude, and I heard him say—you shall hear him say it : " My Lord, since I am again restored, I will hope continually, and will yet praise thee more and more."

II. Now let us turn to another point. Let us in the Spirit's strength DRIVE AWAY THAT WHICH HINDERS US FROM PRAISING GOD MORE AND MORE.

One of the deadliest things is *dreaminess*, sleepiness. A Christian readily falls into this state. I notice it even in the public congregation. Very often the whole service is gone through mechanically. That same dreaminess falls upon many professors and abides with them, and instead of praising God more and more, it is as much as ever they can do to keep up the old strain—and barely that. Let us shake ourselves from all such sleep. Surely if there were any service in which a man should be altogether and wholly awake, it is in praising and magnifying God. A sleepy seraph before the throne of Jehovah, or a cherub nodding during sacred song, it were ridiculous to imagine. And shall such an insult to the majesty of heaven be seen on earth ? No ! Let us say to all that is within us, " Awake ! awake !"

The next hindrance would be *divided objects*. We cannot, however we may resolve, praise God more and more, if, as we grow older, we allow this world to take up our thoughts. If I say, " I will praise God more and more," and yet I am striking out right and left with projects of amassing wealth, or I am plunging myself into greater business cares unnecessarily, my actions belie my resolutions. Not that we would check enterprise. There are periods in life when a man may be enabled to praise God more and more by extending the bounds of his business; but there are persons whom I have known who have praised God right well in a certain condition, but they have not been content to let well alone, and they have been for aggrandising themselves, and they have had to give up their Sabbath-school class, or the village station, or attendance at the visiting committee, or some other form of Christian service, because their money-getting demanded all their strength. Beloved, you shall find it small gain if you gain in this world, but lose in praising God. As we grow older, it is wise to concentrate more and more our energies upon the one thing, the only thing worth living for—the praise of God.

Another great obstacle to praising God more is, *self-content;* and this, again, is a condition into which we may very easily fall. Our belief is, only we must not avow it when we may be overheard, we are all very fine fellows indeed. We may confess when we are praying, and at other times, that we are miserable sinners—and I daresay we have some belief that it is so—but for all that, there is within our minds the conviction that we are very respectable people, and are doing exceedingly well upon the whole; and comparing ourselves with other Christians, it is much to our credit that we are praising God as well as we are. Now, I have put this very roughly, but is it not what the heart has said to us at times? Oh, loathsome thought! that a sinner should grow content with himself. Self-satisfaction is the end of progress. Dear friend, why compare yourself with the dwarfs around you? If you must compare yourself with your fellow men, look at the giants of other days; but, better still, relinquish the evil habit altogether; for Paul tells us it is not wise to compare ourselves among ourselves. Look to our Lord and Master, who towers so high above us in peerless excellence. No, no, we dare not flatter ourselves, but with humble self-condemnation we resolve to praise the Lord more and more.

To *rest on the past* is another danger as to this matter. We did so much for God when we were young. I occasionally meet with drones in the Christian hive, whose boast is that they made a great deal of honey years ago. I see men lying upon their oars to-day, but they startle me with a description of the impetus they gave to the boat years ago. You should have seen them when they were master-rowers, in those former times. What a pity that these brethren cannot be aroused to do their first works; it would be a gain to the church, but it would be an equal benefit to themselves. Suppose God should say, " Rest on the past. I gave you great mercies twenty years ago; live on them." Suppose the eternal and ever beloved Spirit should say, " I wrought a work in you thirty years ago; I withdraw myself, and I will do no more." Where were you then? Yet, my dear brother, if you still have to draw afresh upon the eternal fountains, do, I beseech you, praise the ever-blessed source of all.

May God help us then to shake off all those things which would prevent our praising him ! Possibly there is some afflicted one here, in so low a state, so far pressed by poverty or bodily pain, that he is saying : " I cannot praise God more and more : I am ready to despair." Dear brother, may God give you full resignation to his will, and the greater your troubles the sweeter will be your song. I met in an old divine a short but sweet story, which touched my heart. A poor widow and her little child were sitting together in great want, both feeling the pinch of hunger, and the child looked up into the mother's face, and said :

"Mother, God won't starve us, will he?" "No, my child," said the mother; "I do not think he will." "But, mother," said the child, "if he does, we will still praise him as long as we live; won't we, mother?" May those who are grey-headed be able to say what the child said, and to carry it out. "Though he slay me, yet will I trust in him." We have received good at the hands of the Lord; shall we not also receive evil?" "The Lord gave, and the Lord hath taken away; blessed be the name of the Lord." "I will yet praise thee more and more."

III. Very briefly LET US APPLY OURSELVES TO THE PRACTICAL CARRYING OUT OF THIS RESOLUTION. I have given you arguments for it, and tried to move away impediments. Now for a little help in the performance of it. How shall I begin to praise God more and more?

Earnestness says: "I shall undertake some fresh duty this afternoon." Stop, dear brother, just a minute. If you want to praise God, would not it be as well first to begin with yourself? The musician said: "I will praise God better;" but the pipes of his instrument were foul; he had better look to them first. If the strings have slipped from their proper tension, it will be well to correct them before beginning the tune. If we would praise God more, it is not to be done as boys rush into a bath—head first. No; prepare yourself; make your heart ready. Thou needest the Spirit's aid to make thy soul fit for praising God. It is not every fool's work. Go then to thy chamber, confess the sins of the past, and ask the Lord to give thee much more grace that thou mayst begin to praise him.

If we would praise God more and more, let us improve our private devotions. God is much praised by really devout prayer and adoration. Preachings are not fruits: they are sowings. True song is fruit. I mean this, that the green blade of the wheat may be the sermon, but the wheat-ear is the hymn you sing, the prayer in which you unite. The true result of life is praise to God. "The chief end of man," says the catechism, and I cannot put it better, "is to glorify God, and enjoy him for ever;" and wherein we glorify God in our private devotion, we are answering the true end of our being. If we desire to praise God more, we must ask grace that our private devotions may rise to a higher standard. I am more and more persuaded from my own experience, that in proportion to the strength of our private life with God will be the force of our character, and the power of our work for God amongst men. Let us look well to this.

Again, however, I hear the zealous young man or woman saying: "Well, I will attend to what you have said. I will see to private prayer and to heart work, but I mean to begin some work of usefulness." Quite right; but stay a little. I want to ask you this question: Are you sure that your own personal conduct in what you call your every-day life has as much of the praise of God in it as it might have? It is all a mistake to think that we must come here to praise God. You can praise God in your shops, and in your kitchens, and in your bed-rooms. It is all a mistake to suppose that Sunday is the only day to praise God in. Praise him on Mondays, Tuesdays, Wednesdays, every day, everywhere. All places are holy to holy people, and all engagements holy to holy men, if they do them with holy motives, lifting up their hearts to God; and whether a man swings the blacksmith's hammer, or lays his hand upon the ploughtail, that is true worship which is done as unto the Lord and not unto men. I like the story of the servant-maid, who, when she was asked on joining the church, "Are you converted?" "I hope so, sir." "What makes you think you are really a child of God?" "Well, sir, there is a great change in me from what there used to be." "What is that change?" "I don't know, sir, but there is a change in all things; but there is one thing, *I always sweep under the mats now.*" Many a time she had hidden the dust under the mat. It was not so now; it is a very excellent reason for believing that there is a change of heart when work is conscientiously done. There is a set of mats in all our houses where we are accustomed to put the dirt away ; and when a man gets in his business to sweep from under the mats—you merchants have your mats, you know, when you avoid the evils which custom tolerates but which God condemns, then you have marks of grace within. Oh, to have a conduct moulded by the example of Christ! If any man lived after a holy sort, though he never preached a sermon or even sung a hymn, he would have praised God; and the more conscientiously he acted, the more thoroughly would he have done so.

These inner matters being considered, let us go on to increase our actual and direct service of God. Let us do what we have been doing of Christian teaching, visiting, and so on; but in all let us do more, give more, and labour more. Who among us is working at his utmost, or giving at his utmost? Let us quicken our speed. Or suppose we are already doing so much that all the time we can possibly spare is fully occupied, let us do what we do better. In some Christian churches they do not want more societies, but they want more force put into them. You may trip over the sand of the sea-shore and scarcely leave an impression, but if you take heavy steps there is a deep foot-mark each time. May we in our service of God tread heavily, and leave deep foot-prints on the sands of time. Whatsoever ye do, do it heartily; throw yourselves into it; do it with thy might. "Thou shalt love the Lord thy God with all thine heart, and with all thy soul, and with all thy might." Oh, to be enabled to serve God after this fashion—this would be to praise him more and more! Though I do not say that you can always tell how far a man praises God by the quantity of work that he does for God, yet it is not a bad gauge. It was an old aphorism of Hippocrates, the old physician, that you could judge of a man's heart by his arm ; by which he meant that by his pulse he judged of his heart: and as a rule, though there may be exceptions, you shall tell whether a man's heart beats truly to God, by the work that he does for God. You who are doing much, do more; and you who are doing little, multiply that little, I pray you, in God's strength, and so praise him more and more.

We should praise God much more if we threw more of his praise into our common conversation—if we spoke more of him when we are by the way or when we sit in the house. We should praise him more and more if we fulfilled our consecration, and obeyed the precept, "Whether therefore ye eat, or drink, or whatsoever ye do, do all to the glory of God." We should do well if we added to our godly service more singing. The world sings: the million have their songs; and I must say the taste of the populace is a very remarkable taste just now as to its favourite songs. They are, many of them, so absurd and meaningless as to be unworthy of an idiot. I should insult an idiot if I could suppose that such songs as people sing nowadays would really be agreeable to him. Yet these things will be heard from *men*, and places will be thronged to listen to hear the stuff. Now, why should we, with the grand psalms we have of David, with the noble hymns of Cowper, of Milton, of Watts—why should not we sing as well as they? Let us sing the songs of Zion . they are as cheerful as the songs of Sodom any day. Let us drown the howling nonsense of Gomorrha with the melodies of the New Jerusalem.

But to conclude, I would that every Christian here would labour to be impressed with the importance of the subject which I have tried to bring before you. And when I say every Christian, I may correct myself and say, every person here present. "I will yet praise thee more and more." Why some of you present have never praised God at all! Suppose you were to die to-day, and soon you must: where should you go? To heaven? Where would heaven be to you? There can be no heaven for you. They praise God in the only heaven I have ever heard of. The element of heaven is gratitude, praise, adoration. You do not know anything of this, and therefore it would not be possible for God to make a heaven for you. God can do all things except make a sinful spirit happy, or violate truth and justice. Thou must either praise God or be wretched. O my hearer, there is a choice for thee: thou must either worship the God that made thee, or else thou must be wretched. It is not that he kindles a fire for thee, nor that he casts upon it the brimstone of his wrath, though that be true ; but thy wretchedness will begin within thyself, for to be unable to praise is to be full of hell. To praise God is heaven. When completely immersed in adoration, we are completely filled with felicity ; but to be totally devoid of gratitude is to be totally devoid of happiness. O that a change might come over you who have never blessed the Lord, and may it happen this morning ! May the work of regeneration take place now ! There is power in the Holy Spirit to change thy heart of stone in a moment into a heart of flesh, so that instead of being cold and lifeless, it shall palpitate with gratitude. Seest thou not Christ on the cross dying for sinners? Canst thou look on that disinterested love, and not feel some gratitude for such love as is there exhibited? Oh, if thou canst look to Jesus and trust him, thou shalt feel a flash of life come into thy soul, and with it shall come praise, and then shalt thou find it possible to begin the happy life, and it shall be certain to thee that as thou shalt praise God more and more, so shall that happy life be expanded, be perfected in bliss.

But Christians, the last word shall be to you. Are you praising God more and more ? If you are not, I am afraid of one thing, and that is, that you are probably praising him less and less. It is a certain truth that if we do not go forward in the Christian life, we go backward. You cannot stand still ; there is a drift one way or the other. Now he that praises God less than he did, and goes on to praise him less to-morrow, and less the next day, and so on—what will he get to ? and what is he ? Evidently he is one of those that draw back unto perdition, and there are no persons upon whom a more dreadful sentence is pronounced, often spoken of by Paul, and most terribly by Peter and Jude Those " Trees twice dead, plucked up by the roots;" the " Wandering stars for whom is reserved the blackness of darkness for ever." It would have been infinitely better for them not to have known the way of righteousness, than having known it, after a fashion, to have turned aside ! Better never to have put their hand to the plough, than having done so, after a sort, to turn back from it.

But, beloved, I am persuaded better things of you, and things that accompany salvation, though I thus speak. I pray that God will lead you on from strength to strength, for that is the path of the just. May you grow in grace, for life is proven by growth. May you march like pilgrims towards heaven, singing all the way. The lark may serve us as a final picture, and an example of what we all should be. We should be mounting: our prayer should be, " Nearer, my God, to thee." We should be mounting: our motto might well be, " Higher! higher! higher ! " As we mount, we should sing, and our song should grow louder, clearer, more full of heaven. Upward, brother ! sing as thou soarest. Upward, sing till thou art dissolved in glory. Amen.

6. Praises and Vows Accepted in Zion

"Praise waiteth for thee, O God, in Sion: and unto thee shall the vow be performed. O thou that hearest prayer, unto thee shall all flesh come."—Psalm lxv. 1, 2.

UPON Zion there was erected an altar dedicated to God for the offering of sacrifices. Except when prophets were commanded by God to break through the rule, burnt offering was only to be offered there. The worship of God upon the high places was contrary to the divine command: "Take heed to thyself that thou offer not thy burnt offerings in every place that thou seest: but in the place which the Lord shall choose in one of thy tribes, there thou shalt offer thy burnt offerings, and there thou shalt do all that I command thee." Hence the tribes on the other side of Jordan, when they erected a memorial altar, disclaimed all intention of using it for the purpose of sacrifice, and said most plainly, "God forbid that we should rebel against the Lord, and turn this day from following the Lord, to build an altar for burnt offerings, for meat offerings, or for sacrifices, beside the altar of the Lord our God that is before his tabernacle."

In fulfilment of this ancient type, we also "have an altar whereof they have no right to eat that serve the tabernacle." Into our spiritual worship, no observers of materialistic ritualism may intrude; they have no right to eat at our spiritual altar, and there is no other at which they can eat and live for ever. There is but one altar—Jesus Christ our Lord. All other altars are impostures and idolatrous inventions. Whether of stone, or wood, or brass, they are the toys with which those amuse themselves who have returned to the beggarly elements of Judaism, or else the apparatus with which clerical jugglers dupe the sons and daughters of men. Holy places made with hands are now abolished; they were once the figures of the true, but now that the substance has come, the type is done away with. The all-glorious person of the Redeemer, God and Man, is the great centre of Zion's temple, and the only real altar of sacrifice. He is the church's head, the church's heart, the church's altar, priest, and all in all. "To him shall the gathering of the people be." Around him we all congregate even as the tribes around the tabernacle of the Lord in the wilderness.

When the church is gathered together, we may liken it to the assemblies upon Mount Zion, whither the tribes go up, even the tribes of the Lord, unto the testimony of Israel. There the song went up, not so much from each separate worshipper as from all combined; there the praise as it rose to heaven was not only the praise of each one, but the praise of all. So where Christ is the centre, where his one sacrifice is the altar whereon all offerings are laid; and where the church unites around that common centre, and rejoices in that one sacrifice, there is the true Zion. If we this evening—gathering in Christ's name, around his one finished sacrifice, present our prayers and praises entirely to the Lord through Jesus Christ, we are " come unto Mount Zion, and unto the city of the living God, the heavenly Jerusalem, and to an innumerable company of angels, to the general assembly and church of the firstborn, whose names are written in heaven." This is Zion, even this house in the far-off islands of the Gentiles, and we can say indeed and of a truth, " Praise waiteth for thee, O God, in Zion ; and unto thee shall the vow be performed."

We shall, with devout attention, notice two things: the first *is our holy worship, which we desire to render;* and then the encouragement, *the stimulative encouragement, which God provides for us:* " O thou that hearest prayer, unto thee shall all flesh come."

I. First, let us consider the HOLY OFFERING OF WORSHIP WHICH WE DESIRE TO PRESENT TO GOD. It is twofold : there is praise, and there is also a vow, a praise that waiteth, and a vow of which performance is promised.

Let us think, first of all, of *the praise.* This is the chief ingredient of the adoration of heaven; and what is thought to be worthy of the world of glory, ought to be the main portion of the worship of earth. Although we shall never cease to pray as long as we live here below, and are surrounded by so many wants, yet we should never so pray as to forget to praise. " Thy kingdom come. Thy will be done on earth, as it is heaven," must never be left out because we are pressed with want, and therefore hasten to cry, " Give us this day our daily bread." It will be a sad hour when the worship of the church shall be only a solemn wail. Notes of exultant thanksgiving should ever ascend from her solemn gatherings. " Praise the Lord, O Jerusalem ; praise thy God, O Zion." " Praise ye the Lord. Sing unto the Lord a new song, and his praise in the congregation of saints. Let Israel rejoice in him that made him : let the children of Zion be joyful in their King." Let it abide as a perpetual ordinance, while sun and moon endure, " Praise waiteth for thee, O God, in Zion." Never think little of praise, since holy angels and saints made perfect count it their life-long joy, and even the Lord himself saith, " Whoso offereth praise, glorifieth me." The tendency, I fear, among us has been to undervalue praise as a part of public worship, whereas it should be second to nothing. We frequently hear of prayer-meetings, and but seldom of praise-meetings. We acknowledge the duty of prayer by setting apart certain times for it ; we do not always so acknowledge the duty of praise. I hear of " family prayer;" do I always hear of "family praise?" I know you cultivate private prayer: are you as diligent also in private thanksgiving and secret adoration of the Lord? In everything we are to give thanks; it is as much an apostolic precept as that other, "In everything, by prayer and supplication, make your requests known unto God." I have often said to you, dear brethren, that prayer and praise are like the breathing in and out of the air, and make up that spiritual respiration by which the inner life is instrumentally supported. We take in an inspiration of heavenly air as we pray: we breathe it out again in praise unto God, from whom it came; if, then, we would be healthy in spirit, let us be abundant in thanksgiving. Prayer, like the root of a tree, seeks for and finds nutriment; praise, like the fruit, renders a revenue to the owner of the vineyard. Prayer is for ourselves, praise is for God; let us never be so selfish as to abound in the one and fail in the other. Praise is a slender return for the boundless favours we enjoy; let us not be slack in rendering it in our best music, the music of a devout soul. "Praise the Lord; for the Lord is good: sing praises unto his name; for it is pleasant."

Let us notice the praise which is mentioned in our text, which is to be so large a matter of concern to the Zion of God whenever the saints are met together.

You will observe, first, that it is praise *exclusively rendered to God.* "Praise waiteth for *thee, O God*, in Zion." "Praise for *thee*, and *all* the praise for thee," and no praise for man or for any other who may be thought to be, or may pretend to be, worthy of praise. Have I not sometimes gone into places called houses of God where the praise has waited for a woman—for the Virgin, where praise has waited for the saints, where incense has smoked to heaven, and songs and prayers have been sent up to deceased martyrs and confessors who are supposed to have power with God? In Rome it is so, but in Zion it is not so. Praise waiteth for thee, O *Mary*, in Babylon; but praise waiteth for thee, O *God*, in Zion. Unto God, and unto God alone, the praise of his true church must ascend. If Protestants are free from this deadly error, I fear they are guilty of another, for in our worship we too often minister unto our own selves. We do so when we make the tune and manner of the song to be more important than the matter of it. I am afraid that where organs, choirs, and singing men and singing women are left to do the praise of the congregation, men's minds are more occupied with the due performance of the music, than with the Lord, who alone is to be praised. God's house is meant to be sacred unto himself, but too often it is made an opera-house, and Christians form an audience, not an adoring assembly. The same thing may, unless great care be taken, happen amid the simplest worship, even though everything which does not savour of gospel plainness is excluded, for in that case we may drowsily drawl out the words and notes, with no heart whatever. To sing with the soul, this only is to offer acceptable song! We come not together to amuse ourselves, to display our powers of melody, or our aptness in creating harmony; we come to pay our adoration at the footstool of the Great King, to whom alone be glory for ever and ever. True praise is for God—for God alone.

Brethren, you must take heed lest the minister, who would, above all, disclaim a share of praise, should be set up as a demi-god among you. Refute practically the old slander that presbyter is only priest writ large. Look higher than the pulpit, or you will be disappointed. Look far above an arm of flesh, or it will utterly fail you. We may say of the best preacher upon the earth, "Give God the praise, for we know that this man is a sinner." If we thought that you paid superstitious reverence to us, we would, like Paul and Silas at Lystra, rend our clothes, and cry, "Sirs, why do ye these things? We also are men of like passions with you, and preach unto you that ye should turn from these vanities unto the living God, which made heaven, and earth, and the sea, and all things that are therein." It is not to any man, to any priest, to any order of men, to any being in heaven or earth beside God, that we should burn the incense of worship. We would as soon worship cats with the Egyptians, as popes with the Romanists: we see no difference between the people whose gods grew in their gardens and the sect whose deity is made by their baker. Such vile idolatry is to be loathed. To God alone shall all the praise of Zion ascend.

It is to be feared that some of our praise ascends nowhere at all, but it is as though it were scattered to the winds. We do not always realise God. Now, "he that cometh to God must believe that he is, and that he is the rewarder of them that diligently seek him;" this is as true of praise as of prayer. "God is a Spirit," and they that praise him must praise him "in spirit and in truth," for "the Father seeketh such" to praise him, and only such; and, if we do not lift our eyes and our hearts to him, we are but misusing words and wasting time. Our praise is not as it should be, if it be not reverently and earnestly directed to the Lord of Hosts. Vain is it to shoot arrows without a target: we must aim at God's glory in our holy songs, and that exclusively.

Note, next, that *it should be continual.* "Praise *waiteth* for thee, O God, in Zion." Some translators conceive that the main idea is that of continuance. It remains; it abides; for Zion does not break up when the assembly is gone. We do not leave the holiness in the material house, for it never was in the stone and the timber, but only in the living assembly of the faithful.

> "Jesus, where'er thy people meet,
> There they behold thy mercy-seat;
> Where'er they seek thee, thou art found,
> And every place is hallow'd ground,
>
> For thou within no walls confined,
> Inhabitest the humble mind;
> Such ever bring thee where they come,
> And going, take thee to their home."

The people of God, as they never cease to be a church, should maintain the Lord's praise perpetually as a community. Their assemblies should begin with praise and end with praise, and ever be conducted in a spirit of praise. There should be in all our solemn assemblies a spiritual incense-altar, always smoking with "the pure incense of sweet spices, mingled according to the art of the apothecary": the thanksgiving which is made up of humility, gratitude, 'ove, consecration, and holy joy in the Lord.

It should be for the Lord alone, and it should never go out day nor night. "His mercy endureth for ever:" let our praises endure for ever. He makes the outgoings of the morning to rejoice, let us celebrate the rising of the sun with holy psalm and hymn. He makes the closing in of the evening to be glad, let him have our vesper praise. "One generation shall praise thy works to another, and shall declare thy mighty acts." Could his mercy cease, there might be some excuse for staying our praises: but, even should it seem to be so, men who love the Lord would say with Job, "Shall we receive good at the hand of the Lord, and shall we not also receive evil? The Lord gave, and the Lord hath taken away; and blessed be the name of the Lord." Let our praise abide, continue, remain, and be perpetual. It was a good idea of Bishop Farrar, that, in his own house, he would keep up continual praise to God; and as, with a large family and household, he numbered just twenty-four, he set apart each one for an hour in the day to be engaged specially in prayer and praise, that he might girdle the day with a circle of worship. We could not do that. To attempt it might on our part be superstition; but to fall asleep blessing God, to rise in the night to meditate on him, and when we wake in the morning to feel our hearts leap in the prospect of his presence during the day, this is attainable, and we ought to reach it. It is much to be desired that all day long, in every avocation, and every recreation, the soul should spontaneously pour forth praise, even as birds sing, and flowers perfume the air, and sunbeams cheer the earth. We would be incarnate psalmody, praise enshrined in flesh and blood. From this delightful duty we would desire no cessation, and ask no pause. "Praise *waits* for thee, O God, in Zion;" thy praise may come and go, from the outside world, where all things ebb and flow, for it lies beneath the moon, and there is no stability in it; but amidst thy people, who dwell in thee, and who possess eternal life—in them thy praise perpetually abides.

A third point, however, is clear upon the surface of the words. "Praise *waiteth* for thee"—as though *praise must always be humble.* The servants "wait" in the king's palace. There the messengers stand girt for any mission; the servitors wait, prepared to obey; and the courtiers surround the throne, all eager to receive the royal smile and to fulfil the high command. Our praises ought to stand, like ranks of messengers, waiting to hear what God's will is; for this is to praise him, Furthermore, true praise lies in the actual doing of the divine will, even this,—to pause in sacred reverence until God the Lord shall speak, whatever that will may be; it is true praise to wait subserviently on him. Praises may be looked upon as servants who delight to obey their master's bidding. There is such a thing as an unholy familiarity with God; this age is not so likely to fall into it as some ages have been, for there is little familiarity with God of any sort now; public worship becomes more formal, and stately, and distant. The intense nearness to God which Luther enjoyed—how seldom do we meet with it! But, however near we come to God, still he *is God*, and we are his creatures. He is, it is true, "our Father," but be it ever remembered that he is "our Father which art in heaven." "Our *Father*"—therefore near and intimate: "our Father *in heaven*," therefore we humbly, solemnly bow in his presence. There is a familiarity that runs into presumption:

there is another familiarity, which is so sweetly tempered with humility that it doth not intrude. " Praise waiteth for thee " with a servant's livery on, a servant's ear to hear, and a servant's heart to obey. Praise bows at thy foot-stool, feeling that it is still an unprofitable servant.

But, perhaps, you are aware, dear friends, that there are other translations of this verse. " Praise waiteth for thee," may be read, " Praise is silent unto thee "—" is silent before thee." One of the oldest Latin commentators reads it, " Praise and silence belong unto thee;" and Dr. Gill tells us, that in the King of Spain's Bible, it runs, " The praise of angels is only silence before thee, O Jehovah," so that when we do our best our highest praise is but silence before God, and we must praise him *with confession of shortcomings*. Oh, that we too, as our poet puts it, might,

> " Loud as his thunders speak his praise,
> And sound it lofty as his throne !"

But we cannot do that, and when our notes are most uplifted, and our hearts most joyous, we have not spoken all his praise. Compared to what his nature and glory deserve, our most earnest praise has been little more than silence. Oh, brethren, have you not often felt it to be so? Those who are satisfied with formal worship, think that they have done well when the music has been correctly sung; but those who worship God in spirit, feel that they cannot magnify him enough. They blush over the hymns they sing, and retire from the assembly of the saints mourning that they have fallen far short of his glory. O for an enlarged mind, rightly to conceive the divine majesty; next for the gift of utterance to clothe the thought in fitting language; and then for a voice like many waters, to sound forth the noble strain. Alas ! as yet, we are humbled at our failures to praise the Lord as we would.

> " Words are but air, and tongues but clay,
> And his compassions are divine ;

How, then, shall we proclaim to men God's glory? When we have done our best, our praise is but silence before the merit of his goodness, and the grandeur of his greatness.

Yet it may be well to observe here, that the praise which God accepts, presents itself *under a variety of forms*. There is praise for God in Zion, and it is often spoken; but there is often praise for God in Zion, and it is silence. There are some who cannot sing vocally, but perhaps, before God, they sing best. There are some, I know, who sing very harshly and inharmoniously—that is to say, to our ears ; and yet God may accept them rather than the noise of stringed instruments carefully touched. There is a story told of Rowland Hill's being much troubled by a good old lady who would sit near him and sing with a most horrible voice, and very loudly—as those people generally do who sing badly—and he at last begged her not to sing so loudly. But when she said, "It comes from my heart," the honest man of God retracted his rebuke, and said, " Sing away, I should be sorry to stop you." When praise comes from the heart, who would wish to restrain it. Even the shouts of the old Methodists, their " hallelujahs " and "glorys," when uttered in fervour, were not to be forb.lden; for if these should hold their peace, even the stones would cry out. But there are times when those who sing, and sing well, have too much praise in their soul for it to enclose itself in words. Like some strong liquors which cannot use a little vent, but foam and swell until they burst each hoop that binds the barrel; so, sometimes, we want a larger channel for our soul than that of mouth and tongue, and we long to have all our nerves and sinews made into harpstrings, and all the pores of our body made mouths of thankfulness. Oh, that we could praise with our whole nature, not one single hair of our heads, or drop of blood in our veins, keeping back from adoring the Most High! When this desire for praise is most vehement, we fall back upon silence, and quiver with the adoration which we cannot speak. Silence becomes our praise.

> " A sacred reverence checks our songs,
> And praise sits silent on our tongues."

It would be well, perhaps, in our public service, if we had more often the sweet relief of silence. I am persuaded that silence, ay, frequent silence, is most beneficial; and the occasional unanimous silence of all the saints when they bow before God would, perhaps, better express, and more fully promote, devout feeling than any hymns which have been composed or songs that could be sung. To make silence a part of worship habitually might be affectation and formalism, but to introduce it occasionally, and even frequently into the service, would be advantageous and profitable. Let us, then, by our silence, praise God, and let us always confess that our praise, compared with God's deserving, is but silence.

I would add that there is in the text the idea that praise waits for God *expectantly*. When we praise God, we expect to see more of him by and by, and therefore wait for him. We bless the King, but we desire to draw nearer to him. We magnify him for what we have seen, and we expect to see more. We praise him in his outer courts, for we shall soon be with him in the heavenly mansions. We glorify him for the revelation of himself in Jesus, for we expect to be like Christ, and to be with him where he is. When I cannot praise God for what I am, I will praise him for what I shall be. When I feel dull and dead about the present, I will take the words of our delightful hymn and say,

> " And a new song is in my mouth,
> To long-loved music set;
> Glory to thee for all the grace
> I have not tasted yet."

My praise shall not only be the psalmody of the past, which is but discharging a debt of gratitude, but my faith shall anticipate the future, and wait upon God to fulfil his purposes; and I will begin to pay my praise even before the mercy comes.

Dear brethren and sisters, let us for a moment present our praise to God, each one of us on his own account. We have our common mercies. We call them common, but, oh, how priceless they are. Health to be able to come here and not to be stretched on a bed of sickness, I count this better than bags of gold. To have our reason, and not to be confined in yonder asylum; to have our children still about us and dear relatives spared still to us—to have bread to eat and raiment to put on —to have been kept from defiling our character—to have been preserved to-day from the snares of the enemy! These are godlike mercies, and for all these our praises shall wait upon God.

But oh! take up the thoughts suggested by the psalm itself in the next verse, and you will doubly praise God. "Iniquities prevail against me. As for our transgressions, thou shalt purge them away." Infinite love has made us clean every whit!—though we were black and filthy. We are washed—washed in priceless blood. Praise him for this! Go on with the passage, "Blessed is the man whom thou choosest and causest to approach unto thee." Is not the blessing of access to God an exceeding choice one? Is it a light thing to feel that, though once far off, we are made nigh through the blood of Christ; and this because of electing love! "Blessed is the man whom thou choosest." Ye subjects of eternal choice, can you be silent? Has God favoured you above others, and can your lips refuse to sing? No, you will magnify the Lord exceedingly, because he hath chosen Jacob unto himself, and Israel for his peculiar treasure. Let us read on, and praise God that we have an abiding place among his people—"That he may dwell in thy courts."—Blessed be God we are not to be cast forth and driven out after a while, but we have an entailed inheritance amongst the sons of God. We praise him that we have the satisfaction of dwelling in his house as children. "We shall be satisfied with the goodness of thy house, even of thy holy temple." But I close the psalm, and simply say to you, there are ten thousand reasons for taking down the harp from the willows; and I know no reason for permitting it to hang there idle. There are ten thousand times ten thousand reasons for speaking well of "him who loved us, and gave himself for us." "The Lord hath done great things for us whereof we are glad." I remember hearing in a prayer-meeting this delightful verse mutilated in prayer, "The Lord hath done great things for us, whereof *we desire to be* glad." Oh, brethren, I dislike mauling, and mangling, and adding to a text of Scripture. If we are to have the Scriptures revised, let it be by scholars, and not by every ignoramus. "*Desire* to be glad," indeed? This is fine gratitude to God when he hath done great things for us." If these great things have been done, our souls must be glad, and cannot help it; they must overflow with gratitude to God for all his goodness.

2. So much on the first part of our holy sacrifice. Attentively let us consider the second, namely, *the vow*. "Unto thee shall the vow be performed."

We are not given to vow-making in these days. Time was when it was far oftener done. It may be that had we been better men we should have made more vows; it may possibly be that had we been more foolish men we should have done the same. The practice was so abused by superstition, that devotion has grown half-ashamed of it. But we have, at any rate, most of us bound ourselves with occassional vows. I do confess to-day a vow I have not kept as I should desire; the vow made on my first *conversion*. I surrendered myself, body, soul, and spirit, to him that bought me with a price, and the vow was not made by way of excess of devotion or supererogation, it was but my reasonable service. *You* have done that. Do you remember the love of your espousals, the time when Jesus was very precious, and you had just entered into the marriage bond with him? You gave yourselves up to him, to be his for ever and for ever. O brethren and sisters, it is a part of worship to perform that vow. Renew it to-night, make another surrender of yourselves to him whose you are and whom you serve. Say to-night, as I will, with you, " Bind the sacrifice with cords, even with cords to the horns of the altar." Oh, for another thong to strap the victim to the altar-horn! Does the flesh struggle? Then let it be more fastly bound, never to escape from the altar of God.

Beloved, many of us did, in effect, make a most solemn vow at the time of our *baptism*. We were buried with Christ in baptism unto death, and, unless we were greatly dissembling, we avowed that we were dead in Christ and buried with him; wherein, also, we professed that we were risen with him. Now, shall the world live in those who are dead to it, and shall Christ's life be absent from those who are risen with him? We gave ourselves up there and then, in that solemn act of mystic burial. Recall that scene, I pray you; and as you do it blush, and ask God that your vow may yet be performed. As Doddridge well expresses it :—

> " Baptised into your Saviour's death,
> Your souls to sin must die ;
> With Christ your Lord ye live anew,
> With Christ ascend on high."

Some such vow we made, too, when we *united ourselves to the church of God*. There was an understood compact between us and the church, that we would serve it, that we would seek to honour Christ by holy living, increase the church by propagating the faith, seek its unity, its comfort, by our own love and sympathy with the members. We had no right to join with the church if we did not mean to give ourselves up to it, under Christ, to aid in its prosperity and increase. There was a stipulation made, and a covenant understood, when we entered into communion and league with our brethren in Christ. How about that? Can we say that, as unto God and in his sight, the vow has been performed? Yes, we have been true to our covenant in a measure, brethren. Oh, that it were more fully so! Some of us made another vow, when we gave ourselves, as I trust, under divine call, altogether to the work of the *Christian ministry ;* and though we have taken no orders, and received no earthly ordination, for we are no believers in man-made priests, yet tacitly it is understood that the man who becomes a minister of the church of God is to give his whole time to his work—that body, soul, and spirit should be thrown into the cause of Christ. Oh, that this vow were more fully performed by pastors of the church! You, my brethren, elders and deacons, when you accepted office, you knew what the church meant. She expected holiness and zeal of you. The Holy Ghost made you overseers that you might feed the flock of God. Your office proves your obligation. You are practically under a vow. Has that vow been performed? Have you performed it in Zion unto the Lord ?

Besides that, it has been the habit of godly men to make *vows* occasionally, in times of pain, and losses, and affliction. Did not the psalm we just now sang put it so?—

> " Among the saints that fill thine house,
> My offerings shall be paid ;
> There shall my zeal perform the vows
> My soul in anguish made.
>
> Now I am thine, for ever thine,
> Nor shall my purpose move !
> Thy hand hath loosed my bands of pain,
> And bound me with thy love.
>
> Here in thy courts I leave my vow,
> And thy rich grace record ;
> Witness, ye saints, who hear me now,
> If I forsake the Lord."

You said, " If I am ever raised up, and my life is prolonged, it shall be better spent." You said, also, " If I am delivered out of this great trouble, I hope to consecrate my substance more to God." Another time you said, " If the Lord will return to me the light of his countenance, and bring me out of this depressed state of mind, I will praise him more than ever before." Have you remembered all this ? Coming here myself so lately from a sick bed, I at this time preach to myself. I only wish I had a better hearer ; I would preach to myself in this respect, and say, " I charge thee, my heart, to perform thy vow." Some of us, dear friends, have made vows in time of joy, the season of the birth of the first-born child, the recovery of the wife from sickness, the merciful restoration that we have ourselves received, times of increasing goods, or seasons when the splendour of God's face has been unveiled before our wondering eye. Have we not made vows, like Jacob when he woke up from his wondrous dream, and took the stone which had been his pillow, and poured oil on its top, and made a vow unto the Most High ? We have all had our Bethels. Let us remember that God has heard us, and let us perform unto him our vow which our soul made in her time of joy. But I will not try to open the secret pages of your private note-books. You have had tender passages, which you would not desire me to read aloud: the tears start at their memory. If your life were written, you would say, " Let these not be told ; they were only between God and my soul "—some chaste and blessed love passages between you and Christ, which must not be revealed to men. Have you forgotten how then you said, " I am my beloved's, and he is mine," and what you promised when you saw all his goodness made to pass before you. I have now to stir up your pure minds by way of remembrance, and bid you present unto the Lord to-night the double offering of your heart's praise and of your performed vow. " O magnify the Lord with me, and let us exalt his name together."

II. And now, time will fail me, but I must have a few words upon THE BLESSED ENCOURAGEMENT afforded us in the text for the presentation of these offerings unto God. Here it is,—" O thou that hearest prayer, unto thee shall all flesh come ? "

Observe, here, that *God hears prayer.* It is, in some aspects, the lowest form of worship, and yet he accepts it. It is not the worship of heaven, and it is, in a measure, selfish. Praise is superior worship, for it is elevating; it is the utterance of a soul that has received good from God, and is returning its love to him in acknowledgment. Praise has a sublime aspect. Now, observe, if prayer is heard, then praise will be heard too. If the lower form, on weaker wing as it were, reaches the throne of the majesty on high, how much more shall the seraphic wing of praise bear itself into the divine presence. Prayer is heard of God: therefore our praises and vows will be. And this is a very great encouragement, because it seems terrible to pray when you are not heard, and discouraging to praise God if he will not accept it. What would be the use of it? But if prayer and yet more praise be most surely heard, ah, brethren, then let us continue and abide in thanksgiving. "Whoso offereth praise glorifieth me, saith the Lord."

Observe too according to the text, that *all* prayer, if it be true prayer, is heard of God, for so it is put—"Unto thee shall *all flesh* come." Oh, how glad I am at that word. My poor prayer—shall God reject it? Yes, I might have feared so if he had said, "Unto thee shall all *spirits* come." Behold, my brethren, he takes the grosser part as it were, and looks at prayer in his infinite compassion, perceiving it to be what it is—a feeble thing—a cry coming from poor fallen flesh, and yet he puts it, "Unto thee shall all *flesh* come. My broken prayer, my groaning prayer shall get to thee, though it seems to me a thing of flesh, it is nevertheless wrought in me by thy Spirit. And, O my God, my song, though my voice be hoarse and oftentimes my notes most feeble, shall reach thee. Though I groan because it is so imperfect, yet even that shall come to thee. Prayer, if true, shall be received of God, notwithstanding all its faultiness, through Jesus Christ. Then so it will be with our praises and our vows.

Again, prayer is always and habitually received of God. "O thou that *hearest* prayer." Not that didst hear it or on a certain occasion may have heard it, but thou that *ever* hearest prayer. If he always hears prayer. then he always hears praise. Is not this delightful to think of my praise, though it be but that of a child or a poor unworthy sinner—God does hear it, does accept it, in spite of its imperfections, and does accept it *always?* Oh, I will have another hymn to-morrow, I will sing a new song to-morrow. I will forget my pain, I will forget for a moment all my care, and if I cannot sing aloud by reason of those that are with me, yet will I set the bells of my heart ringing, I will make my whole soul full of praise. If I cannot let it out of my mouth, I will praise him in my soul, because he always hears me. You know it is hard to do things for one who never accepts what you do. Many a wife has said, "Oh! it is hard. My husband never seems pleased. I have done all I can, but he takes no notice of little deeds of kindness." But how easy it is to serve a person who, when you have done any little thing, says, "How kind it was of you" and thinks much of it. Ah, poor child of God, the Lord thinks much of thy praises, much of thy vows, much of thy prayers. Therefore, be not slack to praise and magnify him unceasingly.

71

And this all the more, because we have not quite done with that word, " Unto thee shall *all* flesh come." All flesh shall come because the Lord hears prayer. Then all my praises will be heard and all the praises of all sorts of men, if sincere, shall come unto God. The great ones of the earth shall present praise, and the poorest of the poor also, for thou shalt not reject them.

And, Lord, wilt thou put it so; " Unto thee shall all flesh come," and wilt thou say, " but not such a one?" Wilt thou exclude me? Brethren, fear not that God will reject you. 1 remind you of what I told you the other night concerning a good earnest believing woman, who in prayer said, " Lord, I am content to be the second thou shalt forsake, but I cannot be the first." The Lord says all flesh shall come to him, and it is implied that he will receive them when they come —all sorts of men, all classes and conditions of men. Then he cannot reject me if I go, nor my prayers if I pray, nor my praise if I praise him, nor my vows if I perform them. Come then, let us praise the Lord, let us worship and bow down, let us kneel before the Lord our maker, for we are the people of his pasture and the sheep of his hand.

I have done when I have said this. Dear brethren and sisters, there may be difficulties in your way; iniquities may hinder you, or infirmities; but there is the promise, " thou shalt purge them away." Infirmities may check you, but note the word of divine help, " Blessed is the man whom thou causest to approach unto thee." He will come to your aid, and lead you to himself. Infirmities, therefore, are overcome by divine grace. Perhaps your emptiness hinders you : " He shall be satisfied with the goodness of thy house." It is not your goodness that is to satisfy either God or you, but God's goodness is to satisfy. Come, then, with thine iniquity, come with thine infirmity; come with thy emptiness. Come, dear brethren, if you have never come to God before. Come and confess your sin to God, and ask for mercy ; you can do no less than ask. Come and trust his mercy, which endures for ever ; it has no limit. Think not hardly of him, but come and lay yourself down at his feet. If you perish, perish there. Come and tell your grief; pour out your hearts before him. Bottom upwards turn the vessel of your nature, and drain out the last dreg, and pray to be filled with the fulness of his grace. Come unto Jesus; he invites you, he enables you. A cry from that pew will reach the sacred ear. " You have not prayed before," you say. Everything must have a beginning. Oh that that beginning might come now. It is not because you pray well that you are to come, but because the Lord hears prayer graciously, therefore, all flesh shall come. You are welcome; none can say you nay. Come! 'tis mercy's welcome hour. May the Lord's bands of love be cast about you ; may you be drawn now to him. Come by way of the cross ; come resting in the precious atoning sacrifice, believing in Jesus; and he has said, " Him that cometh unto me, I will in no wise cast out." The grace of our Lord be with you. Amen.

7. Morning and Evening Songs

"To shew forth thy lovingkindness in the morning, and thy faithfulness every night."—Psalm xcii. 2.

IT is a notion of the Rabbis that this Psalm was sung by Adam in Paradise. There are no reasons why we should believe it was so, and there are a great many why we should be sure it was not; for it is not possible that Adam could have sung concerning brutish men and fools, and the wicked springing as grass, while as yet he was the only man, and himself unfallen. Still, at least the first part of the Psalm might have fallen as suitably from the lips of Adam as from our tongues, and if Milton could put into Adam's mouth the language—

> "These are thy glorious works, Parent of good,
> Almighty; thine this universal frame.
> Thus wondrous fair, thyself how wondrous then!"

He might with equal fitness have made him say, "It is a good thing to give thanks unto the Lord, and to sing praises unto thy name, O Most High: to shew forth thy lovingkindness in the morning, and thy faithfulness every night; for thou, Lord, hast made me glad through thy work: I will triumph in the works of thy hands." The Jews have for a long while used this Psalm in the synagogue-worship on their Sabbath, and very suitable it is for the Sabbath-day; not so much in appearance, for there is little or no allusion to any Sabbatic rest in it, but because on that day above all others, our thoughts should be lifted up from all earthly things to God himself. The Psalm tunes the mind to adoration, and so prepares it for Sabbath worship. It supplies us with a noble subject for meditation,—the Lord, the Lord alone; lifting us up even above his works into a contemplation of himself and his mercies toward us. Oh, that always on the Sabbath-day, when we come together, we might assemble in the spirit of praise, feeling that it is good to give thanks unto the name of the Most High: and would God that always when we were assembled we could say,

73

"Thou, Lord, hast made me glad through thy work : I will triumph in the works of thy hands."

There is no doubt that in this second verse there is an allusion to the offering of the morning and the evening lambs, for, in addition to the great Paschal celebration once a year, and the other feasts and fasts, each of which brought Christ prominently before the mind of those Jews who were instructed by the Spirit of God, a lamb was offered every morning and every evening, as if to remind them that they needed daily cleansing for daily sin ; for then there was always a remembrance of sin, seeing that the one great sacrifice which puts away sin for ever had not yet been offered. Though now, in these our days, we need no morning or evening lamb, and the very idea of a repetition or a rehearsal of the sacrifice of Christ is to us most horribly profane and blasphemous, yet would we remember continually the one sacrifice, and never wake in the morning without beholding "the Lamb of God which taketh away the sin of the world," nor fall to sleep at night without turning our eyes anew to him who on the bloody tree was made sin for us.

Our text, however, is meant to speak to us concerning praise. Praise should be the continual exercise of believers. It is the joyful work of heaven, it should be the continual joy of earth ; and we are taught by the text, I think, that while praise should be given only to One who is in heaven, and we should adore perpetually our Triune God, yet there should be variety in our unity. We bless the Lord and the Lord alone ; we have no music but for him, but we do not always praise him after the same fashion. As there were different instruments of music—the ten-stringed instrument or decachord, the psaltery, the harp,—so, too, there are different subjects, a subject for the morning and a subject for the evening ; lovingkindness to be shown forth at one time, and faithfulness to be sung at another. I wish that men studied more the praise they profess to present unto God. I sometimes find, even in our own public song, simple as it is, that there is a want of thought evidently among us : for time is not maintained with the precision which would grow out of thoughtfulness, there is a tendency to sing more slowly, as if devotion were wearying, if not wearisome, and too frequently I fear the singing gets to be mechanical, as if the tune mastered you, and you did not govern the tune by making those inflections and modulations of voice which the sense would suggest, if you sang with all your hearts and with your understandings also. The very posture of some people indicates that they are going through the hymn, but the hymn is not going through their hearts, nor ascending to God on the wings of soaring gratitude. I have also noticed with sad reflections the way in which, if there happen to be a chorus at the close—a "Hallelujah" or "Praise God"—some will drop into their seats as if they had not thought enough to recollect that it was coming, and then, with a jerk, all in confusion, they stand up again ; being so asleep in heart that anything out of the common way is too much for them. Far am I from caring for postures or tones, but when they indicate want of heart, I do care, and so should you. Remember well that there is no more of music to God's ear in any service than there is of heart-love and holy devotion. You may make floods of music

with your organ if you like ; or you may make equally good music--
and some of us think better—with human voices ; but it is not music
to God, either of instrument or of voice, unless the heart be there ;
and the heart is not fully there, the man, the whole man, is not fully
there, unless the soul glows with the praise.

In our private praise, also, we ought to think more of what we are
doing, and concentrate our entire energies for the sacred exercise.
Ought we not to sit down before we pray, and ask our understanding,
" What am I going to pray for ? I bow my knee at my bedside to
pray : ought I not to pause and consider the things I ought to ask for ?
What do I want, and what are the promises which I should plead,
and why is it that I may expect that God should grant me what I
want ? " Should we not pray better if we occupied more time in consideration ? And so when we come to praise we ought not to rush
upon it helter skelter, but engage in it with prepared hearts. I notice
that when musicians are about to discourse sweet music there is a
tuning-up ; there is a preparation ; and there are rehearsals, which
they perform before they go through their music in public ; so our
soul ought to rehearse the subject for which it is about to bless God ;
and we ought to come before the Lord, both in public and in private,
with subjects of praise which our thought has considered, not offering
unto the Lord that which has cost us nothing, but with a warm heart
pouring out before his throne adoration grounded upon subjects of
thanksgiving appropriate to the occasion. So it seems the psalmist
would have us do : " To shew forth thy lovingkindness in the morning,
and thy faithfulness every night." It is not mere praise, but varied
praise, praise with distinct subjects at appointed seasons. Upon this
we are about to speak for a little while.

And we shall speak thus : first, here is *a subject for morning worship ;*
secondly, here is *another for evening devotion ;* and this last, ere we
close our discourse, *we shall try to practise.*

I. First, then, notice MORNING WORSHIP : " To show forth thy
lovingkindness in the morning."

" In the morning." There cannot be a more suitable time for
praising God than in the morning. Everything around is congenial
therewith. Even in this great wilderness of brick the gleams of sunlight in these summer mornings seem like songs, songs without words,
or rather music without sounds : and out in the country, when every
blade of grass twinkles with its own drop of dew, and all the trees
glisten as if they were lit up with sapphire by the rising dawn, and
when a thousand birds awake to praise their Maker, making harmonious concerts, all with all their hearts casting their entire energies into the service of holy song, it seems most fit that the key of
the morning should be in the hand of praise ; and that when the
daylight lifts its eyelid it should look out upon grateful hearts. We
ourselves have newly risen from our beds, and if we are in a right
state of mind we are thankful for the night's sleep.

> " The evening rests our wearied head,
> And angels guard the room :
> We wake, and we admire the bed
> That was not made our tomb."

Every morning is a sort of resurrection. At night we lay us down to sleep, stripped of our garments, as our souls will be of their bodily array when we come to die ; but the morning wakes us, and if it be a Sabbath morning we do not put on our work-day clothes, but find our Sabbath dress ready to hand ; even thus shall we be satisfied when we wake up in our Master's likeness, no more to put on the soiled raiment of earth, but to find it transformed into a Sabbath robe, in which we shall be beautiful and fair, even as Jesus our Lord himself. Now, as every morning brings to us, in fact, a resurrection from what might have been our tomb, and delivers us from the image of death which through the night we wore, it ought to be saluted with thanks-giving. As the great resurrection morning will be awakened with the sound of the trumpet's far-sounding music, so let every morning, as though it were a resurrection to us, awaken us with hymns of joy.

> " All praise to thee who safe hast kept,
> And hast refreshed me while I slept ;
> Grant, Lord, when I from death shall wake,
> I may of endless life partake."

" To show forth thy lovingkindness in the morning." We are full of vigour then ; we shall be tired ere night comes round : perhaps in the heat of the day we shall be fagged ; let us take care, while we are fresh, to give the cream of the morning to God. Our poet says :—

> " The flower, when offered in the bud,
> Is no mean sacrifice."

Let us give the Lord the bud of the day, its virgin beauty, its un-sullied purity. Say what you will about the evening, and there are many points about it which make it an admirable season for devotion, yet the morning is the choice time. Is it not a queenly hour ? See how it is adorned with diamonds more pure than those which flash in the crowns of eastern potentates. The old proverb declares that they who would be rich must rise early ; surely those who would be rich towards God must do so. No dews fall in the middle of the day, and it is hard to keep up the dew and freshness of one's spirit in the worry, and care, and turmoil of midday ; but in the morning the dew should fall upon our fleece till it is filled therewith ; and it is well to wring it out before the Lord, and give him our morning's vigour, our morning's freshness and unction.

You will see, I think, without my enlarging, that there is a fitness in the morning for praising God. But I shall not merely confine the text to the morning of each day ; the same fitness appertains to the morning of our days. Our youth, our first hours of the day of life, ought to be spent in showing forth the lovingkindness of God. Dear young friends, you may rest assured that nothing can happen to you so blessed as to be converted while you are young. I bless God for my having known him when I was fifteen years of age ; but I have often felt like that Irishman who said that he was converted at twenty, and he wished it had been twenty-one years before. I have often felt the same desire. Oh ! if it could have been so, that the very first breath one drew had been consecrated to God ; that it had been possible for the first rational thought to be one of devotion :

that the first act of judgment had been exercised upon divine truth, and the first pulsing of affection had been towards the Redeemer who loved us and gave himself for us ! What blessed reflections would fill the space now occupied with penitent regrets. The first part of a Christian life has charms peculiar to itself,—in some respects

> " That age is best which is the first,
> For then the blood is warmer."

I know the afterpart is riper, it is more mellow ; there is a sweetness about autumn fruit, but the basket of early fruit—the first ripe fruit —this is what God desireth : and blessed are they who, in the morning, show forth the lovingkindness of God !

Or the words may be explained mystically to signify those periods of life which are bright like the morning to us. We have our ups and downs, our ebbs and flows, our mornings and our nights. Now, it is the duty, and the privilege, of our bright days, for us to shew forth God's lovingkindness in them. It may be some of you have had so rough a life that you consider your nights to be more numerous than your days. Others of us could not, even in common honesty, subscribe to such a belief. No, blessed be God, our mornings have been very numerous ; our days of joy and rejoicing, after all, have been abundant—infinitely more abundant than we might have expected they could be, dwelling as we do in the land of sorrows. Oh, when the joy days come, let us always consecrate them by showing forth God's lovingkindness. Do not as some do, who, if they are prospering, make a point of not owning to it. If they make money, for instance—well, they are " doing pretty well." " Pretty well," do they call it ? Time was, when, if they had done half so well, they would have been ready to jump for joy. How often the farmer, when his crop could not be any larger, and when the field is loaded with it, will say, " Well, it is a very fair crop." Is that all ? Oh, what robbery of God ! This talk is far too common on all sides, and ought to be most solemnly rebuked. When we have been enjoying a long stretch of joy and peace, instead of saying that it is so, we speak as if—well, well, God hath dealt very well with us upon the whole, but at the same time he has done for us nothing very remarkable. I saw a tombstone the other day which pleased me ; I do not know that I ever saw an epitaph of that kind before ; I think it was for a person of the age of eighty, and it said of her, " who after a happy and grateful enjoyment of life, died," and so on. Now, that is what we ought to say, but we talk as if, really, we were to be pitied for living, as if we were little better off than toads under a harrow, or snails in a tub of salt. We whine as if our lives were martyrdoms, and every breath a woe. But it is not so. Such conduct slanders the good Lord. Blessed be the Lord for creating us. Our life has mercies, yea innumerable mercies ; and, notwithstanding the sorrows and the troubles of it, there are joys and benedictions past all count. There are mornings in which it becomes us to show forth the lovingkindness of the Lord. See, then, the season, the morning of each day, the morning of our days, and the morning of our brightness and prosperity.

The psalmist suggests that the best topic for praise on such occasions is lovingkindness. And truly I confess that this is a theme which might suit nights as well as days, though doubtless he saw an appropriateness in allotting this topic to the morning. Verily it might suffice for all the day long. Was there ever such a word in any language as that word lovingkindness ? I have sometimes heard Frenchmen talking about their language, and I have no doubt it is a very beautiful tongue ; and Germans glorify the speech of the Fatherland, and I have heard our Welsh friends extolling their unpronounceable language, and crying it up as the very tongue that was spoken in Paradise. Very likely indeed. But I venture to say that no language beneath the sky has a word in it that is richer than this—*loving-kindness.* It is a duplicate deliciousness. There are within it linked sweetnesses long drawn out. *Lovingkindness.* It is a kind of word with which to cast spells which should charm away all fears. It was said of Mr. Whitefield that he could have moved an audience to tears by saying the word " Mesopotamia " ; I think he could have done it better with the word "lovingkindness." Put it under your tongue, now. Let it lie there. LOVINGKINDNESS. *Kindness.* Does that mean kindness ? Some say that it is the root-sense of the word—*kinned-ness,* such feeling as we have to our own kin, for blood is ever thicker than water, and we act towards those who are our kindred as we cannot readily do towards strangers. Now, God has made us of his kin. In his own dear Son he has taken us into his family. We are children of God— " heirs of God and joint-heirs with Christ Jesus ; " and there is a *kinned-ness* from God to us through our great kinsman Jesus Christ. But then the word is only half understood when you get to that, for it is *loving*-kindness. For a surgeon to set a man's limb when it is out of joint or broken is kindness, although he may do it somewhat roughly, and in an off-hand manner ; but if he does it very tenderly, covering the lion's heart with the lady's hand, then he shows *loving*-kindness. A man is picked up on the battle-field, and put into an ambulance and carried to the hospital, that is kindness ; but oh, if that poor soldier's mother could come into the hospital and see her boy suffering, she would show him *loving*-kindness, which is something far more. A child run over in the street outside yonder, and taken to the hospital, would be cared for, I have no doubt, with the greatest kindness ; but, after all, send for its mother, for she will give it *loving*-kindness. And so the Lord dealeth with us. He gives us what we want, in a fatherly manner. He doeth to us what we need, in the tenderest fashion. It is kindness ; it is kinned-ness ; but it is loving-kindness. The very heart of God seems written out in this word. We could hardly apply it in full force to any but to our Father who is in heaven.

Now, here is a subject for us to sing about in the morning.

How shall I begin, with the hope of going through this subject ? It is an endless one. Lovingkindness begins,—ah, I must correct myself : it never did begin. It had no beginning. " I have loved thee with an everlasting love ; therefore with lovingkindness have I drawn thee." Everlasting love, therefore, is what we must begin to sing of. And that everlasting love was infinite in its preparations, for before we had been created the Lord had made a covenant on our account, and resolved

78

to give his only-begotten Son, that we might be saved from wrath through him. The lovingkindness of God our Father appeared in Jesus Christ. Oh, brethren, let us always be talking about this! I wonder why it is, when we meet each other, that we do not begin at once to say, " Brother, have you been thinking over the lovingkindness of the Lord in the gift of his dear Son ?"—for, indeed, it is such a marvellous thing that it ought not to be a nine-days' wonder with us. It ought to fill us with astonishment every day of our lives. Now, if something wonderful happens, everybody's mouth is full of it, and we speak to one another about it at once, while like the Athenians all our neighbours are greedy to hear ; let our mouths, then, be full of the marvellous lovingkindness of God, and for fear we should leave the tale half untold, let us begin early in the morning to rehearse the eternal love manifested in the great gift of Jesus Christ. If we have already spoken about these things, and wish for variety, let us speak concerning the lovingkindness of God to each one of us in bringing us to Jesus. What a history each man's own life is. I suppose that if any one of our lives should be fully written, it would be more wonderful than a romance. I have sometimes seen a sunset of which I have said, " Now, if any painter had depicted that, I should have declared that the sky never looked in that way, it is so strange and singular ;" and in the same way, should some of our lives be fully written, many would say, " It could not have been so." How many have said of Huntingdon's " Bank of Faith," for instance, " Oh, it is a bank of nonsense ;" yet I believe that it is correct, and bears the marks of truth upon its very face. I believe that the man did experience all that he has written, though he may not always have told us everything in the best possible manner. Many other people's lives would be quite as wonderful as his if they could be written. Tell ye, then, the loving-kindness of God to yourself in particular. Rehearse, if to no other ear, to your own ear, and to the ear of God, the wondrous story of how—

> "Jesus sought you when a stranger
> Wandering from the fold of God."

How his grace brought you to himself and so into eternal life. And then, brethren, sing of the lovingkindness of God to yourselves since your new birth. Remember the mercies of God. Do not bury them in the grave of ingratitude. Let them glisten in the light of gratitude. I am sure that you will find this a blessed morning portion, it will sweeten all the day. The psalmist would have you begin the day with it, because you will need all the day to complete it ; indeed, you will want all the day of life and all eternity ; and I am half of Addison's mind—though the expression is somewhat hyperbolical—

> "But, oh, eternity's too short
> To utter half thy praise."

What a blessed subject you have before you—the lovingkindness of the Lord. Not yourself—not yourself. That is a horrible subject to speak upon. When I hear brethren get up and glory in their own attainments and graces, I remember the words of the wise man, " Let another praise thee, and not thine own lips." Above all things, when a man says that he has made great advances in sanctification it is sickening, and clearly proves that he has not learned the meaning of the word "humility." I hope the eyes of our friends will be opened, and that they will come to loathe the devil's meat which now deceives them may we no longer see spiritual self-conceit held up among us as a virtue, but may it be shunned as a deadly evil. No, let my mouth be filled with God's praise, but not with my own.

My brethren, let not our tongues be always occupied with our griefs. If you have a skeleton in your house, why should you always invite every friend who calls upon you to inspect the uncomely thing? No : tell what God has done for you : tell of his lovingkindness. I have heard—and I repeat the story because it ought to be repeated, simple as it is—of a pastor who frequently called upon a poor bedridden woman, who very naturally always told him of her pains and her wants. He knew all about her rheumatics : he had heard of them fifty times, and at last he said to her, "My dear sister, I sympathise with you deeply, and I am never at all tired of hearing your complaints ; but could you not now and then tell me something about what the Lord does for you—something about your enjoyments, how he sustains you under your pain, and so on ? " It was a rebuke well put and well taken ; and ever afterwards there was less said about the griefs and more heard about the blessings. Let us henceforth resolve, Great God, " To show forth thy lovingkindness in the morning."

Thus we have considered the time and the topic, and now we are bound to observe the manner in which we are to deal with the subject. The psalmist says we are to *show it forth*, by which I suppose he means that we are not to keep to ourselves what we know about God's lovingkindness.

Every Christian in the morning ought to shew it forth first in his own chamber before God. He should express his gratitude for the mercies of the night and the mercies of his whole life. Then let him, if it be possible, show it forth in his family ; let him gather them together and worship the Lord, and bless him for his lovingkindness. And then when the Christian goes into the world, let him show forth God's lovingkindness ; I do not mean by talking of it to every one he meets, casting pearls before swine as it would be to some men, but by the very way in which he speaks, acts, and looks. A Christian ought to be the most cheerful of men, so that others should say, "What makes him look so happy? He is not rich : he is not always in good health : he has his troubles ; but he seems to bear all so well and to trip lightly along the pathway of life." By our cheerful conversation we ought to show forth in the morning God's lovingkindness. " Ah," says one, " but when you are depressed in spirit ? " Do not show it if you can help it. Do as your Master said : " appear not unto men to fast." Do not imagine that the appearance of sadness indicates sanctity ; it often means hypocrisy. To conceal one's own griefs for the sake of cheering others betokens a self-denying sympathy which is the highest kind of Christianity. Let us present the sacrifice of praise in whatever company we may be, but when we get among God's own people, then is the time for a whole burnt offering. Among our own kith and kin we may safely open our box of sweets. When we find a brother who can understand the lovingkindness of the Lord let us tell it forth with sacred delight. We have choice treasures which we cannot show to ungodly eyes, for they would not appreciate them ; but when we meet with eyes which God has opened, then let us open the casket, and say, " Brother, rejoice in what God has done for us. See his lovingkindness to me his servant, and his tender mercies which have been ever of old."

Thus, beloved friends, I have set before you a good morning's work ; and I think, if God's Spirit helps us to attend to it, we shall come out of our chambers with our breath smelling sweet with the praises of God. We shall go down into the world without care, much more without anger. We shall go calmly to our work, and meet our cares quietly and happily. The joy of the Lord will be our strength. It is a good rule never to look into the face of man in the morning till you have looked into the face of God ; an equally good rule always to have business with heaven before you have any business with earth. Oh, it is a sweet thing to bathe in the morning in the love of God ; to bathe in it, so that when you come forth out of the ivory chambers of communion wherein you have been made glad, your garments shall smell of the myrrh and aloes and cassia of holiness. Do we all attend to this ? I am afraid we are in too much of a hurry, or we get up too late. Could not we rise a little earlier ? If we could steal even a few minutes from our beds, those few minutes would scatter their influence over the entire day. It is always bad to start on a journey without having looked to the harness, and to the horse's shoes ; and it often happens that the time saved by omitting examination turns out to be a dead loss when the traveller has advanced a little on his journey. Not one minute, but a hundred minutes may be lost by the want of a little attention at first. Set the morning watch with care, if you would be safe through the day ; begin well if you would end well. Take care that the helm of the day is put right, look well to the point you want to sail to, then whether you make much progress or little, it will be so far in the right direction. The morning hour is generally the index of the day.

II. Now, let us turn to the second part of our subject very briefly. The psalmist says, " To show forth thy faithfulness EVERY NIGHT.

Now, the night, beloved, is a peculiarly choice time for praising God's faithfulness. " Oh," says one, " we are very tired." Well, that may be ; but it is a pity that we should be reduced to such a condition that we are too tired to praise God. A holy man of God used always to say, when they said to him, " Can you pray ? " " Thank God, I am never too tired to pray." If anything can arouse us the service of Christ should do it, there should be within us an enthusiasm which kindles at the very thought of prayer. Have you never known an army on the march weary and ready to drop, and the band have played some enlivening tune which has bestirred the men afresh, and they have gone over the last few miles as they could not have done if it had not been for the inspiration of the strain. Let the thought of praising God wake up our wearied energies, and let not God be robbed of his glory at the close of the day. The close of the day is calm, quiet, and fit for devotion. God walked in the garden in the cool of the day, before man fell, and Adam went forth to meet him; Isaac walked in the fields at eventide, and there he received a blessing. The evening is the Sabbath of the day, and should be the Lord's.

Now, notice the topic which is set for the evening; it is *faithfulness*. Why? Why, because we have had a little more experience of our God. We have a day's more experience than we had in the morning; therefore we have more power to sing of God's faithfulness. We can look back now upon the day and see promises fulfilled. May I ask you to look over to-day, my dear brothers and sisters in Christ. Can you not notice some promises which God has kept towards you? Show forth his faithfulness, then. Provision has been given you: he promised to give it; he has given it. Protection has been afforded you: more than you know of, infinitely more. Guidance also has been given in points where you otherwise would have gone very much astray. Illumination has been granted you: comfort also in a season of depression; or upholding in a time of temptation. God has given you much to-day. If he has taken anything away from you, yet still bless his name; it was only what he had given, and he had a right to take it. Look through the day, and you will find that God has acted towards you as he promised that he would act. You have had trouble, you say; did not he say, "In the world ye shall have tribulation"? Has he not spoken concerning the rod of the covenant? Affliction only illustrates his faithfulness. Carefully observe the fulfilled promises of each day: it is a good custom to conclude the day by rehearsing its special mercies. I do not believe in keeping a detailed diary of each day's experience, for one is very apt, for want of something to put down, to write what is not true, or at least not real. I believe there is nothing more stilted or untruthful, as a general rule, than a religious diary; it easily degenerates into self-deceit. Still, most days, if not all our days, reveal singular instances of providence, if we will but watch them. Master Flavel used to say, "He that notices providences shall never be without a providence to notice." I believe we let our days glide by us, unobservant of the wondrous things that are in them, and so miss many enjoyments. As in nature the uneducated person sees but little beauty in the wild flowers—

> " The primrose by the river's brim,
> A yellow primrose is to him,
> And it is nothing more;"

so we, for want of thought, let great mercies go by us; they are trifles to us, and nothing more. Oh, let us change our ways, and think more of what God has done, and then we shall utter a song concerning his faithfulness every night.

Do you notice in the text that word "*every*." It does not say, "to show forth his lovingkindness every morning," though it means that; but concerning the nights it is very distinct. "And his faithfulness *every* night." It is a cold night. Did he not promise winter? and now it has come the cold only proves his faithfulness. It is a dark night; but then it is a part of his covenant that there should be nights as well as days. Supposing that there were no nights and no winters, where were the covenant which God made with the earth?

But every change of temperature in the beautiful vicissitudes of the year, and every variation of light and shade, only illustrate the faithfulness of God. If you happen now to be full of joy, you can tell of divine faithfulness in rendering love and mercy to you ; but if, on the other hand, you are full of trouble, tell of God's faithfulness, for now you have an opportunity of proving it. He will not leave you : he will not forsake you. His word is, "When thou passest through the rivers I will be with thee : the floods shall not overflow thee." Depend upon it that promise will be faithfully fulfilled.

Beloved friends, you who are getting old are nearing the night of life ; and you are peculiarly fitted to show forth the Lord's faithfulness. The young people may tell of his lovingkindness, but the old people must tell of his faithfulness. You can speak of forty or fifty years of God's grace to you, and you can confidently affirm that he has not once failed you. He has been true to every word that he has spoken. Now, I charge you, do not withhold your testimony. If we, young people, should be silent we should be guilty, but we might speak, perhaps, another day ; but for you advanced Christians to be silent will be sinful indeed, for you will not have another opportunity in this world of showing forth the faithfulness of God. Bear witness now, ere your eyes are closed in death ! The faithfulness of God every night is a noble subject for his greyheaded servants.

And this it is our great business to *show forth*. O beloved, do let us publish abroad the faithfulness of God. I wonder sometimes that there should be any doubts in the world about the doctrine of the final perseverance of the saints, and I think the reason why there are any is this —those professors who fall are very conspicuous, everybody knows about them. If a high-flying professor makes a foul end of his boastings, why, that is talked of everywhere. They speak of it in Gath, and publish it in the streets of Askelon. But, on the other hand, those thousands of true believers that hold on their way, they cannot, of course, say much about themselves ; it would not be right they should, but I wish they could sometimes say more about the unfailing goodness and immutable truthfulness of God, to be a check to the effect produced by backsliders, so that the world may know that the Lord doth not cast away his people whom he did foreknow, but that he gives strength to them even in their fainting, and bears them through. If there is any one topic that you Christians ought to speak about thankfully, bravely, positively, continuously, it is the faithfulness of God to you. It is that upon which Satan makes a dead set in the minds of many tempted ones, and therefore to that you should bring the strength of your testimony, that tried saints may know that he doth not forsake his people.

III. And now, to close, I desire in the name of God's people here present, TO SHOW FORTH GOD'S FAITHFULNESS THIS VERY NIGHT.

My brethren, as a church, let us declare how faithful God has been to us ! Our history as a church has been very wonderful. When we were few and feeble, minished and brought low, God appeared for us. Then we began to prosper, and we began also to pray. And what prayers they were ! Surely the more we prayed the more God blessed us. We have now had almost twenty years of uninterrupted blessing. We have had no fits and starts, revivals and retreats, but onward has been our course, in the name of God, a steady, continued progress, like the growth of a cedar upon Lebanon. Up to this time God has always heard prayer in this place. This very building was an answer to prayer. There is scarcely an institution connected with it but what can write upon its banner, " We have been blessed by a prayer-hearing God." It has become our habit to pray, and it is God's habit to bless us. Oh, let us not flag ! Let us not flag ! If we do we shall be straitened in ourselves, but not in God. God will not leave us while we prove him in his own appointed way. If we will but continue mighty in earnest intercession, we may, as a church, enjoy another twenty years, if so it pleases God, of equal or greater prosperity. If ever there was a spot on earth where it became men to speak well of a faithful God, it is the spot whereon I stand, and I do speak of it to his glory. We have used no carnal attractions to gather people together to worship here, we have procured nothing to please their taste by way of elaborate music, fine dresses, painted windows, processions, and the like ; we have used the gospel of Jesus without any rhetorical embellishments, simply spoken as a man speaketh to his friend ; and God has blessed it, and he will bless it still.

Now, dear friends, each one of you can say of yourselves, as well as of the church, that God has been faithful to you. Tell it to your children ; tell them God will save sinners when they come to him, for he saved you. Tell it to your neighbours ; tell them he is faithful and just to forgive us our sins if we confess them to him, and to save us from all unrighteousness, for he forgave you. Tell every trembler you meet with that Jesus will in nowise cast out any that come to him. Tell all seekers that if they seek they shall find, and that to every one that knocks, the door of mercy shall be opened. Tell the most desponding and despairing that Jesus Christ came into the world to save sinners, even the very chief. Make known his faithfulness every night. And when your last night comes, and you gather up your feet in the bed, like Jacob, let your last testimony be to the Lord's faithfulness ; and like glorious old Joshua, end your life by saying, " Not one good thing hath failed of all the Lord God hath promised, but all hath come to pass."

The Lord bless you, dear friends, and give you all to know his lovingkindness and his faithfulness. Amen and Amen.

8. The Philosophy and Propriety of Abundant Praise

"They shall abundantly utter the memory of thy great goodness, and shall sing of thy righteousness."—Psalm cxlv. 7.

THIS is called "David's Psalm of praise," and you will see that all through it he is inflamed by a strong desire that God may be greatly magnified. Hence he uses a variety of expressions, and repeats himself in his holy vehemence. Run your eye down the psalm and notice such words as these : "I will extol thee "; "I will bless thy name "; " Every day will I bless thee "; " I will praise thy name for ever and ever "; " Great is the Lord, and greatly to be praised "; " One generation shall praise thy works to another "; "I will speak of the glorious honour of thy majesty "; " Men shall speak of the might of thy terrible acts," and other words of like import, down to the last verse : " My mouth shall speak the praise of the Lord: and let all flesh bless his holy name for ever and ever." David is not content with declaring that Jehovah is worthy of praise, or with pleading that his praise ought to be felt in the heart, but he will have it publicly spoken of, openly declared, plainly uttered, and joyfully proclaimed in song. The inspired Psalmist, moved by the Holy Ghost, calls upon all flesh, yea, and upon all the works of God to sound forth the praises of the Most High. Will we not heartily respond to the call ?

In following out his design of praise, David had spoken in verse five of the majesty of God, the glorious King. His eye seems to be dazzled by the glorious splendour of the august throne, and he cries, " I will speak of the glorious honour of thy majesty." Then he bethinks himself of the power of that throne of majesty and of the force with which its just decrees are carried out, and so in verse six he exclaims, " Men shall speak of the might of thy terrible acts, and I will declare thy greatness." Here he speaks in brief both as to the majesty and the might of the dread Supreme, but when he turns his thoughts to the divine goodness, he enlarges and uses words which indicate the stress which he lays upon

85

his subject, and his desire to linger over it. "They shall abundantly utter," saith our text, "the memory of thy great goodness." Now, our desire this morning is that we also may praise and magnify the name of the infinite Jehovah without bound or stint, and may especially have our hearts enlarged and our mouths opened wide to speak abundantly of his great goodness. O that in the whole of this congregation the text may become true—"They shall abundantly utter the memory of thy great goodness"; and having uttered it in plain speech may we all rise a stage higher, and with gladsome music sing of his righteousness.

You see our object, an object in which I trust you all sympathise. Come, one and all, and praise the Lord. Is the invitation too wide? Observe the ninth verse: "The Lord is good to all: and his tender mercies are over all his works. All thy works shall praise thee," I will not limit the invitation of the Lord; since you all drink of the river of his bounty, render to him all of you such praises as you can.

But there is a special invitation to his saints. Come ye and *bless* his name with spiritual, inward, enlightened praise. "Bless the Lord, O house of Israel. Ye that fear the Lord, bless the Lord." In your heart of hearts extol, adore, and make him great, for it is written—"Thy saints shall bless thee." Verily this shall not be written in vain, for our souls shall bless the Lord this day as the Holy Ghost shall move within us.

We shall speak upon two things that we may promote the object we have in view. The first is, *the method of securing the abundant utterance of God's praise as to his goodness;* and, secondly, *the motives for desiring to secure this abundant utterance.*

I. THE METHOD OF SECURING THE ABUNDANT UTTERANCE OF THE DIVINE PRAISE CONCERNING HIS GOODNESS. Our text gives us the mental philosophy of abounding praise, and shows us the plan by which such praise may be secured. The steps are such as the best mental philosophy approves. First, we shall be helped to abundant praise *by careful observation*. Notice the text—"They shall abundantly utter the memory of thy great goodness." Now, in order to memory there must first of all be observation. A man does not remember what he never knew; this is clear to all, and therefore the point is virtually implied in the text. In proportion as a fact or a truth makes an impression upon the mind, in that proportion is it likely to abide in the memory. If you hear a sermon, that which you remember afterwards is the point which most forcibly strikes you while you are listening to the discourse. At the time you say, "I will jot *that* down, for I should not like to forget it, for it comes so closely home to me;" and whether you use your pencil or not, memory obeys your wish and makes a record upon her tablets. It is so with the dealings of God towards us. If we want to remember his goodness we must let it strike us; we must notice it, consider it, meditate upon it, estimate it, and allow it to exert its due influence upon our hearts; and then we shall not need to say that "we must try and remember," for we shall remember as a matter of course. The impression being clearly and deeply made will not easily fade away, but we shall see it after many days. The first thing, therefore, towards the plentiful praising of God is a careful observation of his goodness.

Now, see what it is that we are to observe—it is God's goodness. Too many are blind to that blessed object. They receive the bounties of providence but they do not see the hand of God in them. They are fed by his liberality and guided by his care, but they attribute all that they receive to themselves, or to secondary agents. God is not in all their thoughts, and consequently his goodness is not considered. They have no memory of his goodness because they have no observation of it. Some, indeed, instead of observing the goodness of God, complain of his unkindness to them, and imagine that he is needlessly severe. Like the unprofitable servant in the parable, they say, " I knew thee, that thou art an austere man." Others sit in judgment upon his ways, as we find them recorded in Holy Scripture, and dare to condemn the Judge of all the earth. Denying the goodness of Jehovah, they attempt to set up another God than the God of Abraham, Isaac, and Jacob, who for this enlightened nineteenth century is a God much too sternly just. In this house, however, we worship *Jah*, Jehovah the God of Abraham, Isaac, and Jacob, the God and Father of our Lord and Saviour Jesus Christ, and none other than he. In many a place of worship at this day they adore new gods, newly come up, which our fathers knew not; not like unto the God of the Old Testament, who in the opinion of modern philosophers is as much out of date as Jupiter himself. This day we say with David, " This God is our God for ever and ever." " O come let us worship and bow down; let us kneel before Jehovah our Maker. For he is our God, and we are the people of his pasture, and the sheep of his hand." As we find the Lord revealed both in the Old and the New Testament, making no division in the revelation, but regarding it as one grand whole, we behold abundant goodness in him. Mingled with that awful justice which we would not wish to deny, we see surpassing grace, and we delight that God is love. He is gracious and full of compassion ; slow to anger, and of great mercy. We have no complaints to make against him, we wish to make no alteration in his dealings or in his character ; he is our exceeding joy ; our whole heart rejoices in the contemplation of him. " Who is like unto thee, O God ? Among the gods who is like unto thee ?" We are then to consider, what many will not so much as believe, that there is great goodness in Jehovah, the God of creation, providence, and redemption ; the God of Paradise, of Sinai, and of Calvary. We are thoroughly to acquaint ourselves with him as he has made himself known, and we are continually to consider his great goodness, that we may retain the memory of it.

If we are willing to see we shall not lack for opportunities of beholding his goodness every day, for it is to be seen in so many acts that I will not commence the catalogue, since I should never complete it. His goodness is seen in creation ; it shines in every sunbeam, glitters in every dewdrop, smiles in every flower, and whispers in every breeze. Earth and sea and air, teeming with innumerable forms of life, are all full of the goodness of the Lord. Sun, moon, and stars affirm that the Lord is good, and all terrestrial things echo the proclamation. His goodness is also to be seen in the providence which ruleth over all. Let rebellious spirits murmur as they may, goodness is enthroned in Jehovah's kingdom, and evil and suffering are intruders there. God is good towards all his creatures, and especially towards the objects of his eternal love, for whom all things work together for good. It is, however, in the domain of grace that the noblest form of divine goodness is seen. Begin with the goodness which shines in our election, and follow the silver thread through redemption, the mission of the Holy Spirit, the calling, the adoption, the preservation, the perfecting of the chosen, and you will see riches of goodness which will astound you. Dwell where you may within the kingdom of redemption, and you will see rivers, yea, oceans of goodness. I leave your own minds to remember these things, and your own lips abundantly to utter the memory of the Lord's great goodness in the wonders of his salvation; for it is not my design to speak for you, but to stir you up to speak for yourselves.

The point which struck the Psalmist, and should strike us all, is *the greatness* of the goodness. The greatness of the goodness will be seen by the contemplative mind upon a consideration of *the person upon whom the goodness* lights. "Whence is this to me?" will often be the utterance of a grateful spirit. That God should be good to any of his people shows his mercy, but that he should make *me* to be one of his, and deal so well with me, herein his goodness doth exceed itself! Whence is this to me? Is this the manner of man, O Lord? What am I, and what is my father's house? It is great goodness since it visits persons so insignificant, yea more, so guilty and so deserving of wrath. Blessed be God that he is good to persons so ungrateful, to persons who cannot even at the best make any adequate return, who, alas, do not even make such return as they could. Ah, Lord, when I consider what a brutish creature I am it is easy to confess the greatness of thy goodness.

The greatness of the goodness becomes apparent when we think of *the greatness of God the benefactor*. "What is man that thou art mindful of him, or the son of man that thou visitest him?" That God himself should bless his people, that he should come in the form of human flesh to save his people, that he should dwell in us, and walk in us, and be to us a God, a very present help in trouble, is a miracle of love. Is not this great goodness? I can very well understand that the infinity of his benevolence should commit us to the charge of angels, but it is amazing that it should be written, "I the Lord do keep it: I will water it every moment: lest any hurt it, I will keep it night and day." Oh, the greatness of such personal condescension, such personal care. O heir of heaven, from the fountain of all goodness shalt thou drink, and not from its streams alone. God himself is thy portion, and the lot of thine inheritance; thou art not put off with creatures, the Creator himself is thine. Wilt thou not remember this, and so keep alive the memory of his goodness?

The greatness of the goodness is on some occasions made manifest by the *evil from which it rescues us*. Nobody knows so well the blessing of health as he who has but lately been tortured in every limb; then for his restoration he blesses Jehovah Rophi, the healing Lord. None know what salvation from sin means like those who have been crushed beneath the burden of guilt, and have been racked by remorse. Did you ever feel yourself condemned of God, and cast out from his presence? Did the pangs of hell commence within your startled conscience? Did your soul long for death rather than life, while thick clouds and darkness enshrouded your guilty spirit? If so, when the Lord has put away your sin, and said, "Thou shalt not die;" when he has brought you forth from the prison-house, and broken your bonds asunder, and set your feet upon a rock, then has the new song been in your mouth, even praise for evermore. Then have you known it to be great goodness which thus delivered you. We may imagine what the bottom of the sea is like, and conceive what it must be to be borne adown the lower deeps where the weeds are wrapped about the dead men's brows; yet I warrant you that our imagination but poorly realizes what Jonah experienced when the floods compassed him about, and he went down to the bottom of the mountains. When the Lord brought up his life from corruption then had he a strong and vivid memory of the great goodness of God, seeing he had been delivered from so great a death. It is in the storm-life that we learn to praise the Lord for his goodness, and for his wonderful works to the children of men. If I might have it so, I could wish my whole life to be calm as a fair summer's evening, when scarce a zephyr stirs the happy flowers; I could desire that nothing might again disturb the serenity of my restful spirit: but were it to be so I suspect I should know but little of the great goodness of the Lord. The sweet singer in the one hundred and seventh psalm ascribes the song of gratitude not to dwellers at home, but to wanderers in the wilderness; not to those who are always at liberty, but to emancipated captives; not to the strong and vigorous, but to those who barely escape from the gates of death; not to those who stand upon a sea of glass, but to those who are tossed in tempest upon a raging ocean. Doubtless so it is: we should not perceive the greatness of goodness if we did not see the depth of the horrible pit, from which it snatches us. You were almost ruined in business, friend, but you escaped as with the skin of your teeth, then you praised God for his great goodness. Your dear child was given up of the physicians, your wife apparently sickened for death, but both these have been spared to you, and herein you see the heights and depths of mercy. Now, therefore, lay up this great goodness in your memory to be the material for future psalms of praise.

Nor is this the only way of estimating God's great goodness: you may estimate it by *the actual greatness of the benefits bestowed.* He giveth like a king; nay, he giveth like a God. Behold, your God has not given you a few minted coins of gold, but he has endowed you with the mines themselves: he has not, as it were, handed to you a cup of cold water, but he has brought you to the flowing fountain, and made the well itself your own. God himself is ours. "The Lord is my portion, saith my soul." If you must have a little list of what he has given you, ponder the following items:—He has given you a name and a place among his people; he has given you the rights and the nature of his sons; he has given you the complete forgiveness of all your sins, and you have it now; he has given you a robe of righteousness, and you are wearing it now; he has given you a superlative loveliness in Christ Jesus, and you have it now; he has given you access to him, and prevalence at the mercy-seat; he has given you this world and worlds to come; he has given you all that he has; he has given you his own Son, and how shall he now refuse you anything? Oh, he has given like a God. The greatness of his goodness this tongue can never hope to tell, and so I ask you to think it over in a quiet hour at home. As for myself I will speak of my Lord as I find him, for the old proverb bids us do so. Whatever *you* shall say, men and brethren, I have nought to speak but what is good of my God, my King, from my childhood until now. He amazes me with his mercy; he utterly astounds me with his lovingkindness; he causes my spirit almost to swoon away with delight beneath the sweetness of his love. Yet hath he not spared me the rod, nor will he, and blessed be his name for that also. "Shall we receive good at the hand of the Lord, and shall we not also receive evil?" said the patriarch; but we will go beyond that, and assert that evil is no evil when it comes from his hand—everything is good which he ordains. We may not see it to be so at the time, but so it is. Our heavenly Father seems to rise from good to better, and from better to yet better still in infinite progression: he causes the roadway of our life to rise higher and higher, and carries it over lofty mountains of lovingkindness. Our life-path winds ever upward to yet higher summits of abounding mercy: therefore let his praise increase, and the name of the Lord be greater and greater still.

I want to urge you, dear friends, to observe the goodness of God carefully for your souls' good. There is a great difference between eyes and no eyes; yet many have eyes and yet see not. God's goodness flows before them, and they say, "Where is it?" They breathe it and they say, "Where is it?" They sit at the table, and they are fed upon it; they wear it upon their limbs: it is in the very beating of their heart, and yet they say, "Where is it?" Be not thus blind. "The ox knoweth his owner, and the ass his master's crib," let us not be more sottish than beasts of the field, but let us know the Lord and consider well the greatness of his goodness.

I have said that the text contains the philosophy of great praise, and we see this in the second stage of the process, namely, *diligent memory*. That which has made an impression upon the mind by observation is fastened upon the memory. Memory seems to lie in two things—first in retaining an impression, and then in recollecting it at a future time. I suppose that, more or less, everything that happens to us is retained in the mind, but it is not easy to reproduce the fainter impressions when you wish to do so. I know in my own mind a great many things that I am sure I remember, but yet I cannot always recollect them immediately. Give me a quarter of an hour to run through a certain arrangement of ideas, and I shall say, "Oh yes, I have it. It was in my mind, but I could not recall it at the time." Memory collects facts and afterwards recollects them. The matters before us are recorded by memory, but the tablet may be mislaid: the perfection of memory is to preserve the tablet in a well-known place, from which you can fetch it forth at the moment. I have dwelt rather longer upon observation with the view that you may begin aright from the beginning, and, by getting vivid impressions, may be the better able to retain and to recall them. We cannot utter what we have forgotten; hence the use of close observation to make a strong memory touching the Lord's great goodness.

How are we to strengthen our memory as to God's goodness? First, we should be well acquainted with *the documents* in which his goodness is recorded. A man may be said to keep in memory a fact which did not happen in his own time, but hundreds of years before he was born: he remembers it because he has seen the document in which the fact is recorded. In a certain sense this is within the range of memory; it is within the memory of man, the united memory of the race. Beloved, be familiar with the Word of God. Store your memory with the ancient records of his great goodness : drink in the whole narrative of the evangelists, and despise not Moses and the prophets ; lie a-soak in the Psalms and the Song of Solomon, and such like books, till you come to know the well recorded goodness of the Lord. Have his words and deeds of goodness arranged and ready to hand ; let them be as it were at your fingers' ends because they are in your heart's core, and then you will be sure abundantly to utter the memory of his goodness, for "out of the abundance of the heart the mouth speaketh."

Next, if you would strengthen your memory, right diligently observe *the memorials*. There are two in the Christian Church. There is the memorial of your Saviour's death, burial, and resurrection which is set forth in believers' baptism, wherein we are buried and risen with the Lord Christ. Forget not that memorial of his deep anguish, when he was immersed in grief and plunged in agony ; for he bids you observe it. And as for the Holy Supper, never neglect it, but be often at the table, where again you set forth his death till he come. He has bidden you do this in remembrance of him; cherish devoutly the precious memorial. Great events in nations have been preserved upon the memory of future generations by some ordained ceremonial, and the Lord's Supper is of that kind ; therefore observe ye well the table of the Lord, that ye forget not his great goodness. See how the Jews kept their Exodus in mind by means of the Paschal Lamb; how they ate it after the sprinkling of the blood ; how they talked to their children and told them of the deliverance from Egypt, abundantly uttering the memory of God's goodness, and then after supper they sang a hymn, even as our text bids us sing of the righteousness of God. Strengthen your memories, then, by reverent attention to the historical documents and the memorial ordinances.

Still, the most important is the memory of what has happened to yourself, your own *personal experience*. I will not give a penny for your religion unless it has taken effect upon yourself. The power of prayer ! What of that ? Did you ever receive an answer to prayer ? Did you ever wrestle with the angel and come off victorious ? What do you know about prayer if you never did ? You are very orthodox. Yes, but unless the doctrines of grace have brought to your soul the grace of the doctrines, and you have tasted and handled them, what do you know about them ? Nothing certainly to remember. O, dear heart, wert thou ever born again ? Then thou wilt remember his great goodness. Wert thou ever cleansed from thy sin and justified in Christ ? Thou wilt remember his great goodness. Hast thou been renewed in heart so as to hate sin and live in holiness ? If so, thou wilt remember, because thou knowest something which flesh and blood have not revealed unto thee. Let every personal mercy be written upon your personal memory.

I have heard that the science of mnemonics, or the strengthening of the memory, for which I have not a very high esteem, lies in the following of certain methods. According to some, you link one idea with another ; you recollect a date by associating it with something that you can see. Practise this method in the present case. Remember God's goodness by the objects around you which are associated with it. For instance, let your bed remind you of God's mercy in the night watches, and your table of his goodness in supplying your daily needs. My garments when I put them on this morning reminded me of times when my hand was unequal even to that simple task. All around us there are memoranda of God's love if we choose to read them. The memory of some deed of divine goodness may be connected with every piece of furniture in your room. There is the old arm-chair where you wrestled with God in great trouble, and received a gracious answer; you cannot forget it; you do not pray so well anywhere else as you do there; you have become attached to that particular chair. That thumbed Bible,—that particular one I mean: it is getting rather worn now, and is marked a good deal; but, nevertheless, out of that very copy the promises have gleamed forth like the stars in heaven, and therefore it helps your memory to use it. I remember a poor man giving me what I thought great praise. I visited him in the hospital, and he said, " Ah, you seem to have hung this room round with your texts, for everything reminds me of what I have heard you say, and as I lie here I recollect your stories and your sayings." In much the same way we should recollect what God has done for us, by looking at all the various places, circumstances, times, and persons which were the surroundings of his mercy. O for a clear remembrance of the goodness of God.

Memory is sometimes helped by classification. You send a servant to a shop for a variety of articles: she will forget some of them unless you so arrange the order that one suggests another. Take care, then, to set God's mercies in order before you, and reckon them up in number, if you can, and so fix them in your memory.

At other times, when persons have very bad memories, they like to figure down on a bit of paper that which it is important to remember. I have often done so, and have placed the paper where I have never found it again. A thread around the finger, or a knot in a handkerchief, and many other devices have been tried. I do not mind what it is, so long as you try and recollect God's mercy to you by some means or other. Do make some record of his goodness. You know the day in which you lost that money, do you not? " Yes, very well." You recollect the day of the month of Black Friday, or Black Monday, up in the City; you have evil days indelibly noted in the black pocket-book of memory: do you remember as well the days of God's special lovingkindness to you? You should do so. Take pains to make notes of notable benefits, and to mark remarkable blessings, so shall you in future days utter the memory of God's great goodness.

The first two processes for securing abundant praise are observation and remembrance. The next is *utterance;* " They shall abundantly *utter*." The word contains the idea of boiling or bubbling up like a fountain. It signifies a holy fluency about the mercy of God. We have quite enough fluent people about, but they are many of them idlers for whom Satan finds abundant work to do. The Lord deliver us from the noise of fluent women: but it matters not how fluent men and women are if they will be fluent on the topic now before us. Open your mouths; let the praise pour forth; let it come, rivers of it. Stream away! Gush away, all that you possibly can. " They shall abundantly utter the memory of thy great goodness." Do not stop the joyful speakers, let them go on for ever. They do not exaggerate, they cannot. You say they are enthusiastic, but they are not half up to the pitch yet ; bid them become more excited and speak yet more fervently. Go on, brother, go on ; pile it up : say something greater, grander, and more fiery still ! You cannot exceed the truth. You have come to a theme where your most fluent powers will fail in utterance. The text calls for a sacred fluency, and I would exhort you liberally to exercise it when you are speaking of the goodness of God.

"They shall abundantly utter it"—that is, they shall constantly be doing it : they shall talk about God's goodness all day long. When you step into their cottages they will begin to tell you of God's goodness to them ; when you bid adieu to them at night you shall hear more last words upon the favourite theme. Very likely they will repeat themselves, but that does not matter ; you cannot have too much of this truly good thing. Just as the singers in the temple repeated again and again the chorus, " His mercy endureth for ever," so may we repeat our praises. Some of God's mercies are so great and sweet, that if we never had another throughout eternity the recollection of the single favour might for ever remain. The splendour of divine love is so great, that a single manifestation of it is often all that we can bear : to have two such revelations at once would be as overpowering as though God should make two suns when one already fills the world with light. Oh, praise ye the Lord, my brethren and sisters, with boundless exultation : rouse all your faculties to this divine service, and abundantly utter the memory of his goodness.

You cannot praise abundantly unless your memory supplies materials, and on the other hand your memory will lose strength unless you utter what you know. When you went to school and had a lesson to learn you found out that by reading your lesson aloud you learned it more quickly, for your ear assisted your eye. Uttering the divine goodness is a great help to the memory of it. By teaching we learn ; by giving the truth expression we deepen its impression upon our minds.

Now I come to the last part of this admirable process. When we have abundantly uttered, then we are to *sing*. In the old Greek mythology Mnemosynè, the goddess of memory, is the mother of the Muses, and surely where there is a good memory of God's lovingkindness the heart will soon produce a song. But what is surprising in the text is that when the joy is described as mounting from plain utterance to song it takes another theme—" Sing of *thy righteousness*." When the heart is most adoring, and selects the grandest theme for reverent song, it chooses the meeting of goodness and righteousness as its topic. How sweet is that canticle—" Mercy and truth are met together, and righteousness and peace have kissed each other." The atonement is the gem of the heart's poetry. Do not your hearts burn within you at the very mention of the glorious deed of Jesus our great Substitute? Parnassus is outdone by Calvary ; the Castalian spring is dried and Jesus' wounded side has opened another fount of song. The goodness of the Lord to us in all the blessings of his providence we gladly chant, but when we tell of the grace which led our Lord Jesus to bleed and die, " the just for the unjust to bring us to God," our music leaps to nobler heights. Incomparable wisdom ordained a way in which God should be righteous to the sternness of severity, and yet should be good, illimitably good, to those that put their trust in him ; lift up then your music till the golden harps shall find themselves outdone.

Thus, then, we have explained the method of securing an abundant utterance, may the Holy Spirit help us to carry it out.

II. In the second place, we shall very briefly note THE MOTIVES FOR THIS ABUNDANT UTTERANCE. These lie very near to hand. The first is, because we cannot help it. The goodness of God demands that we should speak of it. If the Lord Jesus himself should charge his people to be silent as to his goodness they would scarcely be able to obey the command. They would, like the man that was healed, blaze abroad the mighty work that he had done. But, bless his name, he has not told us to be quiet; he allows us to utter abundantly the memory of his great goodness. The stones of the street would cry out as we went along if we did not speak of his love. Some of you good people seldom speak of the goodness of God; how is this? I wonder you can be so coldly quiet. "Oh," said one in his first love, "I must speak or I shall burst"; and we have sometimes felt the same, when the restrained testimony was as fire within our bones. Is it not a sacred instinct to tell out what we feel within? The news is too good to keep. Indulge to the full the holy propensity of your renewed nature. Your soul says, "Speak," and if etiquette says, "Hush, they will think you a fanatic," regard it not, but speak aloud, and let them think you a fanatic if they please. Sir, play the organ very softly when the subject is your own praise ; but when you come to the praises of God, pull out all the stops; thunders of music are all too little for his infinite deservings.

Another motive for abundantly uttering the praises of God is that other voices are clamorous to drown it. What a noisy world this is, with its conflicting and discordant cries. "Lo here," cries one ; "Lo there," shouts another. This uproar would drown the notes of God's praise unless his people uttered it again and yet again. The more there is said against our God the more should we speak for him. Whenever you hear a man curse, it would be wise to say aloud, "Bless the Lord." Say it seven times for every time he curses, and make him hear it. Perhaps he will want to know what you are at, and you will then have an opportunity of asking what he is at, and he will have more difficulty in explaining himself than you will in explaining yourself. Do try if you can to make up for the injuries done to the dear and sacred name of God by multiplying your praises in proportion as you hear him spoken ill of. I say, unless you give forth abundant utterance, God's praise will be buried under heaps of error, blasphemy, ribaldry, nonsense, and idle talk. Abundantly utter it so that some of it, at least, may be heard.

Praise the Lord abundantly because it will benefit you to do so. How bright the past looks when we begin to praise God for it. We say, "I am the man that hath seen affliction," and we are to fill the cup of memory with gall and wormwood, but when we see the goodness of God in it all, we turn the kerchief with which we wiped our tears into a flag of victory, and with holy praise, in the name of our God, we wave the banneret.

As for the present, if you think of God's mercies, how different it seems. A man comes to his dinner table, and does not enjoy what is there, because he misses an expected dainty ; but if he were as poor as some people he would not turn his nose up, but would bless the goodness which has given him so much more than he deserves. Some I know even among Christians are growlers in general always finding fault. The best things in the world are not good enough for them. Ah, my brother, abundantly utter the memory of God's goodness and you will find nothing to grumble at, nothing to complain about, but everything to rejoice in.

As for the future, if we remember God's goodness how joyfully we shall march into it. There is the same goodness for to-morrow as for yesterday, and the same goodness for old age as for youth ; the same God to bless me when I grow grey as when I was a babe upon my mother's breast. Therefore, forward to the future without hesitation or suspicion, abundantly uttering the lovingkindness of the Lord.

Again, I think we ought to do this because of the good it does to other people. If you abundantly talk of God's goodness you are sure to benefit your neighbours. Many are comforted when they hear of God's goodness to their friends. Draw a long face, and lament the trials of the way ; sit down with sombre brethren, and enjoy a little comfortable misery, and see whether crowds will ask to share your vinegar-cruet.

> "While here our various wants we mourn,
>   United groans ascend on high,"

says Dr. Watts, and I am afraid he speaks the truth, but very few will be led in this way to resolve—" We will go with these people, for we perceive that God is with them." Is it good reasoning if men say, " These people are so miserable that they must be on the way to heaven"? We may hope they are, for they evidently want some better place to live in ; but then it may be questioned if such folks would not be wretched even in heaven. You smile, dear friends, as if you said you would not be much attracted by sanctimonious misery, nor do I think you would. Therefore do not try it yourselves, but on the contrary talk much of the goodness of the Lord, and wear a smiling face, and let your eyes sparkle, and go through the world as if after all you are not slaves under the lash, or prisoners in bonds, but the Lord's free men. We have glorious reasons for being happy ; let us be so, and soon we shall hear persons asking, " What is this? Is this religion? I always thought religious people felt bound to be down in the dumps, and to go mourning and sighing all their days." When they see your joy they will be tempted to come to Christ. There is a blessed seductiveness in a holy, happy life. Praise then his name, praise his name evermore ; abundantly utter the memory of his great goodness, and you will bring many to Christ.

Such happy utterance will help also to comfort your own Christian friends and fellow-sufferers. There is a deal of misery in the world— just now more than usual. Many are sorrowing from various causes ; therefore, my dear friends, be happier than ever you were. That venerable man of God, now in heaven, our dear old father Dransfield, when it was a very foggy morning in November, used always to come into the vestry before the sermon and say, " It is a dreary morning, dear pastor; we must rejoice in the Lord more than usual. Things around us are dark, but within and above all is bright. I hope we shall have a very happy service to-day." He would shake hands with me and smile, till he seemed to carry us all into the middle of summer. What if it is bad weather? Bless the Lord that it is not worse than it is. We are not altogether in Egyptian darkness: the sun does shine now and then, and we are sure it is not blown out. So, when we are sick and ill, let us thank God that we shall not be ill for ever, for there is a place where the inhabitants are no more sick. And now to-day, if your harps have been hanging on the willows, take them down : if you have not praised the Lord as you should, begin to do so. Wash your mouths and get rid of the sour flavour of murmuring about bad trade and bad weather. Sweeten your lips with the pleasant confection of praise. I will tell you this, brethren, if any of you shall confess to me that you have sinned by going too far in blessing God, I will for once become a priest, and give you absolution. I never tried my hand at that business before, but I think I can manage so much. Praise God extravagantly if you can. Try it. I wish you would say within yourself, "I will go beyond all bounds in this matter"; for there are no bounds to the deservings of an ever blessed God.

Lastly, let us praise and bless God because it is the way in which he is glorified. We cannot add to his glory, for it is infinite in itself; but we can make it to be more widely known by simply stating the truth about him. Do you not want to give honour to God? Would you not lay down your life that the whole earth might be filled with his glory? Well, if you cannot cover the earth with his praise as the waters cover the sea, you can at least contribute your portion to the flood. Oh, keep not back your praises, but bless and magnify his name from the rising of the sun to the going down of the same. It will lift earth upward and heavenward if we can all unite in praise : we shall see it rising as it were beneath our feet, and ourselves rising with it, until we shall stand as upon the top of some loftiest Alp that has pierced the vault of heaven, and we shall be among the angels, feeling as they feel, doing as they do, and losing ourselves as they lose themselves in the eternal hallelujah of " Glory, and honour, and majesty, and power, and dominion, and might, be unto him that sitteth upon the throne, and unto the Lamb for ever and ever."

9. Maschil of Ethan

"I will sing of the mercies of the Lord for ever: with my mouth will I make known thy faithfulness to all generations. For I have said, Mercy shall be built up for ever: thy faithfulness shalt thou establish in the very heavens."—Psalm lxxxix. 1, 2.

THIS psalm is one of the very choicest songs in the night. Midst a stream of troubled thoughts there stands a fair island of rescue and redemption, which supplies standing-room for wonder and worship; while the music of the words, like the murmuring of a river, sounds sweetly in our ears. Read the psalm carefully and it will rouse your sympathy, for he who wrote it was bearing bitter reproach, and was almost broken-hearted by the grievous calamities of his nation. Yet his faith was strong in the faithfulness of God, and so he sang of the stability of the divine covenant when the outlook of circumstances was dark and cheerless. Nor did he ever sing more sweetly than he sang in that night of his sorrow. Greatly doth it glorify God for us to sing his high praises in storms of adversity and on beds of affliction. It magnifies his mercy if we can bless and adore him when he takes as well as when he gives. It is good that out of the very mouth of the burning fiery furnace there should come a yet more burning note of grateful praise. I am told that there is a great deal of relief to sorrow in complaining; that the utterance of our murmurs may sometimes tend to relieve our pain or sorrow. I suppose it is so. Certainly it is a good thing to weep, for I have heard it from the mouth of many witnesses. Most of us have felt that there are griefs too deep for tears, and that a flood of tears proves that the sorrow has begun to abate. But, methinks, the best relief for sorrow is to sing: this man tried it, at any rate. When mercy seems to have departed, it is well to sing of departed mercy. When no present blessing appears it is a present blessing to remember the blessing of the years gone by, and to rehearse the praises of God for all his former mercies towards us. Two sorts of songs we ought to keep up, even if the present appears to yield us no theme for sonnets: the song of the past for what God has done, and the song of the future for the grace we have not tasted yet—the covenant blessings held in the pierced hand, safe and sure against the time to come.

Brothers and sisters, I want you at this time to feel the spirit of gratitude within your hearts. What though your mind should be heavy, your countenance sad, and your circumstances gloomy; still let the generous impulse kindle and glow. Oh, come, let us sing unto the Lord. It does not seem to me to be much for us to sing God's praises in fair weather. The shouts of "Harvest home" over the loaded wain are proper, but they are only natural. Who would not sing *then?* What bird in all the country is silent when the sun is rising, and the dews of spring are sparkling? But the choicest choir charms the stars of night, and no note is sweeter even to the human ear than that which comes from the bare bough amidst the abundant snows of dark winter. O sons of sorrow, your hearts are tuned to notes which the joyful cannot reach: yours is the full compass and swell. You are harps upon which the chief player on stringed instruments can display his matchless skill to a larger degree than upon the less afflicted. I pray he may do so now, by leading you to be first in the song. We must all of us follow, and some of us will not readily yield to be outstripped in this holy exercise. Like Elijah, we will try to run before the king's chariot in this matter of praise Accounting ourselves the greatest debtors of all to the grace and mercy of God, we must and will sing loudest of the crowd, and make even

> "Heaven's resounding arches ring
> With shouts of sovereign grace."

I invite your attention to two things. First, we shall look at *the work of the eternal builder*—"Mercy shall be built up for ever"; then, secondly, we shall listen to *the resolve of an everlasting singer*—"I will sing of the mercies of the Lord for ever."

I take the second verse first: it is needful for the handling of our subject. You know, in the *book of common prayer* the rubric prescribes concerning a certain form of words that it is "to be said or sung." We will do both. The first part we will have is the verse which begins "*I have said*"; and then the second part shall be the verse which begins "*I will sing.*" It shall be said and sung too. God grant we may say it in the depth of our heart, and afterwards that our mouth may sing it, and make it known unto all generations. May the Spirit of all grace fill us with his own power.

I. First, then, let us contemplate THE ETERNAL BUILDER, AND HIS WONDERFUL WORK. "I have said, Mercy shall be built up for ever: thy faithfulness shalt thou establish in the very heavens."

I can see a vast mass of ruins. Heaps upon heaps they lie around me. A stately edifice has tottered to the ground. Some terrible disaster has occurred. There it lies—cornice, pillar, pinnacle, everything of ornament and of utility, broken, scattered, dislocated. The world is strewn with the *débris*. Journey where you will the desolation is before your eyes. Who has done this? Who has cast down this temple? What hand has ruined this magnificent structure? Manhood, manhood it is which has been destroyed, and Sin was the agent that effected the Fall. It is man broken by his sin. Iniquity has done it. O thou devastator, what destructions hast thou wrought in the earth! What desolation thou hast made unto the ends of the world! Everywhere is ruin; everywhere is ruin. Futile attempts are made to rebuild this temple upon its own heap, and the Babel towers arise out of the rubbish and abide for a season, but they are soon broken down, and the mountain of decay and corruption becomes even more hopeless of restoration. All that man has done with his greatest effort is but to make a huger display of his total failure to recover his position, to realise his ostentatious plans, or to restore his own fleeting memories of better things. They may build, and they may pile up stone upon stone, and cement them together with untempered mortar, but their rude structure shall all crumble to the dust again, for the first ruin will be perpetuated even to the last. So must it be, for sin destroys all. I am vexed in my spirit and sore troubled as I look at these ruins, fit habitations for the bittern and the dragon, the mole and the bat. Alas for manhood that it should be thus fallen and destroyed!

But what else do I see? I behold the great original Builder coming forth from the ivory palaces to undo this mischief; and he cometh not with implements of destruction, that he may cast down and destroy every vestige, but I see him advancing with plummet and line, that he may rear, set up, and establish on a sure foundation a noble pile that shall not crumble with time, but endure throughout all ages. He cometh forth with mercy. So "I said" as I saw the vision, "Mercy shall be built up for ever." There was no material but mercy with which a temple could be constructed among men. What can meet the guilt of human crimes but mercy? What can redress the misery occasioned by wanton transgression but mercy? Mere kindness could not do it. Power alone —even Omnipotence—could not accomplish it. Wisdom could not even commence until Mercy stood at her right hand. But when I saw Mercy interpose I understood the meaning. Something was to be done that would change the dreary picture that made my heart to groan, for at the advent of Mercy the walls would soon rise, until the roof ascended high and the palace received within its renovated glory the sublime architect who reared it. I knew that now there would be songs instead of sighs, since God had come, and come in mercy. Beloved brethren and sisters, blessed was that day when Mercy, the Benjamin of God, his last-born attribute, appeared. Surely it was the son of our sorrow, but it was the son of his right hand. There had been no need of mercy if it had not been for our sin; thus from direst evil the Lord took occasion to display the greatest good.

When Mercy came—God's darling, for he saith he delighteth in mercy —then was there hope that the ruins of the Fall would no longer be the perpetual misery of men. I said, "Mercy shall be built up." Now, if you closely scan the passage you will clearly perceive that the psalmist has the idea of God's mercy being manifest in building, because a great breach has to be repaired, and the ruins of mankind are to be restored. As for building, it is a very substantial operation. A building is something which is palpable and tangible to our senses. We may have plans and schemes which are only visionary, but when it comes to building, as those know who have to build, there is something real being done, something more than surveying the ground and drawing the model. And oh, what real work God has done for men! What real work in the gift of his dear Son! The product of his infinite purpose now becomes evident. He is working out his great designs after the counsel of his own will. What real work there is in the regeneration of his people. That is no fiction. Mercy is built, and the blessings that you and I have received have not mocked us; they have not been the dream of fanatics, nor the fancy of enthusiasts. God has done real work for you and for me, as we can bear testimony, and as we do bear testimony at this hour. " For I have said, Mercy shall be built." That is no sham, no dream; it is the act and deed of God. Mercy has been built. A thing that is built is a fixed thing. It exists—exists really, and exists according to a substantial plan. It is presumed to be permanent. True, all earthly structures will moulder and decay, and man's buildings will dissolve in the last great fire, but still a building is more durable than a tent, or a run-up lodge in a garden of cucumbers, and " I have said, Mercy shall be built." It is not a movable berth, but a fixed habitation—I have found it so. And have not you? God's mercy began with some of you—no, I must not talk about when it began, but I mean you began to perceive it many years ago now, when these heads that are now bald or grey had locks bushy and black as a raven—when you were curly-headed boys and girls, that clambered on your father's knee. You remember, even then, the mercy of your God, and it has continued with you—a fixed, substantial, real thing. Not the old house at home has been more fixed than the mercy of God. There has been a warm place for you by the fireside from your childhoo until now, and a mother's love has not failed; but more substantial than a house has been the mercy of God to you. You can endorse the declaration of David: " I have said, Mercy shall be built."

A building is an orderly thing as well as a fixed thing. There is a scheme and design about it. Mercy shall be built. God has gone about blessing us with designs that only his own infinite perfections could have completed. We have not seen the design yet in the full proportion. We shall be lost in wonder, love, and praise when we see it all carried out; but we perceive already some lines, some distinct traces of a grand design, and I said, as I caught first one thought of God, and then another, of his mercy toward me, " Mercy shall be built." I see that it shall. This is no load of bricks shot out. It is polished stones builded one upon another. God's grace and goodness toward me have not come to me by chance, or as the blind distribution of a God who cared for all alike, and for none with any special purpose. No, but there has been as much a specialty of purpose to me as if I were the only one he loved, though, praised be his name, he has blessed and is blessing multitudes of others beside me. As I discovered that in all his dealings of mercy there was a plan, I said, " Mercy shall be built," and so it has been. Yea, more, if I had the time, I should like to picture to you the digging out of that foundation of mercy in the olden time, the marking out of the lines of mercy in the predestinating purpose and the ancient covenant of God. Then I would appeal to your experience, and entreat you to observe how progressively, line upon line, the divers promises have been verified to you up till now. With what transport you would say, "Yes, the figure may run, if it likes, on all fours, yea, and may go on as many legs as a centipede, and yet there shall be no spoiling of it, the metaphor is so good. Mercy has been in course of construction, and is now being reared." So the song begins, "Mercy shall be built."

But now he says, "Mercy shall be built up." Will you try to think for a minute upon these words—"built up"? It is not merely a long, low wall of mercy that is formed, to make an inclosure or to define a boundary, but it is a magnificent pile of mercy, whose lofty heights shall draw admiring gaze, that is being built up. God puts mercy on the top of mercy, and he gives us one favour that we may be ready to receive another. There are some covenant blessings that you and I are not ready to receive yet; they would not be suitable to our present circumstances. "I have many things to say unto you, but ye cannot bear them now." Weak eyes that are gradually recovering their use must not have too much light. A man half starved must not be fed at once upon substantial meat: he must have the nutriment gently administered to him. An excess of rain might inundate the land and wash up the plants, while gentle showers would refresh the thirsty soil and invigorate the herbs and the trees. Even so mercy is bestowed upon us in measure. God does not give us every spiritual blessing at once. There are the blessings of our childhood in grace, which we perhaps shall not so much enjoy when we come to be strong men; but then the blessings of the strong man and of the father would crush the child, and God aboundeth toward us in all wisdom and prudence in the distribution of his gifts: and, as I thought of that, I said, "Yes, mercy shall be built up. There shall be one mercy on another."

Would that I had a vivid imagination, and a tongue gifted with eloquence; then I would try to portray the twelve courses of the new Jerusalem, and show how the stones of fair colours came one next to the other, so that the colours set each other off, and blended into a wondrous harmony; but I can clearly see that the mercy of the azure shall not come first, but there shall be the mercy of the emerald to underlie it, and there shall be an advance made in the preciousness of the stones with which God shall build us up, and we cannot tell what the next is to be; certainly not what the next after that is to be, nor the next after that, and the one to follow after that. But as I saw half-a-dozen of the courses of God's mercy, I said, "His mercy shall be built up." I can see it rising tier on tier, and course on course, and it gathers wonders. The longer I gaze the more I am lost in contemplation. Silent with astonishment, spell-bound with the fascinating vision, I think, I believe, I know that—"Mercy shall be built up." Moreover, my expectations are awakened. I am waiting eagerly for the next scene. The designs of mercy are not exhausted; the deeds of mercy are not all told; the display of mercy must reach higher than has ever yet dawned upon my imagination. Its foundations were laid low. In great mercy he gave me a broken heart. That was pure mercy, for God accepts broken hearts; they are very precious in his sight; but it was a higher mercy when he gave me a new heart, which was bound up and united in his fear and filled with his joy. Oh, brethren, let us remember how he showed us the evil of sin, and caused as to feel a sense of shame. That was a choice mercy, but it was a clearer mercy when he gave us a sense of pardon. Oh, it was a blessed day when he gave us the little faith that tremblingly touched his garment's hem. It was better when he gave us faith as a grain of mustard seed that grew. It has been better still when by faith we have been able to do many mighty works for him. We do not know what we shall do yet when he gives us more faith. Far less can we imagine how our powers shall develop in heaven, where faith will come to its full perfection. It will not die, as some idly pretend. There we shall implicitly believe in God. With the place of his throne as the point of our survey, we shall see nothing but his sovereign will to shape events; so with joyful assurance of hope we shall look onward to the advent of our Lord Jesus Christ and the glory that is to follow. We shall sit in heaven, and sing that the Lord reigneth; we shall gaze upon the earth, and behold how it trembles at the coming of the King of kings; and with radiant faces we shall smile at Satan's rage. We do not know what any one of our graces may be built up into, but if you are conscious of any growth in any grace, you have learnt enough to appreciate the oracle that speaketh in this wise—" I have said, Mercy shall be built up for ever."

Once again would I read this verse with very great emphasis, and ask you to notice how it rebukes the proud and the haughty, and how it encourages the meek and lowly in spirit. " I have said mercy shall be built up for ever." In the edification of the saints there is nothing else but mercy. Some people seem to fancy that when we get to a certain point in grace we do not need to sue for mercy. My dear friends, if any of you get into that humour that you say, " I need not make any confession of sin, I need not ask pardon of sin," you are trifling with the very truths of which you seem to be tenacious. I do not care what doctrine it is that brings you there; you are in a dangerous state if you stop there. Get away back directly. Your right position is at the throne of grace, and a throne of grace is meant for people that want grace, and you need grace now; never more than now. Without mercies new every morning, as the manna that fed the Israelites of old, your days will be full of misery. Your Lord and Master taught you to say not only " Our Father which art in heaven," and " Thy kingdom come," but he bade you constantly to pray, " Forgive us our trespasses as we forgive them that trespass against us." " I have no trespasses," says one. Tut, brother, go home and look at your own heart. I will have no argument with you. Take the bandage off your eyes. You are about as full of sin as an egg is full of meat. Among the rest of your many sins there is this rotten egg of an accursed pride as to your own state of heart. I said, whatever you say, " Mercy shall be built up for ever." I expect God to deal with me on the footing of mercy, as long as I live. I do not expect that he shall build me up in any way but according to his grace, and pity, and forgiving love. If there be any creatures in this world that can boast of having got beyond the need of asking for mercy, I have not learnt their secret of self-deception. I do know of some professors who climb so high up the ladder that they come down the other side. I fancy that is very much like the wonderful growing in perfection of which they prate. It means full often going up so high that they are pure saints in their own esteem, but anon they have gone down so low that they are poor lost sheep in the estimation of the churches of Christ. God grant you may not fall by any such process.

"I have said, mercy shall be built up for ever." Brethren, if you and I ever get to the gate of heaven, and stand upon the alabaster doorstep with our finger on the glittering latch, unless the mercy of God carry us over the threshold, we shall be dragged down to hell even from the gates of paradise. Mercy, mercy, mercy! His mercy endureth for ever, because we always want it. As long as we are in this world we shall have to make our appeal to mercy, and cry, "Father, I have sinned. Blot out my transgressions." Well, that is, as I have said, what the text declares, "I have said mercy shall be built up," nothing else but mercy. There will not come a point when the angelic masons shall stop and say, "Now then, the next course is to be merit. So far mercy : now the next course is to be perfection in the flesh ; the next course is to be no need of mercy." No, no, mercy, mercy, mercy, till the very topstone shall be brought forth with shoutings of "grace, grace unto it." "Mercy shall be built up."

Yet onward glance your eye. "I said, mercy shall be built up for ever." For ever? Well, I have been peering back into the past, and I discover that nothing else but mercy can account for my being or my well-being. By the grace of God I am what I am. The psalm of my life, though filled with varied stanzas, has but one chorus,—his mercy endureth for ever. Will you look back, beloved, on all the building of your life and character? Any of it that has been real building—gold and silver and precious stones—has all been mercy, and so the building will go on. The operation is proceeding slowly but surely. What though at this present hour you may be in grievous trouble? Mercy is being built up for you. "Oh, no," say you, "I am tottering, and my days are declining, and I feel I shall be utterly cast down." Yes, you may be very conscious of your own weakness and infirmity ; but the mercy of the Lord is steadfast, its foundation abides firm, not a single stone can be moved from its setting. The work is going on, storm or tempest notwithstanding. There is nothing precarious about the fact that mercy shall be built up for ever. Let not the murky atmosphere that surrounds you blind your eyes—the eyes of your understanding—to this glorious word—"*for ever.*" Rather say, if I am well set in this fabric of mercy my castings down are often the way in which God builds up his mercy. I shall be built up for ever. And oh, if it goes on being built up for ever—I am ravished with the thought, though I cannot give expression to it—what will it grow to? What will it grow to? If it is going to be built up in the case of any one of you, say seventy years, oh it will be a grand pinnacle, an everlasting monument to the Eternal Builder's praise : but you see it will go on; it will be built up for ever. What! never cease? No, never. But shall it never come to a pause? No, mercy shall be built up for ever; it shall go on towering upward. Do you imagine that it will go at a slower rate by-and-by? That is not likely. It is not God's way: he generally hastens his speed as he ripens his purposes. So I suspect that he will go on building up his mercy tier on tier, height on height, for ever. Says one, " Will its colossal altitude pierce the clouds, and rise above the clear azure of the sky?" It will. Read the text: " Thy faithfulness shalt thou establish in the very heavens "—not in the heavens only, but in the " *very heavens* "—the heaven of heavens. He will build up to that height: he will go on building you up, dear brother, dear sister, till he gets you to heaven: he will build you up till he makes a heavenly man of you, till where Christ is, you shall be—and what Christ is, as far as he is man, you shall be ; and with God himself you shall be allied—a child of God, an heir of heaven, a joint heir with Jesus Christ.

I wish I had an imagination, I say again, bold and clear, uncramped by all ideas of the masonry of men, free to expand, and still to cry, "*Excelsior.*" Palaces, methinks, are paltry, and castles and cathedrals are only grand in comparison with the little cots that nestle on the plain. Even mountains, high as the Himalaya range or broad as the Andes, though their peaks be so lofty to our reckoning, are mere specks on the surface of the great globe itself, and our earth is small among the celestial orbs, a little sister of the larger planets. Figures fail me quite : my description must take another turn. I try, and try again, to realize the gradual rising of this temple of mercy which shall be built up for ever. Within the bounds of my feeble vision, I can discern that it has risen above death, above sin, above fear, above all danger ; it has risen above the terrors of the judgment day ; it has outsoared the " wreck of matter and the crash of worlds"; it towers above all our thoughts. Our bliss ascends above an angel's enjoyments, and he has pleasures that were never checked by a pang ; but he does not know the ineffable delight of free grace and dying love. It has ascended above all that I dare to speak of, for even the little I know has about it somewhat that it were not lawful for a man to utter. It is built up into the very arms of Christ, where his saints shall lie emparadised for ever, equal with himself upon his throne, " I said, Mercy shall be built up for ever." The building-up will go on throughout eternity.

Yes, and what is once built up will never fall down, neither in whole nor in part. There is the mercy of it. God is such a Builder that he finishes what he begins, and what he accomplishes is for ever. " The gifts and calling of God are without repentance." He does not do and undo ; or build for his people after a covenant fashion, and then cast down again because the counsel of his heart has changed. So let us sing and praise and bless the name of the Lord. I do hope that, from what little our experience has taught us already, we are prepared to cry, like the psalmist, " I have said, Mercy shall be built up for ever : thy faithfulness shalt thou establish in the very heavens."

II. Well, now, we come back to the first verse. There are first that shall be last, and last that shall be first, so is it with our text. We have looked at the Eternal Builder, let us now listen to AN EVER-LASTING SINGER. " I will sing of the mercies of the Lord for ever: with my mouth will I make known thy faithfulness to all generations."

Here is a good and godly resolution : " *I will sing.*" The singing of the heart is intended, and the singing of the voice is expressed, for he mentions his mouth ; and equally true is it that the singing of his pen is implied, since the psalms that he wrote were for others to sing in generations that should follow. He says, "I will sing." I do not know what else he could do. There is God building in mercy. We cannot assist him in that. We have no mercy to contribute, and what is built is to be all of mercy. We cannot impart anything to the great temple which he is building; yet we can sit down and sing. It seems delightful that there should be no sound of hammer or noise of axe; that there should be no other sound than the voice of song, as when they fabled of the ancient player upon the instruments that he builded temples by the force of song. So shall God build up his church, and so shall he build us as living stones into the sacred structure, and so shall we sit and muse on his mercy till the music breaks from our tongue, and we rise to our feet and stand and sing about it. I will sing of the mercy while the mercy is being built up. "I will sing of the mercies of the Lord."

But will he not soon sink these sweet notes and relapse into silence? No; he says, "I will sing of the mercies of the Lord *for ever*." Will he not grow weary and wish for some other occupation? No; for true praise is a thirsty thing, and when it drinks from a golden chalice it soon empties it, and yearns for deeper draughts with strong desire. It could drink up Jordan at a draught. This singing praise to God is a spiritual passion. The saved soul delights itself in the Lord, and sings on, and on, and on unwearily. "I will sing for ever," saith he. Not, "I will get others to perform, and then I will retire from the service;" but rather, "I will myself sing: my own tongue shall take the solo, whoever may refuse to join in the chorus. I will sing, and with my mouth will I make known thy faithfulness." Oh, that is blessed—that singing personally and individually. It is a blessed thing to be one of a choir in the praise of God, and we like to have others with us in this happy employment; still for all that, the hundred and third Psalm is a most beautiful solo. It begins, "Bless the Lord, O my soul," and it finishes up with "Bless the Lord, O my soul." There must be personal, singular praise, for we have received personal and singular mercies. I will sing, I will sing, I will sing of the mercies of the Lord for ever.

Now note his subject. "I will sing of the *mercies of the Lord*." What, not of anything else? Are the mercies of the Lord his exclusive theme? "*Arma virumque cano*."—"Arms and the man, I sing," says the Latin poet. "Mercies and my God, I sing," says the Hebrew seer. "I will sing of mercies," says the devout Christian. This is the fount of mercy, whereof if a man doth drink he shall sing far better than he that drinketh of the Castalian fount, and on Parnassus begins to tune his harp.

> "Praise the mount, oh, fix me on it,
> Mount of God's unchanging love."

Here we are taught a melodious sonnet, "sung by flaming tongues above." "I will sing of mercies, I will sing of mercies for ever," he says, and I suppose the reason is because God's mercies would be built up for ever. The morning stars sang together when God's work of creation was completed. Suppose God created a world every day, surely the morning stars would sing every day. Ah, but God gives us a world of mercies every day : therefore, let us sing of his mercies for ever. Any one day that you live, my brother, there is enough mercy packed away into it to make you sing not only through that day but through the rest of your life. I have thought sometimes when I have received great mercies of God that I almost wanted to pull up, and to " rest and be thankful," and say to him, " My blessed Lord, do not send me anything more for a little while. I really must take stock of these. Come, my good secretaries, take down notes, and keep a register of all his mercies." Let us gratefully respond for the manifold gifts we have received, and send back our heartiest praise to God who is the giver of every good thing. But, dear me ! before I could put the basketfuls away on the shelf there came waggons loaded with more mercy. What was one to do then, but to sit on the top of the pile and sing for joy of heart ? Then let us lift each parcel and look at each label, and lay them up in the house and say, " Is it not full of mercy ? As for me, I will go and sit, like David, before the Lord, and say, " Who am I, O Lord God ? and what is my house, that thou hast brought me hitherto ?" " And is this the manner of man, O Lord God ?" I will sing of the mercies of the Lord for ever, because I shall never have got through with them. It is true, as Addison puts it—

> " Eternity 's too short
> To utter all thy praise."

You will never accomplish the simple task of acknowledgments, because there will be constantly more mercies coming ; you will always be in arrears. In heaven itself you will never have praised God sufficiently. You will want to begin heaven over again, and have another eternity, if such a thing could be, to praise him for the fresh benefits that he bestows. " For I have said, mercy shall be built up for ever : therefore will I sing of the mercies of the Lord for ever." What a spectacle it will be as you sit in heaven, and watch God building up his mercies for ever, or, if it may be, to wander over all the worlds that God has made ; for I suppose we may do that, and yet still have heaven for our home. Heaven is everywhere to the heart that lives in God. What a wonderful sight it will be to see God going on building up his mercy. Ah, we have not acquired an idea of the grandeur of the plan of mercy. The grandeur of his justice no thought can conceive, no words can paint. Ah, my dear brethren, although there have been expressions and metaphors used about the wrath to come which cannot be found in Scripture, and are not to be justified, yet I am persuaded that there is no exaggeration possible of the inviolability of God's law, of the truthfulness of his threatenings, of the terror of his indignation, or of the holiness of Jehovah, a holiness that shall constrain universal homage ; but you must always take care that you balance all your thoughts. In the retributions of his wrath there shall be a revelation of his righteousness : for no sentence of his majesty will ever cast a shadow over his mercy, and every enemy will be speechless before the equity of his award. They that hate him shall hide their faces from him ; in burning shame they shall depart to perpetual banishment from his presence. Their condemnation will not dim the purity of his atributes.

The glory of the redeemed will also reveal the righteousness of Jehovah, and his saints will be perfectly satisfied when they are conformed to his likeness. On the summit of the eternal hill you shall sit down and survey that mercy-city now in course of construction builded up; it lieth four square, its height is the same as its breadth, ever towering, ever widening, ever coming to that divine completion which, nevertheless, it has, in another sense, already attained. We know that God in his mercy shall be all in all. "I will sing of the mercy of the Lord for ever," for I shall see his mercy built up for ever.

This singing of Ethan was intended to be instructive. How large a class did he want to teach? He intended to make known God's mercy *to all generations.* Dear, dear, if a man teaches one generation, is not that enough? *Modern thought* does not adventure beyond the tithe of a century, and it gets tame and tasteless before half that tiny span of sensationalism has given it time to evaporate. But the echoes of truth are not so transient; they endure, and by means of the printing press we can teach generation after generation, leaving books behind us as this good man has bequeathed this psalm, which is teaching us to-night, perhaps more largely than it taught any generation nearer to him. Will you transmit blessed testimonies to your children's children? It should be your desire to do something in the present life that will live after you are gone. It is one proof to us of our immortality that we instinctively long for a sort of immortality here. Let us strive to get it, not by carving our names on some stone, or writing our epitaphs upon a pillar, as Absalom did when he had nothing else by which to commemorate himself; but get to work to do something which shall be a testimony to the mercy of God, that others shall see when you are gone. Ethan said, "God's mercy shall be built up for ever," and he is teaching us still that blessed fact. Suppose you cannot write, and your influence is very narrow, yet still you shall go on singing of God's praise for ever, and you shall go on teaching generations yet to come. You Sunday-school teachers, you shall be Sunday-school teachers for ever. "Oh," say you, "no, I cannot credit that." Well, but you shall. You know it will always be Sunday when you get to heaven. There will never be any other day there, but one everlasting Sabbath; and through you and by you shall be made known to angels, and principalities, and powers, the manifold wisdom of God. I teach some of you now, and I often think you could better teach me, some of you old experienced saints. You will teach me by-and-by. When we are in glory we shall all of us be able to tell one another something of God's mercy. Your view of it, you know, differs from mine, and mine from my brother's. You, my dear friend, see mercy from one point; and your wife, even though she be one with you, sees it from another point, and detects another sparkle of it which your eye has never caught. So shall we barter and exchange our knowledge in heaven, and trade together and grow richer in our knowledge of God there. "I have said, mercy shall be built up for ever: thy faithfulness shalt thou establish in the very heavens." Then I said, "I will sing of the mercies of the Lord for ever: with my mouth will I make known thy faithfulness to all generations." We will go on exulting in God's mercy so long as we have any being; and that shall be for ever and ever. When we have been in heaven millions of years, we shall not want any other subject to speak of but the mercy of our blessed God, and we shall find auditors with charmed ears to sit and listen to the matchless tale, and some that will ask us to tell it yet again. They will come to heaven, you know, as long as the world lasts, some out of every generation. We shall see them streaming in at the gates more numerously, I hope, as the years roll by, till the Lord comes; and we will continue to tell to fresh comers what the Lord has done for us. We never can stop it; we never can cease; but as the heavens are telling the glory of God, and every star declares in wondrous diversity his praise, so where the stars differ from one another in the glory of God above, the saints shall be for ever telling the story which yet shall remain untold—the love we knew, but which surpassed our knowledge; the grace of which we drank, but yet was deeper than our draughts; the bounty in which we swam until we seemed to lose ourselves in love; the favour which still was greater than our utmost conceptions, and rose above our most eager desires.

God bless you, brethren and sisters, and send you away singing—

> " All that remains for me
> Is but to love and sing,
> And wait until the angels come,
> To bear me to my King."

10. The Happy Duty
of Daily Praise

"I will extol thee, my God, O King; and I will bless thy name for ever and ever. Every day will I bless thee; and I will praise thy name for ever and ever."—Psalm cxlv. 1, 2.

IF I were to put to you the question, "Do you pray?" the answer would be very quickly given by every Christian person, "Of course I do." Suppose I then added, "And do you pray every day?" the prompt reply would be, "Yes; many times in the day. I could not live without prayer." This is no more than I expect, and I will not put the question. But let me change the enquiry, and say, "Do you bless God every day? Is praise as certain and constant a practice with you as prayer?" I am not sure that the answer would be quite so certain, so general, or so prompt. You would have to stop a little while before you gave the reply; and I fear, in some cases, when the reply did come, it would be, "I am afraid I have been negligent in praise." Well, then, dear friend, have you not been wrong? Should we omit praise any more than we omit prayer? And should not praise come daily and as many times in the day as prayer does? It strikes me that to fail in praise is as unjustifiable as to fail in prayer. I shall leave it with your own heart and conscience, when you have asked and answered the question, to see to it in the future that far more of the sweet frankincense of praise is mingled with your daily oblation of devotion.

Praise is certainly not at all so common in family prayer as other forms of worship. We cannot all of us praise God in the family by joining in song, because we are not all able to raise a tune, but it would be well if we could. I agree with Matthew Henry when he says, "They that pray in the family do well; they that pray and read the Scriptures do better; but they that pray, and read, and sing do best of all." There is a completeness in that kind of family worship which is much to be desired.

Whether in the family or not, yet personally and privately, let us endeavour to be filled with God's praise and with his honour all the day. Be this our resolve—"I will extol thee, my God, O King; and I will bless thy name for ever and ever. Every day will I bless thee; and I will praise thy name for ever and ever."

109

Brethren, praise cannot be a second-class business; for it is evidently due to God, and that in a very high degree. A sense of justice ought to make us praise the Lord; it is the least we can do, and in some senses it is the most that we can do, in return for the multiplied benefits which he bestows upon us. What, no harvest of praise for him who has sent the sunshine of his love and the rain of his grace upon us! What, no revenue of praise for him who is our gracious Lord and King! He doth not exact from us any servile labour, but simply saith, "Whoso offereth praise glorifieth me." Praise is good, and pleasant, and delightful. Let us rank it among those debts which we would not wish to forget, but are eager to pay at once.

Praise is an act which is pre-eminently characteristic of the true child of God. The man who doth but pretend to piety will fast twice in the week, and stand in the temple and offer something like prayer; but to praise God with all the heart, this is the mark of true adoption, this is the sign and token of a heart renewed by divine grace. We lack one of the surest evidences of pure love to God if we live without presenting praise to his ever-blessed name.

Praising God is singularly beneficial to ourselves. If we had more of it we should be greatly blest. What would lift us so much above the trials of life, what would help us to bear the burden and heat of the day, so well as songs of praise unto the Most High? The soldier marches without weariness when the band is playing inspiriting strains; the sailor, as he pulls the rope or lifts the anchor, utters a cheery cry to aid his toil; let us try the animating power of hymns of praise. Nothing would oil the wheels of the chariot of life so well as more of the praising of God. Praise would end murmuring, and nurse contentment. If our mouths were filled with the praises of God, there would be no room for grumbling. Praise would throw a halo of glory around the head of toil and thought. In its sunlight the commonest duties of life would be transfigured. Sanctified by prayer and praise, each duty would be raised into a hallowed worship, akin to that of heaven. It would make us more happy, more holy, and more heavenly, if we would say, "I will extol thee, my God, O King."

Besides, brethren, unless we praise God here, are we preparing for our eternal home? There all is praise; how can we hope to enter there if we are strangers to that exercise? This life is a preparatory school and in it we are preparing for the high engagements of the perfected. Are you not eager to rehearse the everlasting hallelujahs?

> "I would begin the music here,
> And so my soul should rise :
> Oh, for some heavenly notes to bear
> My passions to the skies!"

Learn the essential elements of heavenly praise by the practice of joyful thanksgiving, adoring reverence, and wondering love; so that, when you step into heaven, you may take your place among the singers, and say, "I have been practising these songs for years. I have praised God while I was in a world of sin and suffering, and when I was weighed down by a feeble body; and now that I am set free from earth and sin, and the bondage of the flesh, I take up the same strain to sing more sweetly to the same Lord and God."

I wish I knew how to speak so as to stir up every child of God to praise. As for you that are not his children—oh, that you were such! You must be born again ; you cannot praise God aright till you are. "Unto the wicked God saith, What hast thou to do to declare my statutes, or that thou shouldest take my covenant in thy mouth ?" You can offer him no real praise while your hearts are at enmity to him. Be ye reconciled to God by the death of his Son, and then you will praise him. Let no one that has tasted that the Lord is gracious, let no one that has ever been delivered from sin by the atonement of Christ, ever fail to pay unto the Lord his daily tribute of thanksgiving

To help us in this joyful duty of praise we will turn to our text, and keep to it. May the Holy Spirit instruct us by it !

I. In our text we have first of all THE RESOLVE OF PERSONAL LOYALTY :—" I will extol thee, my God, O King." David personally comes before his God and King, and utters this deliberate resolution that he will praise the divine majesty for ever.

Note here, first, that *he pays homage to God as his King.* There is no praising God aright if we do not see him upon the throne, reigning with unquestioned sway. Disobedient subjects cannot praise their sovereign. You must take up the Lord's yoke—it is easy, and his burden, which is light. You must come and touch his silver sceptre and receive his mercy, and own him to be your rightful Monarch, Lawgiver, and Ruler. Where Jesus comes, he comes to reign : where God is truly known, he is always known as supreme. Over the united kingdom of our body, soul, and spirit the Lord must reign with undisputed authority. What a joy it is to have such a King ! " O King," says David : and it seems to have been a sweet morsel in his mouth. He was himself a king after the earthly fashion ; but to him God alone was King. Our King is no tyrant, no maker of cruel laws. He demands no crushing tribute or forced service : his ways are ways of pleasantness, and all his paths are peace. His laws are just and good ; and in the keeping of them there is great reward. Let others exult that they are their own masters ; our joy is that God is our King. Let others yield to this or that passion, or desire ; as for us, we find our freedom in complete subjection to our heavenly King. Let us, then, praise God by loyally accepting him as our King ; let us repeat with exultation the hymn we just now sang—

> " Crown him, crown him,
> King of kings, and Lord of lords."

Let us not be satisfied that he should reign over us alone : but let us long that the whole earth should be filled with his glory. Be this our daily prayer—" Thy kingdom come. Thy will be done, in earth as it is in heaven." Let this be our constant ascription of praise—" For thine is the kingdom, and the power, and the glory, for ever. Amen."

Note that the Psalmist, also, in this first sentence, *praises the Lord by a present personal appropriation of God to himself by faith :* " I will extol thee, my God." That word " my " is a drop of honey ; nay, it is like Jonathan's wood, full of honey ; it seems to drip from every bough, and he that comes into it stands knee-deep in sweetness. " My God " is as high a note as an angel can reach. What is another man's God to me? He must be my God or I shall not extol him. Say, dear heart, have you ever taken God to be your God? Can you say with David in another place, "This God is our God for ever and ever. He shall be our guide, even unto death"? Blessed was Thomas when he bowed down, and put his finger into the print of his Master's wounds, and cried, "My Lord and my God." That double-handed grip of appropriation marked the death of his painful unbelief. Can you say, "Jehovah is my God"? To us there are Father, Son, and Holy Spirit; but these are one God, and this one God is our own God. Let others worship whom they will, this God our soul adores and loves, yea, claims to be her personal possession. O beloved, if you can say, "My God," you will be bound to exalt him! If he has given himself to you so that you can say, "My Beloved is mine" you will give yourself to him, and you will add, "And I am his." Those two sentences, like two silken covers of a book, shut in within them the full score of the music of heaven.

Observe that David *is firmly resolved to praise God.* My text has four "I wills" in it. Frequently it is foolish for us poor mortals to say "I will," because our will is so feeble and fickle; but when we resolve upon the praise of God, we may say, "I will," and "I will," and "I will," and "I will," till we make a solid square of determinations. Let me tell you you will have need to say "I will" a great many times, for many obstacles will hinder your resolve. There will come depression of spirit, and then you must say, "I will extol thee, my God, O King." Poverty, sickness, losses, and crosses may assail you, and then you must say, "I will praise thy name for ever and ever." The devil will come and tell you that you have no interest in Christ; but you must say, "Every day will I bless thee." Death will come, and perhaps you will be under the fear of it; then it will be incumbent upon you to cry, "And I will praise thy name for ever and ever."

> "Sing, though sense and carnal reason
> Fain would stop the joyful song :
> Sing, and count it highest treason
> For a saint to hold his tongue."

A bold man took this motto—"While I live I'll crow"; but our motto is, "While I live I'll praise." An old motto was, "*Dum spiro spero*"; but the saint improves upon it, and cries, "*Dum expiro spero.*" Not only while I live I will hope, but when I die I will hope : and he even gets beyond all that, and determines—"Whether I live or die I will praise my God." "O God, my heart is fixed, my heart is fixed ; I will sing and give praise."

While David is thus resolute, I want you to notice that *the resolution is strictly personal.* He says, "*I* will extol thee." Whatever others do, my own mind is made up. David was very glad when others praised God: he delighted to join with the great congregation that kept holy day; but still he was attentive to his own heart and his own praise. There is no selfishness in looking well to your own personal state and condition before the Lord. He cannot be called a selfish citizen who is very careful to render his own personal suit and service to his king. A company of persons praising God would be nothing unless each individual was sincere and earnest in the worship. The praise of the great congregation is precious in proportion as each individual, with all his heart, is saying, " I will extol thee, my God, O King." Come, my soul, I will not sit silent, because so many others are singing : however many songsters there may be, they cannot sing for me : they cannot pay my private debt of praise, therefore awake, my heart, and extol thy God and King. What if others refuse to sing, what if a shameful silence is observed in reference to the praises of God ; then, my heart, I must bestir thee all the more to a double diligence, that thou mayest with even greater zeal extol thy God and King ! I will sing a solo if I cannot find a choir in which I may take my part. Anyhow, my God, I will extol thee. At this hour men go off to other lords, and they set up this and that new-made god ; but as for me, my heart, I extol thy God and King. At this hour men go off to other lords, and to Jehovah's door-post ; I will not go out from his service for ever. Bind the sacrifice with cords, even with cords to the horns of the altar. Whatever happens, I will extol thee, my God, O King.

Now brothers and sisters, have you been losing your own personality in the multitude. As members of a great church, have you thought " Things will go on very well without me" ? Correct that mistake : each individuality must have its own note to bring to God. Let him not have to say to you, " *Thou* hast bought me no sweet cane with money ; neither hast *thou* filled me with the fat of *thy* sacrifices." Let us not be slow in his praise, since he has been so swift in his grace.

Once more upon this head, while David is thus loyally resolving to praise God, you will observe that *he is doing it all the time.* For the resolution to praise can only come from the man who is already praising God. When he saith, " I will extol thee," he is already extolling. We go from praise to praise. The heart resolves, and so plants the seed, and then the life is affected, and the harvest springs up and ripens. O brethren, do not let us say, " I will extol thee to-morrow " ; or, " I will hope to praise thee when I grow old, or when I have less business on hand." No, no ; thou art this day in debt ; this day own thine obligation. We cannot praise God too soon. Our very first breath is a gift from God, and it should be spent to the Creator's praise. The early morning hour should be dedicated to praise : do not the birds set us the example ? In this matter he gives twice who gives quickly. Let thy praise follow quickly upon the benefit thou dost receive, lest even during the delay thou be found guilty of ingratitude. As soon as a mercy touches our coasts, we should welcome it with acclamation. Let us copy the little chick, which, as it drinks, lifts up its head, as if to give thanks. Our thanksgiving should echo the voice of divine loving-kindness. Before the Lord our King, let us continually rejoice as we bless him, and speak well of his name.

Thus, then, I have set before you the resolve of a loyal spirit. Are you loyal to your God and King ? Then I charge you to glorify his name. Lift up your hearts in his praise, and in all manner of ways make his name great. Praise him with your lips ; praise him with your lives ; praise him with your substance ; praise him with every faculty and capacity. Be inventive in methods of praise : "sing unto the Lord a new song." Bring forth the long-stored and costly alabaster box ; break it, and pour the sweet nard upon your Redeemer's head and feet. With penitents and martyrs extol him ! With prophets and apostles extol him! With saints and angels extol him! Great is the Lord, and greatly to be praised.

II. And now I must conduct you to the second clause of the text, which is equally full and instructive. We have in the second part of it THE CONCLUSION OF AN INTELLIGENT APPRECIATION: "And I will bless thy name for ever and ever." Blind praise is not fit for the all-seeing God. God forbade of old the bringing of blind sacrifices to his altar. Our praise ought to have brain as well as a tongue. We ought to know who the God is whom we praise; hence David says, "I will bless *thy name*"; by which he means—thy character, thy deeds, thy revealed attributes.

First, observe that *he presents the worship of inward admiration:* he knows, and therefore he blesses the divine name. What is this act of blessing? Sometimes "bless" would appear to be used interchangeably with "praise"; yet there is a difference, for it is written, "All thy works shall praise thee, O Lord; and thy saints shall bless thee." You can praise a man, and yet you may never bless him. A great artist, for instance; you may *praise* him, but he may be so ungenerous to you and others that it may never occur to you to *bless* him. Blessing has something in it of love and delight. It is a nearer, dearer, heartier thing than *praise.* "I will bless thy name," that is to say—"I will take an intense delight in thy name: I will lovingly rejoice in it."

The very thought of God is a source of happiness to our hearts; and the more we muse upon his character the more joyous we become. The Lord's name is love. He is merciful and gracious, tender and pitiful. Moreover, he is a just God, and righteous, faithful, and true, and holy. He is a mighty God, and wise and unchanging. He is a prayer-hearing God, and he keepeth his promise evermore. We would not have him other than he is. We have a sweet contentment in God as he is revealed in holy Scripture. It is not everybody that can say this, for a great many professors nowadays desire a god of their own making and shaping. If they find anything in Scripture concerning God which grates upon their tender susceptibilities, they cannot abide it. The God that casts the wicked from his presence for ever—they cannot believe in him; they therefore make unto themselves a false deity, who is indifferent to sin. All that is revealed concerning God is to me abundantly satisfactory; if I do not comprehend its full meaning, I bow before its mystery. If I hear anything of my God which does not yield me delight, I feel that therein I must be out of order with him, either through sin or ignorance, and I say, "What I know not, teach thou me." I doubt not that perfectly holy and completely instructed beings are fully content with everything that God does, and are ready to praise him for all. Do not our souls even now bless the Lord our God, who chose us, redeemed us, and called us by his grace? Whether we view him as Maker, Provider, Saviour, King, or Father, we find in him an unfathomable sea of joy. He is God, our exceeding joy. Therefore we sit down in holy quiet, and feel our soul saying, "Bless the Lord! Bless the Lord!" He is what we would have him to be. He is better than we could have supposed or imagined. He is the crown of delight, the climax of goodness, the sum of all perfection. As often as we see the light, or feel the sun, we would bless the name of the Lord.

114

I think when David said, "I will bless thy name," he meant that *he wished well to the Lord.* To bless a person means to do that person good. By blessing us what untold benefits the Lord bestows! We cannot bless God in such a sense as that in which he blesses us; but we would if we could. If we cannot give anything to God, we can desire that he may be known, loved, and obeyed by all our fellow-men. We can wish well to his kingdom and cause in the world. We can bless him by blessing his people, by working for the fulfilment of his purposes, by obeying his precepts, and by taking delight in his ordinances. We can bless him by submission to his chastening hand, and by gratitude for his daily benefits. Sometimes we say with the Psalmist, "O my soul, thou hast said unto the Lord, Thou art my Lord: my goodness extendeth not to thee; but to the saints that are in the earth, and to the excellent, in whom is all my delight." Oh, that I could wash Jesus Christ's feet! Is there a believer here, man or woman, but would aspire to that office? It is not denied you: you can wash his feet by caring for his poor people, and relieving their wants. You cannot feast your Redeemer; he is not hungry: but some of his people are; feed them! He is not thirsty; but some of his disciples are. Give them a cup of cold water in the Master's name, and he will accept it as given to himself. Do you not feel to-day, you that love him, as if you wanted to do something for him? Arise, and do it, and so bless him. It is one of the instincts of a true Christian to wish to do somewhat for his God and King, who has done everything for him. He loved me, and gave himself for me; should I not give myself for him? Oh, for perfect consecration! Oh, to bless God by laying our all upon his altar, and spending our lives in his service!

It seems, then, dear friends, that David *studied the character and doings of God,* and thus praised him. Knowledge should lead our song. The more we know of God the more acceptably shall we bless him through Jesus Christ. I exhort you, therefore, to acquaint yourselves with God. Study his holy Book. As in a mirror you may here see the glory of the Lord reflected, especially in the person of the Lord Jesus, who is in truth the Word, the very name of the Lord. It would be a pity that we should spoil our praises by ignorance: they that know the name of the Lord will trust him and will praise him.

It appears from this text that David *discovered nothing after a long study of God which would be an exception to this rule.* He does not say, "I will bless thy name in all but one thing. I have seen some point of terror in what thou hast revealed of thyself, and in that thing I cannot bless thee." No; without any exception he reverently adores and joyfully blesses God. All his heart is contented with all of God that is revealed. Is it so with us, beloved? I earnestly hope it is.

I beg you to notice *how intense he grows over this* — "I will bless thy name for ever and ever." You have heard the quaint saying of "for ever and a day." Here you have an advance upon it: it is "for ever," and then another "for ever." He says, "I will bless thy name for ever." Is not that long enough? No; he adds, "and ever." Are there two for-evers, two eternities? Brethren, if there were fifty eternities we would spend them all in blessing the name of the Lord our God. "I will bless thy name for ever and ever." It would be absurd to explain this hyperbolical expression. It runs parallel with the words of Addison, when he says—

> "Through all eternity to thee
> My song of joy I'll raise ;
> But oh, eternity's too short
> To utter all thy praise ! "

Somebody cavilled at that verse the other day. He said, " Eternity cannot be too short." Ah, my dear friend, you are not a poet, I can see ; but if you could get just a spark of poetry into your soul, literalism would vanish. Truly, in poetry and in praise the letter killeth. Language is a poor vehicle of expression when the soul is on fire ; words are good enough things for our cool judgment; but when thoughts are full of praise they break the back of words. How often have I stood here and felt that if I could throw my tongue away, and let my heart speak without these syllables and arbitrary sounds, then I might express myself! David speaks as if he scorned to be limited by language. He must overleap even time and possibility to get room for his heart. " I will bless thy name for ever and ever." How I enjoy these enthusiastic expressions ! It shows that when David blessed the Lord he did it heartily. While he was musing the fire burned. He felt like dancing before the ark. He was in much the same frame of mind as Dr. Watts when he sang—

> "From thee, my God, my joys shall rise
> And run eternal rounds,
> Beyond the limits of the skies,
> And all created bounds."

III. But time will fail me unless I pass on at once to the third sentence of our text, which is, THE PLEDGE OF DAILY REMEMBRANCE. Upon this I would dwell with very great earnestness. If you forget my discourse, I would like you to remember this part of the text. " Every day will I bless thee " : I will not do it now and have done with it; I will not take a week of the year in which to praise thee, and then leave the other fifty-one weeks silent; but "every day will I bless thee." All the year round will I extol my God. Why should it be so ?

The greatness of the gifts we have already received demands it. We can never fully express our gratitude for saving grace, and therefore we must keep on at it. A few years ago we were lost and dead; but we are found and made alive again. We must praise God every day for this. We were black as night with sin ; but now we are washed whiter than snow : when can we leave off praising our Lord for this ? He loved me and gave himself for me : when can the day come that I shall cease to praise him for this ? Gethsemane and the bloody sweat, Calvary and the precious blood, when shall we ever have done with praising our dear Lord for all he suffered when he bought us with his own heart's blood ? No, if it were only the first mercies, the mercy of election, the mercy of redemption, the mercy of effectual calling, the mercy of adoption, we have had enough to begin with to make us sing unto the Lord every day of our lives. The light which has risen upon us warms all our day with gladness; it shall also light them up with praise.

To-day it becomes us to sing of the mercy of yesterday. The waves of

116

love as well as of time have washed us up upon the shore of to-day, and the beach is strewn with love. Here I find myself on a Sunday morning exulting because another six days' work is done, and strength has been given for it. Some of us have experienced a world of loving-kindness between one Sabbath and another. If we had never had anything else from God but what we have received during the last week, we have overwhelming reason for extolling him to-day. If there is any day in which we would leave off praising God, it must not be the Lord's day, for

> " This is the day the Lord hath made,
>   He calls the hours his own ;
>   Let heaven rejoice, let earth be glad,
>   And praise surround the throne."

Oh, let us magnify the Lord on the day of which it can be said—

> " To-day he rose and left the dead,
>   And Satan's empire fell ;
>   To-day the saints his triumphs spread,
>   And all his wonders tell."

When we reach to-morrow shall we not praise God for the blessing of the Sabbath ? Surely you cannot have forgotten the Lord so soon as Monday ! Before you go out into the world, wash your face in the clear crystal of praise. Bury each yesterday in the fine linen and spices of thankfulness.

Each day has its mercy, and should render its praise. When Monday is over, you will have something to praise God for on Tuesday. He that watches for God's hand will never be long without seeing it. If you will only spy out God's mercies, with half an eye you will see them every day of the year. Fresh are the dews of each morning, and equally fresh are its blessings. " Fresh trouble," says one. Praise God for the trouble, for it is a richer form of blessing. " Fresh care," says one. Cast all your care on him who careth for you, and that act will in itself bless you. " Fresh labour," says another. Yes, but fresh strength, too.

There is never a night but what there comes a day after it : never an affliction without its consolation. Every day you must utter the memory of his great goodness.

If we cannot praise God on any one day for what we have had that day, *let us praise him for to-morrow.* " It is better on before." Let us learn that quaint verse :—

> " And a new song is in my mouth,
>   To long-lived music set :—
>   Glory to thee for all the grace
>   I have not tasted yet."

Let us forestall our future, and draw upon the promises. What if to-day I am down ; to-morrow I shall be up ! What if to-day I cast ashes on my head : to-morrow the Lord shall crown me with loving-kindness ! What if to-day my pains trouble me, they will soon be gone ! It will be all the same a hundred years hence, at any rate ; and so let me praise God for what is within measurable distance. In a few years I shall be with the angels, and be with my Lord himself. Blessed be his name !

Begin to enjoy your heaven now. What says the apostle? "For our citizenship is in heaven"—not is to be, but is. We belong to heaven now, our names are enrolled among its citizens, and the privileges of the new Jerusalem belong to us at this present moment. Christ is ours, and God is ours!

> "This world is ours, and worlds to come ;
> Earth is our lodge, and heaven our home."

Wherefore let us rejoice and be exceeding glad, and praise the name of God this very day.

"Every day," saith he, " will I bless thee." *There is a seasonableness about the praising of God every day.* Praise is in season every month. You awoke, the sunlight streamed into the windows, and touched your eyelids, and you said, "Bless God. Here is a charming summer's day." Birds were singing, and flowers were pouring out their perfume ; you could not help praising God. But another day it was dark at the time of your rising ; you struck a match, and lit your candle. A thick fog hung like a blanket over all. If you were a wise man, you said, "Come, I shall not get through the day if I do not make up my mind to praise God. This is the kind of weather in which I must bless God, or else go down in despair." So you woke yourself up, and began to adore the Lord. One morning you awoke after a refreshing night's rest, and you praised God for it: but on another occasion you had tossed about through a sleepless night, and then you thanked God that the weary night was over. You smile, dear friends, but there is always some reason for praising God. Certain fruits and meats are in season at special times, but the praise of God is always in season. It is good to praise the Lord in the daytime : how charming is the lark's song as it carols up to heaven's gate! It is good to bless God at night—how delicious are the liquid notes of the nightingale as it thrills the night with its music? I do therefore say to you right heartily, " Come, let us together praise the Lord, in all sorts of weather, and in all sorts of places." Sometimes I have said to myself, " During this last week I have been so full of pain that I am afraid I have forgotten to praise God as much as I should have done, and therefore I will have a double draught of it now. I will get alone, and have a special time of thankful thought. I would make up some of my old arrears, and magnify the Lord above measure. I do not like feeling that there can ever be a day in which I have not praised him. That day would surely be a blank in my life. Surely the sweetest praise that ever ascends to God is that which is poured forth by saints from beds of languishing. Praise in sad times is praise indeed. When your dog loves you because it is dinner-time, you are not sure of him; but when somebody else tempts him with a bone, and he will not leave you, though just now you struck him, then you feel that he is truly attached to you. We may learn from dogs that true affection is not dependent upon what it is just now receiving. Let us not have a cupboard love for God because of his kind providence; but let us love him and praise him for what he is, and what he has done. Let us follow hard after him when he seems to forsake us, and praise him when he deals hardly with us ; for this is true praise. For my part, though I am not long without affliction,

I have no faults to find with my Lord, but I desire to praise him, and praise him, and only to praise him. Oh, that I knew how to do it worthily! Here is my resolve :—" I will extol thee, my God, O King ; and I will bless thy name for ever and ever. Every day will I bless thee."

IV. The last sentence of the text sets forth, THE HOPE OF ETERNAL ADORATION. David here exclaims, " And I will praise thy name for ever and ever."

I am quite sure when David said that, *he believed that God was unchangeable;* for if God can change, how can I be sure that he will always be worthy of my praise ? David knew that what God had been, he was, and what he was then he always would be. He had not heard the sentence, " Jesus Christ the same yesterday, and to-day, and for ever " ; nor yet that other, " I am the Lord, I change not; therefore ye sons of Jacob are not consumed " ; but he knew the truth contained in both these texts, and therefore he said, " I will praise thy name for ever and ever." As long as God is, he will be worthy to be praised.

Another point is also clear : *David believed in the immortality of the soul.* He says, " I will praise thy name for ever and ever." That truth was very dimly revealed in the Old Testament ; but David knew it right well. He did not expect to sleep in oblivion, but to go on praising; and therefore he said " I will praise thy name for ever and ever." No cold hand fell upon him, and no killing voice said to him, " You shall die, and never praise the Lord again." Oh, no; he looked to live for ever and ever, and praise for ever and ever! Brethren, such is our hope, and we will never give it up. We feel eternal life within our souls. We challenge the cold hand of death to quench the immortal flame of our love, or to silence the ceaseless song of our praise. The dead cannot praise God ; and God is not the God of the dead, but of the living. Among the living we are numbered through the grace of God, and we know that we shall live because Jesus lives. When death shall come, it shall bring no destruction to us : though it shall change the conditions of our existence, it shall not change the object of our existence. Our tongue may be silenced for a little while, but our spirit, unaffected by the disease of the body, shall go on praising God in its own fashion ; and then, by-and-by, in the resurrection. even this poor tongue shall be revived ; and body, soul, and spirit shall together praise the God of resurrection and eternal glory. " I will praise thy name for ever and ever." We shall never grow weary of this hallowed exercise for ever and ever. It will always be new, fresh, delightful. In heaven they never require any change beyond those blessed variations of song, those new melodies which make up the everlasting harmony. On and on, for ever telling the tale which never will be fully told, the saints will praise the name of the Lord for ever and ever.

Of course, dear friends, David's resolve was that, *as long as he was here below* he would never cease to praise God; and this is ours also. Brethren, we may have to leave off some cherished engagements, but this we will never cease from. At a certain period of life a man may have to leave off preaching to a large congregation. Good old John Newton declared that he would never leave off preaching while he had breath in his body ; and I admire his holy perseverance ; but it was a pity that he did not leave off preaching at St. Mary Woolnoth; for he often wearied the people, and forgot the thread of his discourse. He might have done better in another place. Ah, well, we may leave off preaching, but we shall never leave off praising ! The day will come when you, my dear friend, cannot go to Sunday-school : I hope you will go as long as ever you can toddle there; but it may be you will not be able to interest the children, your memory will begin to fail ; but even then you can go on praising the Lord. And you will. I have known old people almost forget their own names, and forget their own children; but I have known them still remember their Lord and Master. I have heard of one who lay dying, and his friends tried to make him remember certain things; but he shook his head. At last one said, " Do you remember the Lord Jesus? " Then the mind came into full play, the eyes brightened, and the old man eloquently praised his Saviour. Our last gasp shall be given to the praise of the Lord.

When once we have passed through the iron gate, and forded the dividing river, then we will begin to praise God in a manner more satisfactory than we can reach at present. After a nobler sort we will sing and adore. What soarings we will attempt upon the eagle wings of love ! What plunges we will take into the crystal stream of praise ! Methinks, for a while, when we first behold the throne, we shall do no more than cast our crowns at the feet of him that loved us, and then bow down under a weight of speechless praise. We shall be overwhelmed with wonder and thankfulness. When we rise to our feet again, we will join in the strain of our brethren redeemed by blood, and only drop out of the song when again we feel overpowered with joyful adoration, and are constrained again in holy silence to shrink to nothing before the infinite, unchanging God of love. Oh, to be there ! To be there soon ! We may be much nearer than we think. I cannot tell what I shall do, but I know this, I want no other heaven than to praise God perfectly and eternally. Is it not so with you ? A heart full of praise is heaven in the bud; perfect praise is heaven full-blown. Let us close this discourse by asking grace from God that, if we have been deficient in praise, we may now mend our ways, and put on the garments of holy adoration. This day and onward be our watchword " Hallelujah! Praise ye the Lord!"

11. A Life-long Occupation

"By him therefore let us offer the sacrifice of praise to God continually, that is, the fruit of our lips giving thanks to his name."—Hebrews xiii. 15.

It is instructive to notice where this verse stands. The connection is a golden setting to the gem of the text. Here we have a description of the believer's position before God. He has done with all carnal ordinances, and has no interest in the ceremonies of the Mosaic law. Brethren, as believers in Jesus, who is the substance of all the outward types, we have, henceforth, nothing to do with altars of gold or of stone : our worship is spiritual, and our altar spiritual.

> "We rear no altar, Christ has died ;
> We deck no priestly shrine."

What then ? Are we to offer no sacrifice ? Very far from it. We are called upon to offer to God a continual sacrifice. Instead of presenting in the morning and the evening a sacrifice of lambs, and on certain holy days bringing bullocks and sheep to be slain, we are to present to God continually the sacrifice of praise. Having done with the outward, we now give ourselves entirely to the inward and to the spiritual. Do you see your calling, brethren?

Moreover, the believer is now, if he is where he ought to be, like his Master, "without the camp." "Let us go forth therefore unto him without the camp, bearing his reproach." What then? If we are without the camp, have we nothing to do? Are we cut off from God as well as from men? Shall we fume and fret because we are not of the world? On the contrary, let us the more ardently pursue higher objects, and yield up our disentangled spirits to the praise and glory of God.

Do we come under contempt, as the Master did? Is it so, that we are "bearing his reproach"? Shall we sit down in despair? Shall we be crushed beneath this burden? Nay, verily; while we lose honour ourselves, we will ascribe honour to our God. We will count it all joy that we are counted worthy to be reproached for Christ's sake. Let us now praise God continually. Let the fruit of our lips be a still bolder confession of his name. Let us more and more earnestly make known his glory and his grace. If reproach be bitter, praise is sweet: we will drown the drops of gall in a sea of honey. If to have our name cast out as evil should seem to be derogatory to us, let us all the more see to it that we give unto the Lord the glory due unto his name. While the enemy reproaches us continually, our only reply shall be to offer the sacrifice of praise continually unto the Lord our God.

Moreover, the apostle says that "Here we have no continuing city." Well, then, we will transfer the continuance from the city to the praise—"Let us offer the sacrifice of praise to God continually." If everything here is going, let it go; but we will not cease to sing. If the end of all things is at hand, let them end; but our praises of the living God shall abide world without end. Set free from all the hamper of citizenship here below, we will begin the employment of citizens of heaven. It is not ours to arrange a new Socialism, nor to set up to be dividers of heritages; we belong to a kingdom which is not of this world, a city of God eternal in the heavens. It is not ours to pursue the dreams of politicians, but to offer the sacrifices of God-ordained priests. As we are not of this world, it is ours to seek the world to come, and press forward to the place where the saints in Christ shall reign for ever and ever.

You see then, brethren, that the text is rather an unexpected one in its connection; but when properly viewed, it is the fittest that could be. The more we are made to feel that we are strangers in a strange land, the more should we addict ourselves to the praises of God, with whom we sojourn. Crucified to the world, and the world crucified to us, let us spend and be spent in the praises of him who is our sole trust and joy. Oh, to praise God, and still to praise him, and never to be taken off from praising him, let the world do what it may!

This morning my great business will be to stir you up, dear friends, as many of you as have been made kings and priests unto God by Jesus Christ, to exercise your holy office. I shall, to that end, first, concerning the Christian, *describe his sacrifice;* secondly, *examine its substance;* thirdly, *commend its exercise;* and fourthly, *commence it at once.*

I. First, then, concerning a believer, let me DESCRIBE HIS SACRIFICE. "By him therefore." See, at the very threshold of all offering of sacrifice to God, *we begin with Christ.* We cannot go a step without Jesus. Without a Mediator we can make no advance to God. Apart from Christ there is no acceptable prayer, no pleasing sacrifice of any sort. "By him therefore"—we cannot move a lip acceptably without him who suffered without the gate. The great High Priest of our profession meets us at the sanctuary door, and we place all our sacrifices into his hands, that he may present them for us. You do not wish it to be otherwise, I am quite sure. If you could do anything without him, you would feel afraid to do it. You only feel safe when he is with you, and you are "accepted in the beloved." Be thankful that at the beginning of your holy service your eyes are turned towards your Lord. You are to offer continual sacrifice, looking unto Jesus. Behold our great Melchizedek meets us! Let us give him tithes of all, and receive his blessing, which will repay us a thousand-fold.

Let us never venture upon a sacrifice apart from him, lest it be the sacrifice of Cain, or the sacrifice of fools. He is that altar which sanctifies both gift and giver; by him therefore let our sacrifices both of praise and of almsgiving be presented unto God.

Next, observe that *this sacrifice is to be presented continually.* " By him therefore let us offer the sacrifice of praise to God *continually.*" Attentively treasure up that word. It will not do for you to say, " We have been exhorted to praise God on the Sabbath-day." No, I have not exhorted you to such occasional duty; " continually," says the text, and that means seven days in a week. I would not have you say, " He means that we are to praise God in the morning when we awake, and in the evening before we fall asleep." Do that, my brethren, unfailingly; but that is not what I have to set before you. " Let us offer the sacrifice of praise to God *continually* "—" *continually* " that is to say, without ceasing. Let us make an analogous precept to that which saith, " pray without ceasing," and say, " praise without ceasing." Not only in this place or that place, but in every place, we are to praise the Lord our God. Not only when we are in a happy frame of mind, but when we are cast-down and troubled. The perfumed smoke from the altar of incense is to rise towards heaven both day and night, from the beginning of the year to the year's end. Not only when we are in the assembly of the saints are we to praise God, but when we are called to pass through Vanity Fair, where sinners congregate. Bless the Lord at all times. Not alone in your secret chamber, which is redolent with the perfume of your communion with God; but yonder in the field, and there in the street, ay, and in the hurry and noise of the Exchange, offer the sacrifice of praise to God. You cannot always be speaking his praise, but you can always be living his praise. The heart once set on praising God will, like the stream which leaps adown the mountain's side, continue still to flow in its chosen course. A soul saturated with divine gratitude will continue, almost unconsciously, to give forth the sacred odour of praise, which will permeate the atmosphere of every place, and make itself known to all who have a spiritual nostril with which to discern sweetness. There is no moment in which it would be right to suspend the praises of God: let us therefore offer the sacrifice of praise to God *continually.* This should be done, not only by some of us—pastor, elders, deacons, and special workers—but by all of you. The apostle says, " Let *us* "; and therein he calls upon all of us who have any participation in the great sacrifice of Christ to go with him without the camp, and then and there to stand with him in our places, and continually offer the sacrifice of praise unto God. You see, then, that the two important points are—always, and always through Christ.

The apostle goes on to tell us what the sacrifice is—*the sacrifice of praise.* Praise, that is, heart-worship, or adoration. Adoration is the grandest form of earthly service. We ascribe unto Jehovah, the one living and true God, all honour and glory. When we see his works, when we hear his Word, when we taste his grace, when we mark his providence, when we think upon his name, our spirit bows in the lowliest reverence before him, and magnifies him as the all-glorious

Lord. Let us abide continually in the spirit of adoration, for this is praise in its purest form.

Praise is heart-trust and heart-content with God. Trust is adoration applied to practical purposes. Let us go into the world trusting God, believing that he orders all things well, resolving to do everything as he commands, for neither his character, nor his decrees, nor his commandments are grievous to us. We delight in the Lord as he is pleased to reveal himself, let that revelation be what it may. We believe not only that God is, but that he is a rewarder of all them that diligently seek him: let us so praise him that we shall not be baffled if our good work brings us no immediate recompense; for we are satisfied that he is not unrighteous to forget our work of faith. Let us praise him by being perfectly satisfied with anything and everything that he does or appoints. Let us take a hallowed delight in him, and in all that concerns him. Let him be to us "God, our exceeding joy." Do you know what it is to delight yourselves in God? Then, in that continual satisfaction, offer him continual praise. Life is no longer sorrowful, even amid sorrow, when God is in it, its soul and crown. It is worth while to live the most afflicted and tried life, so long as we know God, and taste his love. Let him do what seemeth him good, so long as he will but be a God to us, and permit us to call him our Father and our God.

Praise is heart-enjoyment; the indulgence of gratitude and wonder. The Lord has done so much for me that I must praise him, or feel as if I had a fire shut up within me. I may speak for many of you, for you also are saying, "He has done great things for us." Brethren, the Lord has favoured you greatly: before the earth was, he chose you, and entered into covenant with you: he gave you to his Son, and gave his Son to you. He has manifested himself to you as he doth not to the world; even now he breathes a child-like spirit into you, whereby you cry, "Abba, Father." Surely you must praise him! How can you ever satisfy the cravings of your heart if you do not extol him? Your obligations rise above you as high as the heavens above the earth. The vessel of your soul has foundered in this sea of love, and gone down fifty fathoms deep in it. High over its mast-head the main ocean of eternal mercy is rolling with its immeasurable billows of grace. You are swallowed up in the fathomless abyss of infinite love. You are absorbed in adoring wonder and affection. Like Leah when Judah was born, you cry, "Now will I praise the Lord."

Have you not, in addition to this, the praise of heart-feeling, while within you burns an intense love to God? Could you love any-one as you love God? After you have poured out the stream of your love upon the dearest earthly ones, do you not feel you have something more within, which all created vessels could not contain? The heart of man yields love without stint, and the stream is too large for the lake into which it flows, so long as we love a created being. Only the infinite God can ever contain all the love of a loving heart. There is a fitness for the heart, and a fulness for its emotions when Jehovah is the heart's one object of love. My God, I love thee! Thou knowest all things: thou knowest that I love thee. Instead of cavilling at the

Lord because of certain stern truths which we read concerning him, we are enabled in these to worship him by bowing our reason to his revelation. That which we cannot understand we nevertheless believe, and believing, we adore. It is not ours to arraign the Almighty, but to submit to him. We are not his censors, but his servants. We do not legislate, but love. He is good, supremely good in our esteem: and infinitely blessed of our hearts. We do not consider what he ought to be; but we learn what he is, and as such we love and adore him. Thus have I gone roundabout the shell of praise; but what it really is you must each one know for himself.

The text evidently deals with *spoken praise*—"Let us offer the sacrifice of praise to God continually, that is, the fruit of our lips giving thanks to his name"; or, as the Revised Version has it, "the fruit of lips which make confession to his name." So, then, we are *to utter* the praises of God, and it is not sufficient *to feel* adoring emotions. The priesthood of believers requires them to praise God with their lips. Should we not sing a great deal more than we do? Psalms and hymns and spiritual songs should abound in our homes. It is our duty to sing as much as possible; we should praise as much as we pray. "I have no voice!" saith one. Cultivate it till you have. "But mine is a cracked voice!" Ah, well! it may be cracked to human ears, and yet be melodious unto God. To him the music lies in the heart, not in the sound. Praise the Lord with song and psalm. Some few godly men whom I have known have gone about the fields and along the roads humming sacred songs continually. These are the troubadours and minstrels of our King. Happy profession! May more of us become such birds of Paradise! Hear how the ungodly world pours out its mirth! Ofttimes their song is so silly as to be utterly devoid of meaning. Are they not ashamed? Then let us not be ashamed. Children of God, sing the songs of Zion, and let your hearts be joyful before your King. "Is any merry? let him sing psalms."

But if we cannot sing so well or so constantly as we would desire, let us talk. We cannot say that we cannot talk. Perhaps some might be better if they could not talk quite so much. As we can certainly talk continually, let us as continually offer to God the sacrifice of praise, by speaking well of his name. Talk ye of all his wondrous works. Let us abundantly utter the memory of his great goodness. Let us praise the Lord for his goodness, and for his wonderful works to the children of men. Many whom you judge to be irreligious would be greatly interested if you were to relate to them the story of God's love to you. But if they are not interested, you are not responsible for that; only tell it as often as you have opportunity. We charge you, as Jesus did the healed man, "Go home to thy friends, and tell them how great things the Lord hath done for thee." Speak, and speak, and speak again, for the instruction of others: for the confirmation of those who have faith, and for the routing of the doubts of those who believe not. Tell what God has done for you. Does not our conversation want more flavouring with the praise of God? We put into it too much vinegar of complaint, and forget the sugar of gratitude. This year, when the harvest seems to have been snatched from between the jaws of the destroyer, our friends say, "Well, things look a shade better"; and I am glad to get them up even as high as that. Hear the general talk: "Things are very bad. Business is dreadful. Trade never was so bad." When I was a boy things were very bad, never were so bad; and I think ever since they have been so bad that they could not be worse, and yet somehow people live, and even farmers are not all turned to skin and bone. Surely, surely, we had better mend our talk, and speak more brightly and cheerily of what God does for us! How can we offer the sacrifice of praise to God continually if we perpetually rail at his providence? Christian men, if you are ever driven to a murmur, let it be the momentary mistake of your extremity; but come back again to contentment and gratitude, which is your proper and acceptable condition. Hear the word of the Lord, which saith, "Neither murmur ye, as some of them also murmured, and were destroyed of the destroyer."

In fine, praise means this, that you and I are appointed to tell out the goodness of God, just as the birds of spring wake up before the sun and begin singing, and singing, and singing, all of them, with all their might. Become ye the choristers of God. Praise ye the Lord evermore, even as they do who, with songs and choral symphonies, day without night, circle his throne rejoicing. This is your office, and it is a holy and a privileged one.

"Well," saith one, "I cannot force myself to praise." I do not want you to force yourself to it: *this praise is to be natural*. It is called the fruit of the lips. In the Book of Hosea, from which the apostle quotes, our version reads, "The calves of our lips." Whether the word is "calves" in the Hebrew original or not, is a matter in dispute; but the translators of the Septuagint certainly read it "fruit," and this seems more clear and plain. The apostle, quoting it from the Greek translation, has endorsed it as being correct. These lips of ours must produce fruit. Our words are leaves: how soon they wither! The praise of God is the fruit which can be stored up and presented to the Lord. Fruit is a natural product: it grows without force, the free outcome of the plant. So let praise grow out of your lips at its own sweet will. Let it be as natural to you, as regenerated men and women, to praise God as it seems to be natural to profane men to blaspheme the sacred name.

This praise is to be sincere and real. The next verse tells us we are to do good and communicate, and joins this with praise to God. Many will give God a cataract of words, but scarce a drop of true gratitude in the form of substance consecrated. When I am pressed with many cares about the Lord's work, I often wish that some of my brethren would be a little more mindful of its pecuniary needs. I should be much relieved if those who can spare it would help different portions of our home service. It should be the joy of a Christian to use his substance in his Master's service. When we are in a right state of heart we do not want anybody to call upon us to extract a subscription from us, but we go and ask, "Is there anything that wants help?" Is any part of the Lord's business in need just now? The great works, such as the Orphanage and College, are provided for; but I often sigh as I see lesser agencies left without help, not because friends would not aid if they were pressed to do so, but because there is not a ready mind to look out for opportunities. Yet that ready mind is the very fat of the sacrifice. I long to see everywhere Christian friends who will not stay to be asked, but will make the Lord's business their business, and take in hand some branch of work in the church, or among the poor, or for the spread of the gospel. Brethren, let your gift be an outburst of a free and gracious spirit, which takes a delight in showing that it does not praise God in word only, but in deed and in truth. In this church let us excel in generous gifts. As the year ripens to its close see that everything is provided in the house of the Lord, and that there is no lack in any quarter. This practical praising of the Lord is the life-office of every true believer. See ye to it.

II. We will, secondly, for a few minutes EXAMINE THE SUBSTANCE OF THIS SACRIFICE. "Let us offer the sacrifice of praise to God continually."

To praise God continually will need *a childlike faith in him.* You must believe his word, or you will not praise his name. Doubt snaps the harp-strings. Question mars all melody. Trust him, lean on him, enjoy him—you will never praise him else. Unbelief is the deadly enemy of praise.

Faith must lead you into *personal communion with the Lord.* It is to him that the praise is offered, and not to our fellow-men. The most beautiful singing in the world, if it be intended for the ears of musical critics, is nothing worth. Only that is praise which is meant for God. O thou my Lord, my song shall find thee! Every part of my being shall have its attribute to sing. I will sing unto the Lord, and unto the Lord alone. You must live in fellowship with God, or you cannot praise him.

You must have also an overflowing content, *a real joy in him.* Dear brothers and sisters, be sure that you do not lose your joy. If you ever lose the joy of religion, you will lose the power of religion. Do not be satisfied to be a miserable believer. An unhappy believer is a poor creature; but he who is resigned to being so is in a dangerous condition. Depend upon it, greater importance attaches to holy happiness than most people think. As you are happy in the Lord you will be able to praise his name. Rejoice in the Lord, that you may praise him.

There must also be *a holy earnestness* about this. Praise is called a sacrifice because it is a very sacred and solemn thing. People who came to the altar with their victims came there with the hush of reverence, the trembling of awe. We cannot praise God with levity. He is in heaven, and we are upon the earth: he is thrice holy, and we are sinful: we must put off our shoe in lowly reverence, and worship with intense adoration, or else he cannot be pleased with our sacrifices. When life is real, life is earnest: and it must be both real and earnest when it is spent to the praise of the great and ever-blessed God.

To praise God continually, you need to cultivate *perpetual gratitude,* and surely it cannot be hard to do that! Remember, every misery averted is a mercy bestowed; every sin forgiven is a favour granted; every duty performed is also a grace received. The people of God have an inexhaustible treasury of good things provided for them by the infinite God, and for all this they should praise him. I

127

pray you, be not only a little grateful, but overflow with it. Let your praises be like the waters of fountains which are abundantly supplied. Let the stream leap up to heaven in bursts of enthusiasm; let it fall to earth again in showers of beneficence; let it fill the basin of your daily life, and run over into the lives of others, and thence again in a cataract of glittering joy let it still descend.

In order to this praise you will need *a deep and ardent admiration of the Lord God*. Admire the Father—think much of his love; acquaint yourself with his perfections. Admire the Son of God, the altogether lovely One; and as you mark his gentleness, self-denial, love, and grace, suffer your heart to be wholly enamoured of him. Admire the patience and condescension of the Holy Ghost, that he should visit you, and dwell in you, and bear with you. It cannot be difficult to the sanctified and instructed heart to be filled with a great admiration of the Lord God. This is the raw material of praise. An intelligent admiration of God, kindled into flame by gratitude, and fanned by delight and joy, must ever produce praise. Living in personal converse with God, and trusting him as a child trusts its father, it cannot be difficult for the soul continually to offer the sacrifice of praise to God through Jesus Christ.

III. I have been very brief upon that point because I want, in the third place, to COMMEND THIS BLESSED EXERCISE.

"Offer the sacrifice of praise to God continually," because in so doing *you will answer the end of your being*. Every creature is happiest when it is doing what it is made for. A bird that is made to fly abroad pines in a cage; an eagle would die in the water, even as a fish that is made to swim perishes on the river's bank. Christians are made to glorify God; and we are never in our element till we are praising him. The happiest moments you have ever spent were those in which you lost sight of everything inferior, and bowed before Jehovah's throne of light with reverent joy and blissful praise. I can say it is so with me, and I doubt not it is so with you. When your whole soul is full of praise, you have at last reached the goal that your heart is aiming at. Your ship is now in full sail: your car is on the tram-lines. Your life moves smoothly and safely on. This is the groove along which it was made to slide. Before, you were trying to do what you were not made to do; but now you are at home. For the praise of God your new nature was fashioned, and it finds rest therein. Keep to this work. Do not degrade yourself by a less divine employ.

Praise God again, because *it is his due*. Should Jehovah be left unpraised? Praise is the quit-rent which he asks of us for the enjoyment of all things; shall we be slow to pay? Will a man rob God? When it is such a happy work to give him his due, shall we deny it? It blesses us to bless the Lord. Shall we stint God in the measure of his glory? He does not stint us in his goodness. Come, my brother, my sister, if you have become sorrowful of late, shake off your gloom, and awake all your instruments of music to praise the Lord! Let not murmuring and complaining be so much as mentioned among saints. Give unto the Lord the glory due unto his name. Shall not the Lord be praised? Surely the very stones and rocks must break their everlasting silence in indignation if the children of God do not praise his name.

Praise him, dear brethren, continually, for *it will help you in everything else*. A man full of praise is ready for all other holy exercises. Such is my bodily pain and weakness, that I could not have forced myself to preach this morning if I had not felt that I must come hither to bid you praise God. I thought that my pain might give emphasis to my words. I do praise the Lord : I must praise him. It is a duty which I hope to perform in my last moments, the Holy Spirit helping me. So you see praise helps me to preach. Whenever you go forth to any service, even though it be nothing better than taking down the shutters, and waiting behind the counter, you will do it all the better for being in the spirit of praise and gratitude. If you are a domestic servant, and can praise God continually, you will be a comfort in the house; and if you are a master, and are surrounded with the troubles of life, if your heart is always blessing the Lord, you will keep up your spirits, and you will not be sharp and ill-tempered with those around you. Come, brethren, this is both meat and medicine—this praising the Lord. Ye birds of heaven, strange to say, this singing will plume your wings for flight! The praises of God put wings upon pilgrims' heels, so that they not only run, but fly.

This will *preserve us from many evils*. When the heart is full of the praise of God, it has not time to find fault and grow proudly angry with its fellows. Somebody has said a very nasty thing about us. Well, well; we will answer him when we have got through the work we have in hand, namely, praising God continually. At present we have a great work to do, and cannot come down to wrangle. Self-love and its natural irritations die in the blaze of praise. If you praise God continually, the vexations and troubles of life will be cheerfully borne. Praise makes the happy man the strong man. The joy of the Lord is your strength. Praising God makes us to drink of the brook by the way, and lift up the head. We cannot fear while we can praise. Neither can we be bribed by the world's favour, nor cowed by its frown. Praise makes men, yea, angels of us : let us abound in it.

Brethren, let us praise God because *it will be a means of usefulness*. I believe that a life spent in God's praise would in itself be a missionary life. That matronly sister who never delivered a sermon, nor even a lecture, in all her days, has lived a quiet, happy, useful, loving life, and her family have learned from her to trust the Lord. Even when she shall have passed away, they will feel her influence, for she was the angel of the house. Being dead, she yet will speak. A praiseful heart is eloquent for God. Mere verbiage, what is it but as autumn leaves, which will be consumed in smothering smoke? But praise is golden fruit to be presented in baskets of silver unto the dresser of the vineyard.

Praise God, brethren, because *this is what God loves*. Notice how the next verse puts it : "With such sacrifices God is well pleased." Would we not do anything and everything to please God? It seems too good to be true that we can impart any pleasure to the ever-blessed One; yet it is so, for he hath declared that he is well pleased with the praises and the gifts of his children. Therefore let us withhold nothing from our dear Father, our blessed God. Can I please him? Tell me what it is, I will do it straight away. I will not deliberate, but without reserve make haste. If I deliberate, it shall be that I may make the service twice as large, or perform it in more careful style; for if I may praise him, it shall be honour, yea, it shall be heaven to me.

To close this commendation, remember that *this will fit you for heaven.* Our hymn expresses a frequent aspiration—

> "I would begin the music here,
> And so my soul should rise."

You can begin the music here—begin the hallelujahs of glory by praising God here below. Think of how you will praise him when you see his face, and never, never sin. Exceedingly magnify the Lord even now, and rehearse the music of the skies. In glory you may rise to a higher key, but let the song be the same even here. Praise him! Praise him! Praise him more and more! Rise on rounds of praise up the ladder of his glory, till you reach the top, and are with him to praise him better than ever before. Oh, that our lives may not be broken, but may be all of a piece: one psalm, for ever rising, verse by verse, into the eternal hallelujahs!

IV. I have brought you thus far, and so I come to the closing point, which is, LET US COMMENCE AT ONCE. What does the text say? It says, "Let *us* offer the sacrifice of praise continually." The apostle does not say, "By-and-by get to this work, when you are able to give up business, and have retired to the country, or when you are near to die;" but now, at once, he says, "Let *us* offer the sacrifice of praise."

Listen! Who is speaking? Whose voice do I hear? Ah! I know, it is the apostle Paul. He says, "Let us offer the sacrifice of praise"! Where are you, Paul? His voice sounds from within a low place. I believe he is shut up in a dungeon. Lift up your hand, O venerable Paul! I can hear the clanking of a fetter. Yes; Paul cries, "Let *us* offer the sacrifice of praise. I, Paul the aged, in prison in Rome, wish you to join with me in a sacrifice of praise to God." Amen. We will do so. O Paul, we are not in prison, and we are not all aged, and none of us are galled with fetters on our wrists; but we can join heartily with you in praising God this morning; and we do so. Come, let *us* praise God.

> "Stand up and bless the Lord,
> Ye people of his choice;
> Stand up and bless the Lord your God,
> With heart and soul and voice."

You have heard Paul's voice, now hear mine. Join with me, and let *us* offer the sacrifice of praise. Brothers and sisters, we have known each other for many a year, and we have worked together in different ways for the Lord; and as a church and people we have received great favours from the Lord's hand. Come, let us join together with heart and hand to bless the name of the Lord, and worship joyfully before him. With words and with gifts let us offer the sacrifice of praise continually. If I were to select certain of the members, and call upon them one by one, I should say, "Come, brother So-and-so, let us offer the sacrifice of praise." I am sure that the brother would get up, and unite with me very cordially, as in a brotherly duet we praised the Lord our God. I will not at this present call upon any of you; but if I did say, "Sister So-and-so, let us offer praise to God," many of you would reply, "Ah, Pastor! if nobody else can praise him, we can, and we will." Well, well, kindly take it as done, so far as the outward expression is concerned; but inwardly let us at once offer the sacrifice of praise to God by Jesus Christ. Let us stir one another up to praise. Let us spend to-day, and to-morrow, and all the rest of our days in praising God. If we catch one another a little grumbling, or coldly silent, let us, in kindness to each other, give the needful rebuke. It will not do; we must praise the Lord. Just as the leader of an orchestra taps his baton to call all to attention, and then to begin singing, so I this morning arouse you and bestir you to offer the sacrifice of praise unto the Lord.

The apostle has put us rather in a fix: he compels us to offer sacrifice. Did you notice what he said in the tenth verse? He says, "We have an altar." It is not a material altar, but a spiritual one; yet "we have an altar." May the priests of the old law offer sacrifice on it? Answer, "Whereof they have no right to eat that serve the tabernacle." They ate of the sacrifices laid on the altars of the old law, but they have no right here. Those who keep to ritualistic performances, and outward ceremonials, have no right here. Yet we have an altar. Brothers and sisters, can we imagine that this altar is given us of the Lord to be never used? Is no sacrifice to be presented on the best of altars? We have an altar—what then? If we have an altar, do not allow it to be neglected, deserted, unused. It is not for spiders to spin their webs upon; it is not meet that it should be smothered with the dust of neglect. "We have an altar." What then? "Let us offer the sacrifice of praise to God continually." Do you not see the force of the argument. Practically obey it.

Beside the altar we have a High Priest. There is the Lord Jesus Christ, dressed in his robes of glory and beauty, standing within the veil at this moment, ready to present our offerings. Shall he stand there, and have nothing to do? What would you think of our great High Priest waiting at the altar, with nothing to present which his redeemed had brought to God? No, "by him therefore let us offer the sacrifice of praise to God continually." Bring hither abundantly, ye people of God, your praises, your prayers, your thank-offerings, and present them to the Ever-blessed!

Well may you do so if you will read the connection; for the passage brings before you many things which should compel you to praise God. Behold your Saviour in his passion, offered without the gate! Gaze upon his five bleeding wounds, his sacred head so wounded, his face so full of anguish, his heart bursting with the agony of sin! Can you see that sight, and not praise God? Behold redemption accomplished, sin pardoned, salvation purchased, hell vanquished, death abolished, and all this achieved by your blessed Lord and Master! Can you see all this, and not praise him? His precious blood falling on you, and making you clean, bringing you near to God, making you acceptable before the infinite holiness of the Most High! Can you see yourself thus favoured, and behold the precious blood which did it, and not praise his name?

Yonder in the distance, seen dimly, perhaps, but yet not doubtfully, behold "a city that hath foundations, whose builder and maker is God." White-robed, the purified are singing to their golden harps, and you will soon be there. When a few more days or years are passed, you will be among the glorified. A crown and a harp are reserved for you. Will you not begin to praise God, and glorify him for the heaven which is in store for you? With these two sights so wonderfully contrasted—the Passion and the Paradise—Jesus in his humiliation and Jesus in his glory; and yourself a sharer in both these wondrous scenes—surely if you do not begin to offer the perpetual sacrifice of thanksgivings and praise unto God, you must be something harder than stone. God grant us to commence this day those praises which shall never be suspended throughout eternity!

Oh, that you, who have never praised God before, would begin now! Alas! some of you have no Christ to praise, and no Saviour to bless. Yet you need not so abide. By faith you may lay hold upon Jesus, and he then becomes yours. Trust him, and he will justify your trust. Rest in the Lord, and the Lord is your rest. When you have trusted, then waste no time, but at once commence the business for which you were created, and redeemed, and called. Fill the censer with the sweet spices of gratitude and love, and lay on the burning coals of earnestness, and fervency. Then, when praise begins to rise from you like pillars of smoke, swing the censer to and fro in the presence of the Most High, and more and more laud, bless, and magnify the Lord that liveth for ever. Let your heart dance at the sound of his name, and let your lips show forth his salvation. The Lord anoint you this day to the priesthood of praise, for Christ's sake! Amen.

12. Praise for the Gift of Gifts

"Thanks be unto God for his unspeakable gift."—2 Corinthians ix. 15.

In the chapter from which my text is taken, Paul is stirring up the Christians at Corinth to be ready with liberal gifts for the poor saints at Jerusalem. He finishes by reminding them of a greater gift than any they could bring, and by this one short word of praise, "Thanks be unto God for his unspeakable gift," he sets all their hearts a-singing. Let men give as liberally as they may, you can always proclaim the value of their gift: you can cast it up, and reckon its worth; but God's gift is unspeakable, unreckonable. You cannot fully estimate the value of what God gives. The gospel is a gospel of giving and forgiving. We may sum it up in those two words; and hence, when the true spirit of it works upon the Christian, he forgives freely, and he also gives freely. The large heart of God breeds large hearts in men, and they who live upon his bounty are led by his Spirit to imitate that bounty, according to their power.

However, I am not going, on the present occasion, to say anything upon the subject of liberality. I must get straight away to the text, hoping that we may really drink in the spirit of it, and out of full hearts use the apostle's language with intenser meaning than ever as we repeat his words: "Thanks be unto God for his unspeakable gift." I shall commence by saying that *salvation is altogether the gift of God*, and as such is to be received by us freely. Then I shall try to show that *this gift is unspeakable;* and, in the third place, that *for this gift thanks should be rendered to God*. Though it is unspeakable, yet we should speak our praise of it. In this way you will see, as of old preachers used to say, the text naturally falls apart.

I. We begin with the thought that SALVATION IS ALTOGETHER THE GIFT OF GOD. Paul said, "Thanks be unto God for his unspeakable gift." Over and over and over again, have we to proclaim that salvation is wholly of grace: not of works nor of wages, but is the gift of God's great bounty to undeserving men. Often as we have preached

133

this truth, we shall have to keep on doing so as long as there are men in the world who are self-righteous, and as long as there are minds in the world so slow to grasp the meaning of the word " grace ", that is, "free favour", and as long as there are memories that find it difficult to retain the idea of salvation being God's free gift.

Let us say, simply and plainly, that salvation must come to us as a gift from God, for salvation comes to us by the Lord Jesus, and *what else could Jesus be ?* The essence of salvation is the gift of God's Only-begotten Son to die for us, that we might live through him. I think you will agree with me that it is inconceivable that men should ever have merited that God should give his Only-begotten Son to them. To give Christ to us, in any sense, must have been an act of divine charity ; but to give him up to die on yonder cruel and bloody tree, to yield him up as a sacrifice for sin, must be a free favour, passing the limits of thought. It is not supposable that any man could deserve such love. It is plain that if man's sins needed a sacrifice, he did not deserve that a sacrifice should be found for him. The fact of his need proves his demerit and his guiltiness. He deserves to die ; he may be rescued by Another dying for him ; but he certainly cannot claim that the eternal God should take from his bosom his Only-begotten and Well-beloved Son, and put him to death. The more you look that thought in the face, the more you will reject the idea that, by any possible sorrow, or by any possible labour, or by any possible promise, a man could put himself into the position of deserving to have Christ to die for him. If Christ is to come to save sinners, it must be as a gift, a free gift of God. The argument, to my mind, is conclusive.

Besides that, over and over again, in God's Word, *we are told that salvation is not of works*. Although there are many who cling to the notion of man's works as a ground of salvation, yet as long as this Book stands, and there are eyes to read it, it will bear witness against the idea of human merit, and it will speak out plainly for the doctrine that men are saved by faith, and not by works. Not once only, but often, it is written, " The just shall live by faith ; " moreover, we are told, " Therefore it is of faith, that it might be by grace." The very choice of the way of salvation by believing, rather than by works, is made by God on purpose that he might show that grace is a gift. " Now to him that worketh is the reward not reckoned of grace, but of debt : but to him that worketh not, but believeth on him that justifieth the ungodly, his faith is counted for righteousness." Faith is that virtue, that grace, which is chosen to bring us salvation, because it never takes any of the glory to itself. Faith is simply the hand that takes. When the beggar receives alms, he does not bless the hand that takes, but blesses the hand that gives ; therefore do we not praise the faith that receiveth, but the God who giveth the unspeakable gift. Faith is the eye that sees. When we see an object, we delight in the object, rather than in the eye that sees it ; therefore do we glory, not in our faith, but in the salvation which God bestows. Faith is appointed as the porter to open the gate of salvation, because that gate turns upon the hinges of free grace.

In the next place, be it always remembered, that we cannot be saved by the merit of our own works, because *holy works are themselves a gift*, the work of the grace of God. If thou hast faith, and joy, and hope, who gave them to thee? These did not spring up spontaneously in thy heart. They were sown there by the hand of love. If thou hast lived a godly life for years, if thou hast been a diligent servant of the church and of thy God, in whose strength hast thou done it? Is there not One who works all our works in us? Could you work out your own salvation with fear and trembling if God did not first work in you both to will and to do of his good pleasure? How can that, then, claim a reward, which is, in itself, the gift of God? I think the ground is cut right away from those who would put confidence in human merit, when we show, first of all, that, in Scripture, salvation is clearly said to be "not of works, lest any man should boast"; and, secondly, that even the good works of believers are the fruit of a renewed life; for "we are his workmanship, created in Christ Jesus unto good works, which God hath before ordained that we should walk in them."

> "All that I *was*, my sin, my guilt,
>   My death, was all mine own;
> All that I *am*, I owe to thee,
>   My gracious God, alone."

Further, if salvation were not a free gift, *how else could a sinner get it?* I will pass over some of you, who fancy that you are the best people in the world. It is sheer fancy, mark you, without any truth in it. But I will say nothing about you. There are, however, some of us, who know that we were not the best people in the world; we who sinned against God, and knew it, and who were broken in pieces under a sense of our guilt. I know, for one, that there would have been no hope of heaven for me, if salvation had not been the free gift of God to those who deserved it not. After ministering among you for nearly thirty-seven years, I stand exactly where I stood when first I came to Christ, a poor sinner and nothing at all, but taking Christ as the free gift of God to me, as I took him at first, when, yet but a lad, I fled to him for salvation. Ask any of the people of God who have been abundant in service, and constant in prayer, whether they deserve aught at the hand of God, and those who have most to be thankful for will tell you that they have nothing that they have not received. Ask these, whom God has honoured to the conversion of many, whether they lay any claim to the grace of God, whether they have any merit, and whether in their hand they dare bring a price, and seek to buy of God his love; they will loathe the very thought. There is no way to heaven for you and me, my friend convinced of sin, unless all the way we are led by grace, and unless salvation is the gift of God.

But, once more: *look at the privileges which come to us through salvation!* I cannot, as I value those privileges, conceive for a minute that they are purchasable, or that they come to us as the result of our desert. They must be a gift; they are so many and so glorious as to be altogether outside the limit of our furthest search, and beyond the height of our utmost reach. We cannot by our efforts compass any salvation of any sort; but if we could, it certainly would not be such a salvation as this. Let us look, then, at our privileges.

Here comes, first, "the forgiveness of sins, according to the riches of his grace." He that believes in Christ has no sin. His sin is blotted out. It has ceased to be. Christ has finished it, and he is unto God as though he had never sinned. Can any sinner deserve that?

> "Here's pardon for transgressions past,
> It matters not how black their cast,
> And oh, my soul, with wonder view,
> For sins to come, here's pardon too!"

Can any sinner bring a price that will purchase such a boon as that? No; such mercy must be a gift.

Next, everyone that believes in Christ is justified, and looked upon by God as being perfectly righteous. The righteousness of Christ is imputed to him, and he is "accepted in the Beloved." By this he becomes not only innocent, that is, pardoned, but he becomes praise-worthy before God. This is justification. Can any guilty man deserve that? Why, he is covered with sin, defiled from head to foot! Can he deserve to be arrayed in the sumptuous robe of the divine righteousness of Christ, and "be made the righteousness of God in him"? It is inconceivable. Such a blessing must be the gift of infinite bounty, or it can never come to man.

Furthermore, beloved, remember that "now are we the sons of God." Can you realize that truth? As others are not, believers are, the sons of God. He is their Father, and the spirit of adoption breathes within their heart. They are children of his family, and come to him as children come to a father, with loving confidence. Think of being made a son of God, a son of him that made the heavens, a son of him who is God over all, blessed for ever. Can any man deserve that? Certainly not; this also must come as a gift.

Sonship leads on to heirship. "If children, then heirs; heirs of God, and joint-heirs with Christ." My brother, if thou art a believer, all things are thine, this world, and worlds to come. Could you ever desire all that? Could such an inheritance have come to you through any merits of your own? No, it must be a gift. Look at it, and the blaze of its splendour will strike all idea of merit blind.

Further than that, we are now made one with Christ. Oh, tell everywhere this wonder which God hath wrought for his people! It is not to be understood; it is an abyss too deep for a finite mind to sound. Every believer is truly united to Christ: "For we are members of his body, of his flesh, and of his bones." Every believer is married to Christ, and none of them shall ever be separated from him. Seeing, then, that there is such a union between us and Christ, can you suppose that any man can have any claim to such a position apart from the grace of God? By what merit, even of a perfect man, could we deserve to become one with Christ in an endless unity? Such a surpassing privilege is out of the line of purchase. It is, and can only be, the gift of God. Oneness with Christ cannot come to us in any other way.

Listen yet again. In consequence of our union with Christ, God the Holy Spirit dwells in every believer. Our bodies are his temple. God dwelleth in us, and we dwell in God. Can we deserve that?

Even a perfect keeping of the law would not have brought to men the abiding of the Holy Ghost in them. It is a blessing that rises higher than the law could ever reach, even if it had been kept.

Let me say, furthermore, that if you possess a blessed peace, as I trust you do, if you can say—

> "My heart is resting, O my God;
> I will give thanks and sing;
> My heart is at the secret source
> Of every precious thing;"

that divine peace must surely be the gift of God. If there is a great calm within your soul, an entire satisfaction with Christ your Lord, you never deserved that priceless boon. It is the work of his Holy Spirit, and must be his free gift.

And when you come to die, as you may—unless the Lord comes, as he will—the grace that will enable you fearlessly to face the last enemy will not be yours by any right of your own. If you fall asleep, as I have seen many a Christian pass away, with songs of triumph, with the light of heaven shining on your brow, almost in glory while yet you are in your bed, why, you cannot deserve that! Such a death-bed must be the free gift of God's almighty grace. It cannot be earned by merit; indeed, it is just then that every thought of merit melts away, and the soul hides itself in Christ, and triumphs there.

If this does not convince you, look once more. Let a window be opened in heaven. See the long lines of white-robed saints. Hark to their hallelujahs. Behold their endless, measureless delight. Did they deserve to come there? Did they come to their thrones and to their palms of victory by their own merits? Their answer is, "We have washed our robes, and made them white in the blood of the Lamb;" and from them all there comes the harmonious anthem, "*Non nobis, Domine*,"—"Not unto us, O Lord, not unto us; but unto thy name give glory, for thy mercy and for thy truth's sake." From first to last, then, we see that salvation is all the gift of God. And what can be freer than a gift, or more glorious than the gift of God? No prize can approach it in excellence, no merit can be mentioned in the same hour. O my brethren, we are debtors indeed to the mercy of God! We have received much, and there is more to follow; but it is all of grace from first to last. We know but little yet at what a cost these gifts were purchased for us; but we shall know it better by-and-by, as McCheyne so sweetly sings:—

> "When this passing world is done,
> When has sunk yon glaring sun;
> When I stand with Christ in glory,
> Looking o'er life's finished story,
> Then, Lord, shall I fully know—
> Not till then, how much I owe.

> "When I stand before the throne.
> Dressed in beauty not my own;
> When I see thee as thou art,
> Love thee with unsinning heart;
> Then, Lord, shall I fully know,
> Not till then, how much I owe."

II. Now I would try to lead your thoughts in another direction as we consider that THIS GIFT IS UNSPEAKABLE. Do not think it means that we cannot speak about this gift. Ah, how many times have I, for one, spoken upon this gift during the last forty years! I have spoken of little else. I heard of one who said, "I suppose Spurgeon is preaching that old story over again." Yes, that is what he is doing; and if he lives another twenty years, and you come here, it will be "the old, old story" still, for there is nothing like it. It is inexhaustible; it is like an Artesian well that springeth up for ever and ever. We can speak about it; yet it is unspeakable. What mean we, then, by saying it is unspeakable? Well, as I have said already, Christ Jesus our Lord is the sum and substance of salvation, and of God's gift. O God, this gift of thine is unspeakable, and it includes all other gifts beside!

> "Thou didst not spare thine only Son,
> But gav'st him for a world undone,
> And freely with that Blessed One—
> Thou givest all."

Consider, first, that Christ is unspeakable *in his person*. He is perfect man, and glorious God. No tongue of seraph, or of cherub, can ever describe the full nature of him whose name is "Wonderful, Counsellor, the mighty God, the everlasting Father, the Prince of peace." This is he whom the Father gave "for us men, and for our sakes." He was the Creator of all things, for "without him was not anything made that was made," yet he was "made flesh and dwelt among us." He filleth all things by his omnipresence; yet he came and tabernacled on the earth. This is that Jesus, who was born of Mary, yet who lived before all worlds. He was that Word, who "was in the beginning with God, and the Word was God." He is unspeakable. It is not possible to put into human language the divine mystery of his sacred being, truly man and yet truly God. But how great the wonder of it! Soul, God gave God for thee! Dost thou hear it? To redeem thee, O believing man, God gave himself to be thy Saviour; surely, that is an unspeakable gift.

Christ is unspeakable, next, *in his condescension*. Can any one measure or describe how far Christ stooped, when, from the throne of splendour, he came to the manger to be swaddled and lie where the horned oxen fed. Oh, what a stoop of condescension was that! The Infinite becomes an infant. The Eternal is dandled on a woman's knee. He is there in the carpenter's shop, obedient to his parents; there in the temple sitting among the doctors, hearing them and asking them questions; there in poverty, crying, "The Son of man hath not where to lay his head;" and there, in thirst, asking of a guilty woman a drink of water. It is unspeakable. That he, before whom the hosts of heaven veiled their faces, should come here among men, and among the poorest of the poor—that he who dwelt amidst the glory and bliss of the land of light, should deign to be a Man of sorrows and acquainted with grief, passes human thought! Such a Saviour is a gift unspeakable.

But if unspeakable so far, what shall I say of the fashion of Christ *in his death?* Beloved, I cannot speak adequately of Gethsemane and the bloody sweat, nor of the Judas kiss, nor of the traitorous flight of the disciples. It is unspeakable. That binding, scourging, plucking of the beard, and spitting in the face! Man's tongue cannot utter the horror of it. I cannot tell you truly the weight of the false accusations, the slanders, and the blasphemies that were heaped on him; nor would I wish to picture the old soldier's cloak flung over his bleeding shoulders, and the crown of thorns, the buffeting, the mailed fists, and the shame and sorrow he endured, as he was thrust out to execution. Do you wish to follow him along the streets, where weeping women lifted up their hearts in tender sympathy for the Lord of love about to die? If you do, it must be in silence, for words but feebly tell how much he bore on the way to the cross.

> "Well might the sun in darkness hide,
> And shut his glories in,
> When God, the mighty Maker, died
> For man, the creature's sin."

Oh, it was terrible that HE should be nailed to the gibbet, that HE should hang there to be ridiculed by all the mob of Jerusalem! The abjects flouted him, the meanest thought him meaner than themselves. Even dying thieves upbraided him. His eyes are choked, they become dim with blood. He must die. He says, "It is finished." He bows his head. The glorious Victim has yielded up his life to put away his people's sin. This is God's gift to you, divine, unspeakable, O ye sons of men!

But that is not all. Christ is unspeakable *in his glory*. When we think of his resurrection, of his ascending to heaven, and of his glory at the right hand of God, words languish on our lips; but in everyone of these positions, he is the gift of God to us; and when he shall come with all the glory of the Father, he will still be to his people the *Theo-dora*, the gift of God, the great unspeakable benediction to the sons of men. I wish that the people of Christ had this aspect of the Lord's glory more continually on their hearts, for though he seems to tarry, yet will he come again the second time, as he promised.

> "With that blessed hope before us,
> Let no harp remain unstrung;
> Let the mighty Advent chorus
> Onward roll on every tongue.
> Maranatha,
> Come, Lord Jesus, quickly come!"

To me, one of the most wonderful aspects of this gift is Christ *in his chosen;* all the Father gave him, all for whom he died, these he will glorify with himself, and they shall be with him where he is. Oh, what a sight will that be when we shall see the King in his beauty, and all his saints beautiful in his glory, shining like so many stars around him who is the Sun of them all! Then, indeed, shall we see what an unspeakable gift did God give to men, when, through that gift, he makes his saints all glorious, even as he predestinated them, "to be conformed to the image of his Son, that he might be the First-born among many brethren."

But we do not need to wait until we see his face to know his glory. Brethren, Christ is unspeakable as the gift of God *in the heart here.* "Oh," say you, "I trust I have felt the love of God shed abroad in my heart!" I rejoice with you, but could you speak it? Often, when I have tried to preach the love of Christ, I have not been able to preach it rightly, because I did not feel it as I ought; but oftener still, I have not been able to tell it out because I felt it so much. I would fain preach in that manner always, and feel Christ's love so much that I could speak it but little. Oh, child of God, if you have known much of Christ, you have often had to weep out your joys instead of speaking them, to lay your finger on your mouth, and be silent because you were overpowered by his glory. See how it was with John: "When I saw him, I fell at his feet as dead." Why did you not preach, John? If he were here to-night, he would say, "I could not preach then, the splendour of the Lord made me dumb. I fell at his feet as dead." This is one reason why the gift of God is unspeakable, because, the more you know about it, the less you can say about it. Christ overpowers us; he makes us tongue-tied with his wondrous revelations. When he reveals himself in full, we are like men that are blinded with excess of vision. Like Paul, on the Damascus road, we are forced to confess, "I could not see for the glory of that light." We cannot speak of it fully. All the apostles and prophets and saints of God have been trying to speak out the love of God as manifested in Christ; but yet they have all failed. I say, with great reverence, that the Holy Ghost himself seems to have laboured for expression, and, as he had to use human pens and mortal tongues, even he has never spoken to the full the measure and value of God's unspeakable gift. It is unspeakable to men by God himself. God can give it; but he cannot make us fully understand it. We have need to be like God himself to comprehend the greatness of his gift when he gives us his Son.

Though we make constant effort, it is unspeakable, even *throughout a long life*. Do you ministers, who have been a long time in one place, ever say to yourselves, "We shall run dry for subjects by-and-by"? If you preach Christ, you never will run short. If you have preached ten thousand sermons about Christ, you have not yet left the shore; you are not out in the deep sea yet. Dive, my brother! With splendour of thought, plunge into this great mystery of free grace and dying love; and when you have dived the farthest, you will perceive that you are as far off the bottom as when you first touched the surface. It is an endless theme; it is unspeakable!

> "Oh, could I speak the matchless worth,
> Oh, could I sound the glories forth
> Which in my Saviour shine!
> I'd soar and touch the heavenly strings,
> And vie with Gabriel while he sings
> In notes almost divine."

But I can neither speak it nor sing it as I ought; yet would I finish Medley's hymn, and say,—

> "Well, the delightful day will come
> When my dear Lord will bring me home,
> And I shall see his face;
> Then with my Saviour, Brother, Friend,
> A blest eternity I'll spend,
> Triumphant in his grace."

But, even then, Christ will be still *in heaven for ever* a gift unspeakable. Perhaps we shall have another talk together, friends, on this subject when we get there. One good woman said to me, "We shall have more time in eternity than we have now;" to which I replied, "I do not know whether there is any time in eternity, the words look like a contradiction." "Oh, but," said she; "I shall get a talk with you, anyhow; I have never had one yet." Well, I dare say we shall commune up there of these blessed things, when we shall know more about them. As we are to be there for ever and ever, we shall need some great subjects with which to keep up the conversation: what vaster theme can we have than this? Addison, in one of his verses, says—

> " But, oh! eternity's too short
> To utter half thy praise,"

and I have heard simpletons say that the couplet was very faulty; "you cannot make eternity short," they say. That shows the difference between a poet and a critic. A critic is a being all teeth, without any heart; and a poet is one who has much heart, and who sometimes finds that human language is not sufficient to express his thoughts. We shall never have done with Christ in heaven. Oh, my Lord, thy presence will make my heaven!

> " Millions of years my wondering eyes,
> Shall o'er thy beauties rove;
> And endless ages I'll adore
> The glories of thy love."

This wondrous gift of God is an utterly inexhaustible, unspeakable subject.

III. Now, lastly, I come to this point, that FOR THIS GIFT THANKS SHOULD BE RENDERED. The text says, "Thanks be unto God for his unspeakable gift." By this the apostle not only meant that he gave thanks for Christ; but he thus calls upon the church, and upon every individual believer, to join him in his praise. Here do I adopt his language, and praise God on my own behalf, calling upon all of you who know the preciousness of Christ, the gift of God, to unite with me in the thanksgiving. Let us as with one heart say it now, "Thanks be unto God for his unspeakable gift."

Some cannot say this, for they never think of the gift of God. You who never think of God, how can you thank God? There must be "think" at the bottom of "thank." Whenever we think, we ought to thank. But some never think, and therefore never thank. Beloved friend, what are you at? That Christ should die; is it nothing to you? That God "gave his Only-begotten Son, that whosoever believeth in him should not perish, but have everlasting life;" is that nothing to you? Let the question drop into your heart. Press it home upon yourself. Will you say that you have no share in this gift? Will you deliberately give up any hope you may have of ever partaking of the grace of God? Are you determined now to say, "I do not care about Christ"? Well, you would hardly like to say that; but why do you practically declare this to be your intention, if you do not want to say it? Oh, that you might now so think of Christ as to trust him at once, and begin to raise this note of praise!

Some, on the other hand, do not thank God because they are always delaying. Have I not hearers here to-night who were here ten years ago, and were rather more hopeful then than they are now? "There is plenty of time," say you; but you do not say this about other matters. I admired the children, the other day, when the teacher said, "Dear children, the weather is unsettled. You can go out next Wednesday; but do you not think that it would be better to stop a month, so that we could go when the weather is more settled?" There was not a child that voted for stopping a month. All the hands were up for going next Wednesday. Now, imitate the children in that. Do not make it seem as if you were in no hurry to be happy; for as he that believeth in Christ hath eternal life, to postpone having it is an unworthy as well as an unwise thing to do. No, you will have it, I hope, at once. There is a man here who is going to be a very rich man when his old aunt dies. You do not wish that she should die, I am sure; but you sometimes wonder why some people are spared to be ninety, do you not? You are very poor now, and you wish that some of this money could come to you at once; you are not for putting that off. Why should you put off heavenly riches and eternal life? I beseech you to believe in Christ now; then you will be filled with thankfulness and joy.

Some cannot say, "Thanks be unto God for his unspeakable gift," for they do not know whether they have it or not. They sometimes think that they have; they oftener fear that they have not. Never tolerate a doubt on this subject, I implore you. Get full assurance. "Lay hold on eternal life." Get a grip of it. Know Christ: trust Christ wholly: and you have God's word for it, "He that heareth my word, and believeth on him that sent me, hath everlasting life, and shall not come into condemnation, but is passed from death unto life." Then you can say, "Thanks be unto God for his unspeakable gift."

Now, dear friends, let me ask you to join me in this exercise. Let us first unitedly *thank God for this gift*. Put out of your mind the idea that you ought to thank Christ, but not thank the Father. It was the Father that gave Christ. Christ did not die to make his Father love us, as some say that we preach. We have always preached the very opposite, and we have quoted that verse of Kent—

> " 'Twas not to make Jehovah's love
> Towards the sinner flame,
> That Jesus, from his throne above,
> A suffering man became.

> " 'Twas not the death which he endured,
> Nor all the pangs he bore,
> That God's eternal love procured,
> For God was love before."

He gave his Son because he had already loved us. Christ is the exhibition of the Father's love, and the revelation of Christ is made because of "the love of the Spirit." Therefore, "thanks be unto God"—the Father, the Son, the Holy Ghost—"for his unspeakable gift."

While you saved ones, every one, raise your note of gratitude, be very careful to *thank God only*. Do not be thinking by whose means you were converted, and begin to thank the servant instead of the Lord whom he serves. Let the man who was used as the instrument in God's hand be told, for his comfort, of the blessing God sent you through him; but thank God, and thank only God, that you were led to lay hold on Christ, who is his unspeakable gift.

Moreover, *thank God spontaneously*. Look at the apostle, and imitate him. When he sounded this peal of praise, his mind was occupied at the time about the collection for the poor saints; but, collection or no collection, he will thank God for his unspeakable gift. I like to see thanks to God come up at what might seem to be an untimely moment. When a man does not feel just as happy as he might be, and yet says, "Thank God," it sounds refreshingly real. I like to hear such a bubbling up of praise as in the case of old Father Taylor, of New York, when he broke down in the middle of a sentence. Looking up at the people, he said, "There now! the nominative has lost its verb; but, hallelujah! I am on the way to glory;" and so he went on again. Sometimes we ought to do just like that. Take an opportunity, when there comes a little interval, just to say, "Whether this is in tune or not, I cannot help it: thanks be unto God for his unspeakable gift."

Lastly, as you receive the precious gift, *thank God practically*. Thank God by doing something to prove your thanks. It is a poor gratitude which only effervesces in words, and shirks deeds of kindness. Real thankfulness will not be in word only, but in deed too, and so it will prove that it is in truth.

"Well, what could I do that would please God?" you say. First, I should think you could look for his lost children. That is sure to please him. Go to-night, and see whether you cannot find one of the erring whom you might bring back to the fold. Would you not please a mother, if she had lost her baby, and you set to work to find it? We want to please God. Seek the lost ones, and bring them in.

If you want to please God, next, succour his poor saints. If you know anything of them, help them. Do something for them for Christ's sake. I knew a woman who used always to relieve anybody that came to her door in the dress of a sailor. I do not think that half those who came to her ever had been to sea at all; but, still, if they came to the door as sailors, she used to say, "Ah! my dear boy was a sailor. I have not seen him for years. He is lost somewhere at sea; but for dear Jack's sake, I always help every sailor that comes to my door." It is a right feeling, is it not? I remember, when I first came to London from my country charge, I used to think that, if I came across a dog or a cat that came from Waterbeach, I would like to feed it. So, for love of Christ, love Christ's poor people. Whenever you find them, say, "My Lord was poor, and so are you, and for his dear sake I will help you."

If you want to please God, next, bear with the evil ones. Do not lose your temper; I mean, by that, do not get angry with the unthankful and the evil. Let your anger be lost in praise for the gift unspeakable. Please God by bearing with evil men, as he bears with you. But if you have a very bad temper, I hope that, in another sense, you may lose it, and never find it any more.

And, lastly, if you want to please God, watch, like the Thessalonians, "for his Son from heaven." The Lord Jesus is coming again, in like manner as he departed, and there is no attitude with which God is more delighted in his saved people than with that of watching for the time when "unto them that look for him shall he appear the second time, without sin unto salvation."

Beloved, may God help you thus to magnify his Son; and to him shall be all the praise! Let us again lift up our glad hallelujah: "Thanks be unto God for his unspeakable gift." Amen.